How to Start a Business in California

John J. Talamo
Mark Warda
Attorneys at Law

SPHINX® PUBLISHING
AN IMPRINT OF SOURCEBOOKS, INC.®
NAPERVILLE, ILLINOIS
www.SphinxLegal.com

First edition, 2001
Third Printing, June, 2002
Published by: **Sphinx® Publishing, an Imprint of Sourcebooks, Inc.®**

<u>Naperville Office</u>
P.O. Box 4410
Naperville, Illinois 60567-4410
630-961-3900
Fax: 630-961-2168
www.sourcebooks.com
wwwSphinxLegal.com

This publication is designed to provide accurate and authoritative information in regard to the subject matter covered. It is sold with the understanding that the publisher is not engaged in rendering legal, accounting, or other professional service. If legal advice or other expert assistance is required, the services of a competent professional person should be sought.

From a Declaration of Principles Jointly Adopted by a Committee of the
American Bar Association and a Committee of Publishers and Associations

This product is not a substitute for legal advice.

Disclaimer required by Texas statutes.

Library of Congress Cataloging-in-Publication Data

Talamo, John
    How to start a business in California : with forms / John J. Talamo, Mark Warda
      p. cm. -- (Legal survival guides)
    Includes bibliographical references and index.
    ISBN 1-57248-146-3
   1. Business enterprises--Law and legislation--California--Popular works. 2. Business enterprises--Law and legislation--California--Forms. 3. Business Law--California. I. Warda, Mark. Title. III. Series.

KFC337.Z9 T35 2001
346.794'065--dc21
                                                 2001017034

Printed and bound in the United States of America.
VHG Paperback — 10 9 8 7 6 5 4 3

CONTENTS

Using Self-Help
Law Books

Before using a self-help law book, you should realize the advantages and disadvantages of doing your own legal work and understand the challenges and diligence that this requires.

THE GROWING TREND

Rest assured that you won't be the first or only person handling your own legal matter. For example, in some states, more than seventy-five percent of the people in divorces and other cases represent themselves. Because of the high cost of legal services, this is a major trend and many courts are struggling to make it easier for people to represent themselves. However, some courts are not happy with people who do not use attorneys and refuse to help them in any way. For some, the attitude is, "Go to the law library and figure it out for yourself."

We write and publish self-help law books to give people an alternative to the often complicated and confusing legal books found in most law libraries. We have made the explanations of the law as simple and easy to understand as possible. Of course, unlike an attorney advising an individual client, we cannot cover every conceivable possibility.

COST/VALUE ANALYSIS

Whenever you shop for a product or service, you are faced with various levels of quality and price. In deciding what product or service to buy, you make a cost/value analysis on the basis of your willingness to pay and the quality you desire.

When buying a car, you decide whether you want transportation, comfort, status, or sex appeal. Accordingly, you decide among such choices as a Neon, a Lincoln, a Rolls Royce, or a Porsche. Before making a decision, you usually weigh the merits of each option against the cost.

When you get a headache, you can take a pain reliever (such as aspirin) or visit a medical specialist for a neurological examination. Given this choice, most people, of course, take a pain reliever, since it costs only pennies; whereas a medical examination costs hundreds of dollars and takes a lot of time. This is usually a logical choice because it is rare to need anything more than a pain reliever for a headache. But in some cases, a headache may indicate a brain tumor and failing to see a specialist right away can result in complications. Should everyone with a headache go to a specialist? Of course not, but people treating their own illnesses must realize that they are betting on the basis of their cost/value analysis of the situation. They are taking the most logical option.

The same cost/value analysis must be made when deciding to do one's own legal work. Many legal situations are very straight forward, requiring a simple form and no complicated analysis. Anyone with a little intelligence and a book of instructions can handle the matter without outside help.

But there is always the chance that complications are involved that only an attorney would notice. To simplify the law into a book like this, several legal cases often must be condensed into a single sentence or paragraph. Otherwise, the book would be several hundred pages long and too complicated for most people. However, this simplification necessarily leaves out many details and nuances that would apply to special or unusual situations. Also, there are many ways to interpret most legal questions. Your case may come before a judge who disagrees with the analysis of our authors.

Therefore, in deciding to use a self-help law book and to do your own legal work, you must realize that you are making a cost/value analysis. You have decided that the money you will save in doing it yourself outweighs the chance that your case will not turn out to your satisfaction. Most people handling their own simple legal matters never have a problem, but occasionally people find that it ended up costing them more to have an attorney straighten out the situation than it would have if they had hired an attorney in the beginning. Keep this in mind while handling your case, and be sure to consult an attorney if you feel you might need further guidance.

LOCAL RULES   The next thing to remember is that a book which covers the law for the entire nation, or even for an entire state, cannot possibly include every procedural difference of every jurisdiction. Whenever possible, we provide the exact form needed; however, in some areas, each county, or even each judge, may require unique forms and procedures. In our state books, our forms usually cover the majority of counties in the state, or provide examples of the type of form which will be required. In our national books, our forms are sometimes even more general in nature but are designed to give a good idea of the type of form that will be needed in most locations. Nonetheless, keep in mind that your state, county, or judge may have a requirement, or use a form, that is not included in this book.

You should not necessarily expect to be able to get all of the information and resources you need solely from within the pages of this book. This book will serve as your guide, giving you specific information whenever possible and helping you to find out what else you will need to know. This is just like if you decided to build your own backyard deck. You might purchase a book on how to build decks. However, such a book would not include the building codes and permit requirements of every city, town, county, and township in the nation; nor would it include the lumber, nails, saws, hammers, and other materials and tools you would need to actually build the deck. You would use the book as your guide, and then do some work and research involving such matters as whether you need a permit of some kind, what type and grade of wood are available in your area, whether to use hand tools or power tools, and how to use those tools.

Before using the forms in a book like this, you should check with your court clerk to see if there are any local rules of which you should be aware, or local forms you will need to use. Often, such forms will require the same information as the forms in the book but are merely laid out differently or use slightly different language. They will sometimes require additional information.

CHANGES IN THE LAW
Besides being subject to local rules and practices, the law is subject to change at any time. The courts and the legislatures of all fifty states are constantly revising the laws. It is possible that while you are reading this book, some aspect of the law is being changed.

In most cases, the change will be of minimal significance. A form will be redesigned, additional information will be required, or a waiting period will be extended. As a result, you might need to revise a form, file an extra form, or wait out a longer time period; these types of changes will not usually affect the outcome of your case. On the other hand, sometimes a major part of the law is changed, the entire law in a particular area is rewritten, or a case that was the basis of a central legal point is overruled. In such instances, your entire ability to pursue your case may be impaired.

Again, you should weigh the value of your case against the cost of an attorney and make a decision as to what you believe is in your best interest.

INTRODUCTION

Each year about a hundred thousand new corporations are registered in California and thousands more partnerships and proprietorships open for business. California is booming! Nearly 1,000 people move to the state each day and the demand for new products and services keeps growing. Some have said California is now what California was in the '60s—a thriving, trend-setting center of activity where little shops can bloom into expansive enterprises.

The best way to take part in this boom is to run your own business. Be your own boss and be as successful as you dare to be.

But if you don't follow the laws of the state, your progress can be slowed or stopped by government fines, civil judgments, or even criminal penalties.

This book is intended to give you the framework for legally opening a business in California. It also includes information on where to find special rules for each type of business. If you have problems which are not covered by this book, you should seek out an attorney who can be available for your ongoing needs.

In order to cover all of the aspects of any business you are thinking of starting, you should read through this entire book, rather than skipping to the parts that look most interesting. There are many laws that may not sound like they apply to you but which do have provisions that will affect your business.

In recent years the government bureaucracies have been amending and lengthening their forms regularly. The forms included in this book were the most recent available at the time of publication. It is possible that some may be revised at the time you read this book, but in most cases previous versions of the forms will still be accepted.

DECIDING TO START A BUSINESS 1

If you are reading this book, then you have probably made a serious decision to take the plunge and start your own business. Hundreds of thousands of people make the same decision each year and many of them become very successful. Some merely make a living, while others become billionaires. Unfortunately, a lot of them also fail. Knowledge can only help your chances of success. You need to know why some succeed while others fail. Some of what follows may seem obvious, but to someone wrapped up in a new business idea, some of this information is occasionally overlooked.

KNOW YOUR STRENGTHS

The last thing a budding entrepreneur wants to hear is that he is not cut out for running his own business. Those "do you have what it takes" quizzes are ignored with the fear that the answer might be one the entrepreneur does not want to hear. But even if you lack some skills, you can be successful if you know where to get them.

You should consider all of the skills and knowledge that running a successful business means and then decide whether you have what it takes. If you do not, it does not necessarily mean you are doomed to be an employee all your life. Perhaps you just need a partner who has the skills you lack, or perhaps you can hire someone with the skills you need. You can structure your business to avoid areas where you are weak. If those do not work, maybe you can learn the skills.

For example, if you are not good at dealing with employees (either you are too passive and get taken advantage of, or too tough and scare them off), you can:

- ☞ handle product development yourself and have a partner or manager deal with employees;
- ☞ take seminars in employee management; or
- ☞ structure your business so that you don't need employees, either by using independent contractors or setting yourself up as an independent contractor.

Here are some of the factors to consider when planning your business:

- ☞ If it takes months or years before your business turns a profit, do you have the resources to hold out? Businesses have gone under or have been sold just before they were about to take off, and staying power is an important ingredient to success.

- ☞ Are you willing to put in a lot of overtime to make your business a success? Owners of businesses do not set their own hours; the business sets them for the owner. Many business owners work long hours seven days a week, but they enjoy running their business more than family picnics or fishing.

- ☞ Are you willing to do the dirtiest or most unpleasant work of the business? Emergencies come up and employees are not always dependable. You might need to mop up a flooded room, spend a weekend stuffing 10,000 envelopes or work Christmas if someone calls in sick.

- ☞ Do you know enough about the product or service? Are you aware of the trends in the industry and what changes new technology might bring? Think of the people who started typesetting or printing businesses just before type was replaced by laser printers.

☛ Do you know enough about accounting and inventory to manage the business? Do you have a good "head for business?" Some people naturally know how to save money and do things profitably. Others are in the habit of buying the best and the most expensive of everything. The latter can be fatal to a struggling new business.

☛ Are you good at managing employees?

☛ Do you know how to sell your product or service? You can have the best product on the market but people do not beat a path to your door. If you are a wholesaler, shelf space in major stores is hard to get, especially for a new company without a record, a large line of products, or a large advertising budget.

☛ Do you know enough about getting publicity? The media receive thousands of press releases and announcements each day and most are thrown away. Do not count on free publicity to put your name in front of the public.

KNOW YOUR BUSINESS

Not only do you need to know the concept of a business, but you need the experience of working in a business. Maybe you always dreamed of running a bed and breakfast or having your own pizza place. Now that you are laid off you think it is time to use your savings to fulfill your dream. Have you ever worked in such a business? If not, you may have no idea of the day-to-day headaches and problems of the business. For example, do you really know how much to allow for theft, spoilage, and unhappy customers?

You might feel silly taking an entry-level job at a pizza place when you'd rather start your own, but it might be the most valuable preparation you could have. Working in a business as an employee is one of the best ways to be a success at running such a business. A few weeks of seeing how a business operates could mean the difference between success and failure. New people with new ideas who work in old stodgy industries have been known to revolutionize them with obvious improvements that no one before dared to try.

DO THE MATH

Conventional wisdom says you need a business plan before committing yourself to a new venture, but lots of businesses are started successfully without owners even knowing what a business plan is. They have a great concept, they put it on the market, and it takes off. But you at least need to do some basic calculations to see if the business can make a profit. Here are some examples:

☛ If you want to start a retail shop, figure out how many people are close enough to become customers, and how many other stores will be competing for those customers. Visit some of those other shops and see how busy they are. Without giving away your plans to compete, ask some general questions like "how's business?" and maybe they will share their frustrations or successes.

☛ Whether you sell a good or a service, do the math to find out how much profit is in it. For example, if you plan to start a house painting company, find out: 1) what you will have to pay to hire painters; 2) what it will cost you for all of the insurance; 3) what bonding and licensing you will need; and 4) what the advertising will cost you. Figure out how many jobs you can do per month and what other painters are charging. In some industries in different areas of the country there may be a large margin of profit, or there may be almost no profit.

☛ Find out if there is a demand for your product or service. Suppose you have designed a beautiful new kind of candle and your friends all say you should open a shop because "everyone will want them." Before making a hundred of them and renting a store, bring a few to craft shows or flea markets and see what happens.

☞ Figure out what the income and expenses would be for a typical month of your new business. List monthly expenses such as rent, salaries, utilities, insurance, taxes, supplies, advertising, services, and other overhead. Then figure out how much profit you will average from each sale. Next, figure out how many sales you will need to cover your overhead and divide by the number of business days in the month. Can you reasonably expect that many sales? How will you get those sales?

Most types of businesses have trade associations which often have figures on how profitable its members are. Some even have start-up kits for people wanting to start businesses. One good source of information on such organizations is the *Encyclopedia of Associations* published by Gale Research Inc. and is available in many library reference sections. They can also be reached by typing "encyclopedia of association" on an Internet search (don't forget the quotation marks or similar qualifying designation for the search engine you use). Producers of products to the trade often give assistance to small companies getting started. Contact the largest suppliers of the products your business will be using and see if they can be of help. To help you prepare a business plan, see *Your First Business Plan* listed among other useful resources at the end of this book.

Sources for Further Guidance

The following offices offer free or low cost guidance for new businesses:

SCORE
California is a haven for retired people and many of them, members of SCORE (the Service Corps of Retired Executives), are glad to give free guidance to new businesses. The SCORE website on the Internet is **http://www.score.org/**. SCORE offices may be found at:

Los Angeles Score
330 North Brand Boulevard
Suite 190
Glendale, CA 91203-2304

Phone: 818-552-3206
Fax: 818-552-3323

San Francisco SCORE
455 Market Street, 6th Floor
San Francisco, CA 94105

Phone: 415-744-6827
Fax: 415-744-6750

Orange County SCORE
200 W. Santa Ana Blvd.
Suite 700
Santa Ana, CA 92701

Phone: 714-550-7369
Fax: 714-550-0191

San Diego SCORE
550 West C Street, Suite 550
San Diego, CA 92101-3500

Phone: 619-557-7272
Fax: 619-557-5894

Santa Barbara SCORE
P.O. Box 30291
Santa Barbara, CA 93130

Phone: 805-563-0084

Ventura SCORE
5700 Ralston Street, Suite 310
Ventura, CA 93001

Phone: 805-658-2688
Fax: 805-658-2252

Palm Springs SCORE
650 E. Tahquitz Canyon Way
Suite D
Palm Springs, CA 92262-6682

Phone: 760-320-6682
Fax: 760-323-9426

Central California SCORE
2719 N. Air Fresno Drive
Suite 200
Fresno, CA 93727-1547

Phone: 209-487-5605
Fax: 209-487-5636

Sacramento SCORE
9845 Horn Rd., #260B
Sacramento, CA 95827

Phone: 916-361-2322
Fax: 916-361-2164

Stockton SCORE
401 N. San Joaquin Street
Room 114
Stockton, CA 95202

Phone: 209-946-6293

Central Coast SCORE
509 West Morrison Ave.
Santa Maria, CA 93454

Phone: 805-347-7755

Hemet SCORE
1700 E. Florida Avenue
Hemet, CA 92544-4679

Phone: 805-652-4390
Fax: 909-929-8543

East Bay SCORE
519 17th Street
Oakland, CA 94612

Phone: 510-273-6611
Fax: 510-273-6015

Shasta SCORE
c/o Cascade SBDC
737 Auditorium Drive
Redding, CA 96099

Phone: 916-225-2770

Yosemite SCORE
c/o SCEDO
1012 11th Street, Suite 300
Modesto, CA 95354

Phone: 209-521-6177
Fax: 209-521-9373

Golden Empire SCORE
1706 Chester Ave., #200
Bakersfield, CA 93301

Phone: 661-322-5881
Fax: 661-322-5663

Monterey Bay SCORE
Monterey Peninsula Chamber of Commerce
380 Alvarado, P.O. Box 1770
Monterey, CA 93940

Phone: 831-648-5360

Greater Chico Area SCORE
1324 Mangrove Street
Suite 114
Chico, CA 95926

Phone: 530-342-8932
Fax: 530-342-8932

Antelope Valley SCORE
4511 West Ave., M-4
Quartz Hill, CA 93536

Phone: 805-272-0087

Tuolumne County SCORE
39 N. Washington St.
Sonora, CA 95370

Phone: 209-588-0128
Fax: 209-588-0673

San Luis Obispo SCORE
4111 Broad St., Suite A
San Luis Obispo, CA 93401

Phone: 805-547-0779

Silicon Valley SCORE
84 W. Santa Clara St.
Suite 100, Entrepreneur Ctr.
San Jose, CA 95113

Phone: 408-288-8479
Fax: 408-494-0214

SMALL BUSINESS DEVELOPMENT CENTERS

Educational programs for small businesses are offered through the Small Business Development Centers at many California colleges and universities. You should see if they have any that could help you in any areas in which you are weak.

Lead Small Business Development Center
** *Specialized Center*
# *Historical Black College/University*

California Small Business
Development Center
CALIFORNIA TRADE AND COMMERCE
AGENCY*
Ms. Kim Neri, State Director
801 K Street, Suite 1700
Sacramento, CA 95814
916-324-5068
Fax: 916-322-5084
website: http://commerce.ca.gov/business/
small/starting/sb_sbdcl.html

Central Coast Small Business
Development Center
Ms. Theresa Thomae, Director
6500 Soquel Drive
Aptos, CA 95003
831-479-6136
Fax: 831-479-6166
email: tethomae@cabrillo.cc.ca.us
website: http://www.businessonline.org

Sierra College
Small Business Development Center
Ms. Mary Wollesen, Director
560 Wall Street, Suite J
Auburn, CA 95603
530-885-5488
Fax: 530-823-2831
email: sbdcinfo@sbdcsierra.org
website: http://www.sbdcsierra.org

Weill Institute Small Business
Development Center
Mr. Jeffrey Johnson, Director
1706 Chester Ave., Ste. 200
Bakersfield, CA 93301
661-322-5881
Fax: 661-322-5663
email: weill@lightspeed.net
website:
http://www.kccd.cc.ca.us/sbdc.html

Butte College
Small Business Development Center
Ms. Sophie Konuwa, Director
260 Cohasset Road, Suite A
Chico, CA 95926
530-895-9017
Fax: 530-895-9099
email: konuwaso@butte.cc.ca.us
website: http://www.bcsbdc.org/

Southwestern College**
International Trade Center
Small Business Development Center
Ms. Mary Wylie, Director
900 Otay Lakes Road, Bldg. 1600
Chula Vista, CA 91910
619-482-6391
Fax: 619-482-6402
email: mwylie@sbditc.org
Mr. Ken M. Clark, Small Business Programs
email : kmcsbdc@sbditc.org
Mr. Victor M. Castillo, Center Operations
Manager
email: victor@sbditc.org
website: http://www.sbditc.org

North San Diego County SBDC
Ms. Carole Enmark, Director
1823 Mission St.
Oceanside, CA 92054
760-754-6575
Fax: 760-754-0664
email: cenmark@mcc.miracosta.cc.ca.us
website: http://www.sandiegosmallbiz.com

Commerce Small Business
Development Center
The Citadel
Mr. Wendell Watts, Clerical Specialist
500 Citadel Dr., Suite 213
Commerce, CA 90040
323-887-9627
Fax: 323-887-9670

Contra Costa Small Business
Development Center
Ms. Beverly Hamile, Director
2425 Bisso Lane, Suite 200
Concord, CA 94520
925-646-5377
Fax: 925-646-5299
email: bhamile@hotmail.com

North Coast Small Business
Development Center
Ms. Frank Clark, Director
520 E Street
Eureka, CA 95501
707-445-9720
Fax: 707-445-9652
email: fransbdc@northcoast.com

Imperial Valley Satellite
Small Business Development Center
Ben Solomon, Director
1240 State Street
El Centro, CA 92243
760-312-9800
Fax: 760-312-9838
email: ivsbdc@quix.net

Export SBDC of Southern California
Ms. Gladys Moreau, Director
222 North Sepulveda, Ste. 1690
El Segundo, CA 90245
310-606-0166
Fax: 310-606-0155
email: info@exportsdbc.org
website: http://www.exportsbdc.org

North Coast
Small Business Development Center
Ms. Fran Clark, Director
520 E Street
Eureka, CA 95501
707-445-9720
Fax: 707-445-9652
email: fransbdc@northcoast.com

West Company Coast Office
Small Business Development Center
306 Redwood Avenue
Fort Bragg, CA 95437
707-964-7571
Fax: 707-964-7571

Central California SBDC
Mr. Dennis Winans, Director
3419 West Shaw Avenue, Suite 102
Fresno, CA 93711
800-974-0664
559-275-1223
Fax: 559-275-1499
email: Dennisw@ccsbdc.org
website: http://www.ccsbdc.org

Glendale/Pasadena Satellite
Small Business Development Center
Mr. Robert Pindroh, Manager
330 N. Brand, Suite 190
Glendale, CA 91203
818-552-3254
Fax: 818-552-3322
email: sbdcgln@ibm.net

Gavilan College Small Business
Development Center
Mr. Peter Graff, Director
7436 Monterey Street
Gilroy, CA 95020
408-847-0373
Fax: 408-847-0393
email: 1.nolan@gilroy.com
website: http://www.gavilansbdc.org

Venture Point Tech Coast SBDC
Jay DeLong, Director
2 Park Plaza, Suite 100
Irvine, CA 92614
949-794-7244
Fax: 949-476-0763
email: jdelong@ocbc.org

Export SBDC Outreach Center
United States Export Assistance Center
One World Trade Center, Suite 1670
Long Beach, CA 90831
562-980-4550
Fax: 562-980-4561

Los Angeles/Watts
Small Business Development Center
One Stop Capital Shop
Kashif Rasheed, Clerical Specialist
10221 Compton Ave., Suite 103
Los Angeles, CA 90008
213-473-5111
Fax: 213-473-5115
email: sbdcla@ibm.net

Southwest Los Angeles County
Small Business Development Center
Susan Hunter, Director
2377 Crenshaw Blvd., Suite 120
Torrance, CA 90501
310-787-6466
Fax: 310-782-8607
email: shunter@elcamino.cc.ca.us
website: http://swlasbdc.org/

Amador County Outreach
Satellite Small Business Development Center
1500 S. Highway 19
P.O. Box 1077
Jackson, CA 95642
209-223-0351
Fax: 209-223-2261

Lake County Satellite
Small Business Development Center
55 First St., 3rd Floor, MS-J
P.O. Box 1566
Lakeport, CA 95453
707-263-0330
Fax: 707-263-8516
email: lakesbdc@jps.net

Alpine County Outreach
Chamber of Commerce & Visitor Authority
3 Webster Str.
P.O. Box 265
Markleeville, CA 96120
530-694-2475
Fax: 530-694-2478

Yuba College Small Business
Development Center
Mr. James Hunter, Director
330 Ninth Str.
P.O. Box 262 (mailing)
Marysville, CA 95901
530-749-0153
Fax: 530-749-0155
email: phpd@aol.com

Valley Sierra–Merced Satellite
Small Business Development Center
Satellite Manager/Business Consultant
2000 M Street
Merced, CA 95340
800-323-2623
website: http://www.smallbizcenter.org

Valley Sierra Small Business
Development Center
Kelly Beardon, Director
1012 Eleventh Str., Suite 400
Modesto, CA 95354
209-521-6177
Fax: 209-521-9373
email: bearden@scedco.org
website: http://www.smallbizcenter.org

Napa Valley College
Small Business Development Center
Ms. Sue Jensen, Interim Director
1556 First Str., Suite 103
Napa, CA 94559
707-253-3210
Fax: 707-253-3068
email: sjensen@campus.nvc.cc.ca.us
website: http://www.napasbdc.org/

Inland Empire Business Incubator
Mr. John O'Brien, Incubator Manager
155 S. Memorial Drive
San Bernardino, CA 92408
909-382-0065
Fax: 909-382-8543

East Bay Small Business Development Center
Mr. Faheem Hameed, Director
519 17th Street, Suite 210
Oakland, CA 94612
510-893-4114
Fax: 909-893-5532
email: fhameed@ebsbdc.org

Coachella Valley/Palm Springs Satellite
Small Business Development Center
Mr. Brad Mix, Business Consultant
500 S. Palm Canyon Drive, Suite 222
Palm Springs, CA 92264
760-864-1311
Fax: 760-864-1319

Eastern Los Angeles County
Small Business Development Center
Mr. Cope Norcross, Director
300 W. Second Str., Suite 203
Pomona, CA 91766
909-629-2247
Fax: 909-629-8310
email: sbdcpom@attglobal.net
website: http://vclass.mtsac.edu/sbdc

Cascade Small Business Development Center
Mr. Bob Nash, Acting Director
737 Auditorium Drive, Suite A
Redding, CA 96001
530-225-2770
Fax: 530-225-2769
email: bnash@scedd.org
website: http://www.scedd.org

Inland Empire Small Business
Development Center
Mr. Michael Stull, Director
1157 Spruce Street
Riverside, CA 92507
800-750-2353
909-781-2345
Fax: 909-781-2353
email: mstull@iesbdc.org
website: http://www.iesbdc.org

Greater Sacramento
Small Business Development Center
Erik Krause, Interim Director
1410 Ethan Way
Sacramento, CA 95825
916-563-3210
Fax: 916-563-3266
email: krausee@exi.do.losrios.cc.ca.us
website: http://www.sbdc.net

San Francisco Small Business
Development Center
Mr. Romanus Wolter, Director
455 Van Ness Ave., Sixth Floor
San Francisco, CA 94105
415-908-7501
Fax: 415-974-6035
email: sbdcsf@pacbell.net

South Central Coast
Small Business Development Center
Mr. David Ryal, Director
3566 South Higuera, Suite 100
San Luis Obispo, CA 93401
877-549-8349
805-549-0401
Fax: 805-543-5198
email: sccsbdc@fix.net
website:
http://www.cuesta.cc.ca.us/commty/sbdc.htm

Orange County Small Business
Development Center
Vacant, Director
901 East Santa Ana Boulevard, Suite 101
Santa Ana, CA 92701
714-564-5202
Fax: 714-647-1168
email: hazelina@aol.com
website:
http://www.rancho.cc.ca.us/home/sac.bisc/
html/ocsbdc.html

Westside Small Business Development Center
3233 Donald Douglas Loop South, Suite C
Santa Monica, CA 90405
310-398-8883
Fax: 310-398-3024

Redwood Empire
Small Business Development Center
Mr. Ken Dean, Director
606 Healdsburg Ave.
Santa Rosa, CA 95401
707-524-1770
Fax: 707-524-1772
email: kdean@santarosa.edu
website: http://www.santarosa.edu/sbdc

San Joaquin Delta College
Small Business Development Center
Ms. Gillian Murphy
445 North San Joaquin Street
Stockton, CA 95202
209-943-5089
Fax: 209-943-8325
email: gmurphy@sjdccd.cc.ca.us
website: http://www.inreach.com/sbdc

Solano County Small Business
Development Center
Ms. Beth Pratt, Director
424 Executive Court North, Suite C
Suisun, CA 94585
707-864-3382
Fax: 707-864-8025
email: epratt@solano.cc.ca.us
website: http://www.solanosbdc.com

Silicon Valley Small Business
Development Center
Mr. Elza Minor, Director
298 S. Sunnyvale Ave., Suite 204
Sunnyvale, CA 94086
408-736-0680
Fax: 408-736-0679
email: eminor@siliconvalley-sbdc.org
website: http://www.siliconvalley-sbdc.org/

West Company Small Business
Development Center
Ms. Sheilah Rogers, Executive Director
367 N. State St., Suite 201
Ukiah, CA 95482
707-468-3553
Fax: 707-468-3555
email: westco@pacific.net

North Los Angeles County
Small Business Development Center
Ms. Nicole Schramm, Acting Director
4717 Van Nuys Blvd., Suite 201
Van Nuys, CA 91403
818-907-9922
Fax: 818-907-9890
email: vnsbdc@vedc.org
website: http://www.vedc.org/sbdc.htm

Export SBDC Satellite Center
Mr. Ray Bowman, Manager
5700 Ralston St., Suite 310
Ventura, CA 93003
805-644-6191
Fax: 805-658-2252
email: esbdc@primenet.com

Gold Coast Small Business
Development Center
Mr. Jose Vega, Satellite Manager
5700 Ralston St., Suite 310
Ventura, CA 93003
805-658-2688
Fax: 805-658-2252
email: gcsbdc@vedc.org

High Desert/Victorville Satellite
Small Business Development Center
Mr. David Schulte, Satellite Manager/Business
Consultant
15490 Civic Drive, Suite 102
Victorville, CA 92392
760-951-1592
Fax: 760-951-8929
email: ddschulte@eee.org

Central California–Visalia Satellite
Small Business Development Center
Mr. Randy Mason, Satellite Manager/Business
Consultant
720 W. Mineral King Ave.
Visalia, CA 93291
559-625-3051
Fax: 559-625-3053
email: wendim@ccsbdc.org
website: http://www.ccsbdc.org

CALIFORNIA BUSINESS INFORMATION CENTERS

The following business Information Centers are available in the San Francisco, Los Angeles, and San Diego areas.

U.S. Small Business Administration
Business Information Center
Attn: Ken Davis
3600 Wilshire Blvd., Suite L100
Los Angeles, CA 90010
213-251-7253 voice
213-251-7255
kendavis@friendlyuser.com

U.S. Small Business Administration
San Diego District Office
Attn: Ron Serafine
550 West C Street, Suite 550
San Diego, CA 92101-3500
619-557-7250 ext. 1126 voice
619-557-5894 fax
ronaldserafine.sba.gov

Business Information Center
Southwestern College
Attn: Ken Clark
900 Otay Lake Road, Bldg. 1600
Chula Vista, CA 91910
619-482-6393 voice
619-482-6402 fax

The Entrepreneur Center
U.S. Small Business Administration
Attn: Kathleen Butler-Tom
455 Market St., 6th floor
San Francisco, CA 94105-2420
415-744-4244 voice
415-744-6812 fax
kathleen.butler.tom@sba.gov

ONE STOP CAPITAL SHOP

The One Stop Capital Shop is a new addition to SBA assistance. These locations will be the most complete of all, and will offer every service in one place. They are being located in *empowerment zones* to help "small disadvantaged businesses." They will enable those who previously had little chance to start a business to receive extensive training as well as links to financing. The following are the One Stop Capital Shops that are available as of this writing.

ONE STOP CAPITAL SHOP
Watts Civic Center
10221 Compton Ave., Suite 103
Los Angeles, CA 90002
Voice:213-473-5111
Contact: Kashif Rasheed

ONE STOP CAPITAL SHOP
Dufwin Towers
519 17th Street
Oakland, CA 94612
Voice: 510-273-6020 Elkin
Fax: 510-238-7999 Elkin
Voice: 510-273-6010 King
Fax: 510-238-6015 King
E-mail: michael.elkin@sba.gov
       rose.king@sba.gov
Facilitator: Michael Elkin
BIC Coordinator: Rose King

MISCELLANEOUS

There are also centers that provide help specifically in the area of exports as well as help to Native Americans and women.

U.S. Export Assistance Center

U.S. Export Assistance Center
One World Trade Center, Suite 1670
Long Beach, CA 90831

General	562/980-4550	
Fax	202/481-2732	
Joseph Sachs	562/980-4557	joseph.sachs@sba.gov
Sandra Edwards	562/980-4559	sandra.edwards@sba.gov
Martin Selander	562/980-4570	martin.selander@sba.gov
Shannon Pezzente	562/980-4550	shannon.pezzente@sba.gov

U.S. Export Assistance Center
101 Park Center Drive, 1001
San Jose, CA 95113

General	408/271-7300	
Fax	408/271-7307	
Ray C. Monahan	408/271-7300 x106	raymond.monahan@sba.gov

California Tribal Business Information Centers (TBIC)

Karuk Community Development Corp.
Attn: Tracy Burcell
63427 Highway 96
Happy Camp CA 96039
(530) 493-5135 Voice
(530) 493-5378 Fax
email: kcdc@sisqtel.net

Tribal Business Information Center
Attn: Emil Fischer
650 N. Tahquitz Canyon Way
Palm Springs CA 92262
(760) 318-0457 Voice
(768) 837-7161 Fax
email: efischer@popnetusa.com

Women's Business Centers

Renaissance Entrepreneurship Center
Janet Lees, Executive Director
275 Fifth Street
Status: Currently Funded Center
San Francisco, CA 94103-4120
Class: 2-Sophomore
Telephone: 415-541-8580
First Year Funding: 1999
Fax: 415-541-8589
Projected Final Funding Year: FY 2003
email: claudia@rencenter.org; janet@rencenter.org

Renaissance comprises a unique, multicultural marketplace of entrepreneurs. Diversity--ethnic, social and economic--is a critical factor of the center's success. This diversity generates energy that fosters networking and results in business income: 60 percent of Renaissance graduates report doing business with one another. A 10-year impact study by the Federal Reserve Board of San Francisco in 1997 revealed that 87 percent of businesses started through this program are still in operation (compared to the national average of 38 percent). Services include an incubator facility, loan packaging and links to credit resources, core business planning, introduction to business, and advanced action-planning classes. Graduates of Renaissance programs receive a one-year free membership to the San Francisco Chamber of Commerce, as well as continuing peer support, mentoring, listings of events and access to a business expo. (This information was taken from: **http://www.rencenter.org/**).

West Company - Fort Bragg Center
Joy Calonico, Project Director
306 East Redwood Avenue, Suite 2
Status: Currently Funded Center/ Graduated
Fort Bragg, CA 95437
Class: 6-Sustainability Center
Telephone: 707-964-7571
First Year Funding: 1990 / 2000
Fax: 707- 964-7576
Projected Final Funding Year: FY 2004
email: westcofb@mcn.org
website: http://www.westcompany.org

West Company - Ukiah Office Center
Joy Calonico, Project Director
367 North State Street, Suite 201
Status: Sustainability /
Currently Funded Center
Ukiah, CA 95482

Class: 6-Sustainability
Telephone: 707-468-3553
First Year Funding: 1990 / 2000
Fax: 707-468-3555
Projected Final Funding Year: FY 2004
email: toni@westcompany.org; joy@westcompany.org
website: http://www.westcompany.org

WEST Company serves micro-enterprise owners in rural Northern California, targeting low-income women and minorities through its centers in Ukiah and Fort Bragg. WEST Company provides business planning and management assistance at every stage of business ownership from feasibility through expansion. Services include business-plan training, individual consulting, access to capital through individual microloans, business-network formation, and assistance with business applications using technology. (This information was taken from: **http:// www.online.wbc.gov/docs/wbcs/CAUKiah.html**).

Women's Enterprise Development Corporation (WEDC) -
Long Beach
Circe Cox, Project Manager
235 East Broadway, Suite 506
Status: Sustainability /
Currently Funded Center
Long Beach, CA 90802
Class: 6-Sustainability
Telephone: 562-983-3747
First Year Funding: 1992 / 2000
Fax: 562-983-3750
Projected Final Funding Year: FY 2004
email: ccox@wedc.org; bbrandon@wedc.org;
wedc1@wedc.org;
wedc1@aol.com
website: http://www.wedc.org

Women's Enterprise Development Corporation/ San
Gabriel Valley Women's Business Center
JinBin Wang Bacon, Project Director
10507 Valley Boulevard, Suite 810
Status: Currently Funded Center
El Monte, CA 91731
Class: 2-Sophomore
Telephone: 626-401-1190
First Year Funding: 1999
Fax: 626-401-1192
Projected Final Funding Year: FY 2003
email: wedc1@wedc.org; wedc1@aol.com
website: http://www.wedc.org

WEDC, previously known as California AWED, began in 1989 with SBA funding to assist the growing number of women business owners in Los Angeles. A 1999 award targets the unique needs of the San Gabriel Valley area of Southern California. The center focuses on serving the fast-growing Latina and Asian populations, providing business training and business assistance in Mandarin, Spanish, and English. Programs and activities include entrepreneurial training at the startup, mid-size and rapid-growth levels; meetings and consultations; procurement and contracting assistance, direct micro-lending assistance and assistance in procuring SBA loans; and entrepreneurship services for youths. In addition to a full-time facility, WEDC uses a "circuit rider" project manager for outreach. (This information was taken from: **http://www.onlinewbc.gov/docs/wbcs/CALongBeach.html**).

Women's Initiative for Self Employment (WI)
Oakland Center
Laura Hoover, Program Director
1611 Telegraph Ave., Suite 702
Status: Sustainability /
Currently Funded Center
Oakland, CA 94612
Class: 6-Sustainability
Telephone: 510-287-9970 x71
First Year Funding: 1993 / 2000
Fax: 510-451-3428
Projected Final Funding Year: FY 2004
email: lhoover@womensinitiative.org
website: http://www.womensinitiative.org

Women's Initiative for Self Employment (WI) - San Francisco Center
Barbara Johnson, Executive Director
1390 Market Street, Suite 113
Status: Graduated Center
San Francisco, CA 94102
Class: Graduate
Telephone: 415-247-9473
First Year Funding: 1993
Fax: 415-247-9471
Projected Final Funding Year: FY N/A
email: bjohnson@womensinitiative.org
website: http://www.womensinitiative.org

Women's Initiative for Self Employment (WI) Spanish Center
Mercedes Sansores, Executive Director
1398 Valencia St.
Status: Graduated Center
San Francisco, CA 94110
Class: Graduate
Telephone: 415-826 5090

First Year Funding: 1993
Fax: 415-826-1885
Projected Final Funding Year: FY N/A
email: msansores@womensinitiative.org
website: http://www.womensinitiative.org

The Women's Initiative provides business training and technical assistance in English and Spanish to low-income women in the San Francisco Bay Area. The English-language program consists of a two-week business assessment workshop, a 14-week business skills workshop and a four-week workshop on writing a business plan. The Spanish language program parallels the English but is in modular format. WI also offers business support services, including one-to-one consultations, peer networking, support groups and special seminars. (This information was taken from: **http://www.womensinitiative.org/**).

Sandy Licata, President
9875 Widmer Road
Status: Currently Funded Center
Lenexa, KS 66215
Class: 1-Freshman
Telephone: 913-492-5922
First Year Funding: 2000
Fax: 913-888-6928
Projected Final Funding Year: FY 2004
Email: licata97@swbell.net; slicata@KansasWBC.com; kcleaver@KansasWBC.com
Web site: www.KansasWBC.com
email: info@womenbiz.org
website: http://www.womenbiz.org

The Women's Business Center, Inc., is a collaborative organization that encourages and supports women in all phases of enterprise development. The center provides access to educational programs, financing alternatives, technical assistance, advocacy and a network of mentors, peer advisors, and business and professional consultants. By encouraging women in their business ventures, WBC fosters economic development. WBC addresses the needs of women business owners through several targeted programs: seminars for women entrepreneurs; a WBC newsletter, monthly peer advisory meetings, "Internet for Small Business" workshops, and "The Entrepreneur's Network." (This information was taken from: **http://www.womenbiz.org/info.html**).

For more information contact either the Office of Women's Business Ownership at 202-205-6673 or the Small Business Administration at 800-8-ASK-SBA.

Choosing and Starting a Form of Business

2

Basic Forms of Doing Business

The four most common forms for a business in California are *sole proprietorship*, *partnership*, *corporation* and *limited partnership*. Laws have been passed in recent years which allowed creation of two new types of enterprises: *limited liability companies*, and *limited liability partnerships*. These offer new benefits for certain kinds of businesses. The characteristics, advantages, and disadvantages of each form are as follows:

SOLE
PROPRIETORSHIP

Characteristics. A proprietorship is one person doing business in his or her own name or under a fictitious name.

Advantages. Simplicity is just one advantage. There is also no organizational expense, and no extra tax forms or reports. Since there is only one owner, there is complete control. Taxes are personal rather than corporate, so there is no double taxation.

Disadvantages. The proprietor is personally liable for all debts and obligations. There is also no continuation of the business after death. Business affairs are easily mixed with personal affairs. The blessing of complete control comes with the burden of making all decisions and needing all the skills necessary to run a business—including raising money.

GENERAL PARTNERSHIP

Characteristics. This involves two or more people carrying on a business together and sharing the profits and losses.

Advantages. Partners can combine expertise and assets. A general partnership allows liability to be spread among more persons. Also, the business can be continued after the death of a partner if bought out by a surviving partner.

Disadvantages. Each partner is liable for acts of other partners within the scope of the business. This means that if your partner harms a customer or signs a million-dollar credit line in the partnership name, you can be personally liable. Even if left in the business, all profits are taxable. There are two more disadvantages: all parties share control, and the death of a partner may result in liquidation. In a general partnership, it is often hard to get rid of a bad partner.

CORPORATION

Characteristics. A corporation is an artificial legal "person" which carries on business through its directors and officers for its shareholders. This legal person carries on business in its own name and shareholders are not personally liable for its acts. The California Corporations Code (Cal. Corp. Code) embodies the law necessary to form and operate a corporation in California.

An *S corporation* is a corporation that has filed Internal Revenue Service (IRS) Form 2553 choosing to have all profits taxed to the shareholders, rather than to the corporation. An S corporation files a tax return but pays no federal or state tax. The profit shown on the S corporation tax return is reported on the owners' tax returns.

A C *corporation* is any corporation that has not elected to be taxed as an S corporation. A C corporation pays income tax on its profits. The effect of this is that when dividends are paid to shareholders they are taxed twice–once as corporate tax and once as a tax on shareholders.

A *professional corporation* is a corporation formed by a professional such as a doctor or accountant. California has special rules for professional corporations that differ slightly from those of other corporations. These rules are included in California Corporations Code, Sections 13400-13410. There are also special tax rules for professional corporations.

A *nonprofit corporation* is usually used for organizations such as churches and condominium associations. However, with careful planning, some types of businesses can be set up as nonprofit corporations and can save in taxes. While a nonprofit corporation cannot pay dividends, it can pay its officers and employees fair salaries. Some of the major American nonprofit organizations pay their officers well over $100,000 a year. California's special rules for nonprofit corporations are included in several different sections of the Corporations Code, organized by the type of corporation, such as religious, charitable, medical or legal.

Advantages. If properly organized, shareholders have no personal liability for corporate debts and lawsuits; and officers usually have no personal liability for their corporate acts. The existence of a corporation may be perpetual. There are tax advantages allowed only to corporations. There is prestige in owning a corporation. Two other excellent advantages are: capital may be raised by issuing stock, and it is easy to transfer ownership upon death. A small corporation can be set up as an S corporation to avoid corporate taxes but still retain corporate advantages. Some types of businesses can be set up as nonprofit corporations which provide significant tax savings.

Note: A corporation theoretically allows shareholders to avoid personal liability for borrowed money. As a practical matter, you may be asked to personally guarantee (make yourself liable for) loans, leases, inventory and equipment purchased on credit, or other obligations of the corporation. Only when your corporation has sufficient assets to satisfy creditors will you be able to use only your corporate identity.

Disadvantages. The start-up costs for forming a corporation are certainly a disadvantage; plus there are certain formalities such as annual meetings, separate bank accounts and tax forms. Unless a corporation registers as an S corporation, it must pay federal income tax separate from the tax paid by the owners, and it must pay California income tax as set forth in the California

Revenue and Taxation Code, (Cal. Rev. and Tax. Code), Sections 23151-23155. Over the years, there have occasionally been proposals to tax S corporations with an exemption for small operations, but none of these have passed the legislature.

LIMITED
PARTNERSHIP

Characteristics. A limited partnership has characteristics similar to both a corporation and a partnership. There are *general partners* who have the control and personal liability, and there are *limited partners* who only put up money and whose liability is limited to what they paid for their share of the partnership (like corporate stock).

Advantages. Capital can be contributed by limited partners who have no control of the business or liability for its debts.

Disadvantages. A great disadvantage is high start-up costs. Also, an extensive partnership agreement is required because general partners are personally liable for partnership debts and for the acts of each other. (One solution to this problem is to use a corporation as the general partner.) Limited partnerships may be found in the Corporate Code under the Uniform Limited Partnership Act, beginning with Section 15501, and the California Revised Limited Partnership Act, beginning with Section 15611.

Note: A limited partnership is not a good way to structure your new business if you want to avoid personal liability. The reason is that the limited liability protection is lost if you take an active role in managing the business. You probably don't want to start your business by turning over control to someone else.

LIMITED
LIABILITY
COMPANY

Characteristics. A limited liability company (or LLC) is like a limited partnership without general partners. The owners are called *members.* An LLC has characteristics of both a corporation and a partnership. An LLC may be treated as either a partnership or a corporation for both federal and California tax purposes. For California tax purposes, it will be treated as a partnership if it lacks two or more of the following corporate characteristics:

☛ Limited liability of members

☛ Continuity of life (it continues with a change in owners)

☛ Free transferability of interests

☛ Centralized management

It may be taxed as a corporation if it possesses more than two of these corporate characteristics.

Certain professions are prohibited from forming limited liability companies. For forms and more information, contact the Secretary of State, Limited Liability Companies, at 916-653-3794. General provisions governing LLCs are found in California Corporations Code, commencing with Section 17000. For information about taxation of LLCs, see California Revenue and Taxation Code, Sections 17941-17946.

Advantages. The LLC offers the members the limited liability of corporate shareholders, and the tax advantages of a partnership. It offers more tax benefits and flexibility than an S corporation because it may pass through more depreciation and deductions. It may have different classes of ownership, an unlimited number of members, and aliens as members. If it owns appreciated property, it has more favorable tax treatment upon dissolution than an S corporation. The LLC is also extremely flexible in structure and operational aspects, since those are not dictated strictly by statute as they are for corporations, without the restrictions applicable to limited partnerships and S corporations.

Disadvantages. There are higher start-up costs than for a corporation. Because of the flexibility in structural and operational aspects, the governing documents are more complex. The LLC is a relatively new type of business entity. Therefore the law governing them is not as well established as for partnerships and corporations.

LIMITED
LIABILITY
PARTNERSHIP

Characteristics. The limited liability partnership (or LLP) is a specialized type of partnership for accountants, attorneys, and architects. It is like a general partnership, but with limited liability. The LLP was devised to allow partnerships of these professionals to limit their personal liability without losing the tax advantages of the partnership structure. However, the law does not allow these professionals to limit their liability for negligence in their professional function (i.e., for malpractice).

Advantages. The LLP offers the flexibility and tax benefits of a partnership, with the protection from liability of a corporation.

Disadvantages. Start-up and annual fees are higher than for a corporation. Other disadvantages are the same as for the LLC.

START-UP PROCEDURES

SOLE PROPRIETORSHIP

In a sole proprietorship, all accounts, property, and licenses are taken in the name of the owner. See chapter 3 for using a fictitious name.

PARTNERSHIP

To form a partnership, a written agreement should be prepared to spell out rights and obligations of the parties. It may be registered with the Secretary of State, but this is not required. If you do register, the filing fee is $70.

CORPORATION

To form any corporation, *articles of incorporation* must be filed with the Secretary of State in Sacramento along with $100 in filing fees and $300-$800 in pre-paid taxes. For further instructions, you may contact the main office at 1500 11th Street, Sacramento, CA 95814 or by calling 916-657-5448. You may also contact one of the branch offices listed below. An organizational meeting is then held. At the meeting, officers are elected, stock issued and other formalities are complied with in order to avoid the corporate entity being set aside later. Licenses and accounts are titled in the name of the corporation.

LIMITED PARTNERSHIP

A written limited partnership agreement must be registered with the Secretary of State in Sacramento. The form used is relatively simple to fill out (instructions come with it), but the law governing the duties of the partnership and the rights of the limited partners is complex. If you wish to use this form of business, start with a lawyer and accountant.

LIMITED LIABILITY COMPANY

Two or more persons or business entities may form a limited liability company by filing articles of organization with the Secretary of State in Sacramento and paying the $70 filing fee. Licenses and accounts are in the name of the company, and the members must enter into an operating agreement after filing the articles of organization. (Corp. Code, Section 17050.) You would be wise to contact an attorney or accountant to assist you with this form of business.

LIMITED LIABILITY PARTNERSHIP

Two or more persons may form a *limited liability partnership* by filing a registration with the Secretary of State in Sacramento and paying the $70 filing fee. A registration contains the following: 1) the name of the partnership; 2) the address of its principal office; 3) the name and address of the agent for service of process on the limited liability partnership in California; 4) a brief statement of the business in which the partnership engages; 5) any other matters that the partnership determines to include; 6) that the partnership is registering as a registered limited liability partnership. Licenses and accounts are in the name of the company. (Cal. Corp. Code, beginning with Section 16951.)

As stated earlier, this form of business is limited to accountants, attorneys, and architects in California. This is a relatively new form of business in California, so do not try to start one without a lawyer and an accountant. (Cal. Corp. Code, beginning with Section 16951.)

BUSINESS START-UP CHECKLIST

❏ Make your plan
   ❏ Obtain and read all relevant publications on your type of business
   ❏ Obtain and read all laws and regulations affecting your business
   ❏ Calculate whether your plan will produce a profit
   ❏ Plan your sources of capital
   ❏ Plan your sources of goods or services
   ❏ Plan your marketing efforts
❏ Choose your business name
   ❏ Check other business names and trademarks
   ❏ Register your name, trademark, etc.
❏ Choose the business form
   ❏ Prepare and file organizational papers
   ❏ Prepare and file fictitious name if necessary
❏ Choose the location
   ❏ Check competitors
   ❏ Check zoning
❏ Obtain necessary licenses
   ❏ City?   ❏ State?
   ❏ County?   ❏ Federal?
❏ Choose a bank
   ❏ Checking
   ❏ Credit card processing
   ❏ Loans
❏ Obtain necessary insurance
   ❏ Worker's Comp   ❏ Automobile
   ❏ Liability   ❏ Health
   ❏ Hazard   ❏ Life/disability
❏ File necessary federal tax registrations
❏ File necessary state tax registrations
❏ Set up a bookkeeping system
❏ Plan your hiring
   ❏ Obtain required posters
   ❏ Obtain or prepare employment application
   ❏ Obtain new hire tax forms
   ❏ Prepare employment policies
   ❏ Determine compliance with health and safety laws
❏ Plan your opening
   ❏ Obtain all necessary equipment and supplies
   ❏ Obtain all necessary inventory
   ❏ Do all necessary marketing and publicity
   ❏ Obtain all necessary forms and agreements
   ❏ Prepare your company policies on refunds, exchanges, returns

Business Comparison Chart

	Sole Proprietorship	General Partnership	Limited Partnership	Limited Liability Co.	Corporation C or S	Nonprofit Corporation
Liability Protection	No	No	For limited partners	For all members	For all shareholders	For all members
Taxes	Pass through	Pass through	Pass through	Pass through	S corps. pass through C corps. pay tax	None on income—Employees pay on wages
Minimum # of members	1	2	2	1	1	3
Startup fee	None	$100	$125	$285	$145	$75
Annual fee	None	None	None	None	None	None
Diff. classes of ownership	No	Yes	Yes	Yes	S corps. No C corps. Yes	No ownership Diff. classes of membership
Survives after Death	No	No	Yes	Yes	Yes	Yes
Best for	1 person low-risk business or no assets	low-risk business	low-risk business with silent partners	All types of businesses	All types of businesses	Educational

YOUR BUSINESS NAME 3

PRELIMINARY CONSIDERATIONS

Before deciding upon a name for your business, you should be sure that it is not already being used by someone else. Many business owners have spent thousands of dollars on publicity and printing, only to throw it all away because another company owned the name. A company that owns a name can take you to court and force you to stop using that name. It can also sue you for damages if it thinks your use of the name cost it a financial loss.

If you will be running a small local shop with no plans for expansion, you should at least check out whether the name has been trademarked. If someone else is using the same name anywhere in the country and has registered it as a federal trademark, they can sue you. If you plan to expand or to deal nationally, then you should do a thorough search of the name.

The first places to look are the local phone books and official records of your county. Next, you should check with the Secretary of State's office in Sacramento to see if someone has registered a corporate name the same as, or confusingly similar to, the one you have chosen. This can be done by calling the Name Availability Unit at 916-654-7960.

To do a national search, you should check trade directories and phone books of major cities. These can be found at many libraries and are usually reference books which cannot be checked out. The *Trade Names Directory* is a two volume set of names compiled from many sources, published by Gale Research Co.

If you have a computer with Internet access, you can use it to search all of the yellow page listings in the U.S. at a number of sites at no charge. One website, **http://www.infoseek.com**, offers free searches of yellow pages for all states at once.

To be sure that your use of the name does not violate someone else's trademark rights you should have a trademark search done of the mark in the United States Patent and Trademark Office (USPTO). In the past, this required a visit to their offices or the hiring of a search firm. But in 1999, the USPTO put its trademark records online and you can now search them at: **http://www.uspto.gov/tmdb/index.html**. If you do not have access to the internet you might be able to search at a public library or to have a library employee order an online search for you for a small fee. If this is not available to you, you can have the search done through a firm. One such firm is Government Liaison Services, Inc., P. O. Box 10648, Arlington, VA 22210. Tel. 703-524-8200. They also offer searches of 100 trade directories and 4,800 phone books.

No matter how thorough your search is, there is no guarantee that there is not a local user somewhere with rights to the mark. If, for example, you register a name for a new chain of restaurants and later find out that someone in Tucumcari, New Mexico has been using the name longer than you, that person will still have the right to use the name, just in his local area. If you do not want his restaurant to cause confusion with your chain, you can try to buy him out. Similarly, if you are operating a small business under a unique name, and a law firm in New York writes and offers to buy the right to your name, you can assume that some large corporation wants to start a major expansion under that name.

The best way to make sure a name you are using is not already owned by someone else is to make up a name. Names such as Xerox, Kodak and Exxon were made up and didn't have any meaning prior to their use. Remember that there are millions of businesses and even something you make up may already be in use. Do a search anyway.

FICTITIOUS NAMES

In California, as in most states, unless you do business in your own legal name, you must register the name you are using as a *fictitious name*. You must also register if you are using your own name, but in some manner imply that others may also be involved in your business. For example, if your name is *John Doe* and you are operating your own plumbing business, you may operate your business as *John Doe, Plumber*, without registering. But any other name would have to be registered, such as:

Doe Plumbing   *John Doe Plumbing*
John Doe and Associates   *West Coast Plumbing*
John the Plumber   *Plumber John*

Even if your business is a corporation, you must register if you are using a name that is different from your corporate name. For example, if your corporation is *XYZ, Inc.*, but is conducting business under the name *California Pizza Station*, registration would be required.

There are also certain words and abbreviations that you may not use. Unless your business is incorporated, you cannot use the words "corporation" or "incorporated," nor the abbreviations "corp." or "inc." Similarly, unless your business is a limited liability company, you cannot use the words "limited liability company," nor the abbreviations "Ltd.," "Co.," "LLC," or "LC." (California Business and Professional Code (Cal. Bus. and Prof. Code), Section 17910.5.)

The California Business and Professional Code contains the requirements for registering a fictitious name, which is done by obtaining and filing a Fictitious Business Name Statement with the clerk of the county in which you have your principal place of business. This must be done within forty days after you begin doing business. A registration is good for five years, and must be renewed by filing a new Fictitious Business Name Statement before the current one expires.

Within thirty days of filing, you must publish your Fictitious Business Name Statement for four weeks in a row in a local newspaper. Each of the four publications must be at least five days apart, not counting the day of publication. A sample completed Fictitious Business Name Statement may be found on page 36. A blank form with instructions may be found in the appendix. (see form 2, p.231.) Be sure to check with your county court clerk before filing to ensure you have the proper form.

CORPORATE NAMES

A corporation does not have to register a fictitious name because it already has a legal name. When filing a corporate name, you must use the words "incorporated," "corporation," or their abbreviations. (Cal. Corp. Code, Section 202(a).) For example:

| Incorporated | Inc. |
| Corporation | Corp. |

If the name of the corporation does not contain one of the above words or abbreviations, it will be rejected by the Secretary of State. It will also be rejected if the name is already taken by, or is similar to, the name of another corporation; or if it uses a forbidden word such as "Bank" or "Trust." To check on a name, you may call the corporate name information number in Sacramento. Keep trying; they are often busy. You can also check their website:

http://www.ss.ca.gov/

If a name you pick is taken by another company, you may be able to change it slightly and have it accepted. For example, if there is already a *Tri-City Upholstery, Inc.*, and it is in a different county, you may be allowed to use *Tri-City Upholstery of Kern County, Inc.* However, even if this is approved by the Secretary of State, you might still get sued by the other company if your business is close to theirs or there is a likelihood of consumer confusion.

Also, do not have anything printed until your corporate papers are returned to you. Sometimes a name is approved over the phone, but rejected when submitted. Once you have chosen a corporate name and know it is available, you should immediately register the name.

PROFESSIONAL CORPORATIONS

Professionals such as doctors can form a corporation in which to practice. The law covering these corporations is found in the California Corporations Code, Section 13400; as well as Sections 200 through 202, which cover the minimum requirements for stock operations.

DOMAIN NAMES

With the Internet being so new and changing so rapidly, all of the rules for Internet names have not yet been worked out. Originally, the first person to reserve a name owned it, and enterprising souls bought up the names of most of the Fortune 500 corporations. Then a few of the corporations went to court and the rule was developed that if a company had a trademark for a name, that company could stop someone else from using it if the other person did not have a trademark.

You cannot yet get a trademark merely for using a domain name. Trademarks are granted for the use of a name in commerce. Once you have a valid trademark, you will be safe using it for your domain name.

In the next few years there will probably be several changes to the domain name system to make it more flexible and useful throughout the world. One proposed change is the addition of more *top level domains* (TLDs) which are the last parts of the names, like *com* and *gov*. Some of the suggested additions are *firm, store, web, arts, rec, nom,* and *info*. This should free up a lot of names.

If you wish to protect your domain name, the best thing to do at this point is to get a trademark for it. To do this, you would have to use it on your goods or services. The following section gives some basic information about trademarks. To find out if a domain name is available, go to **http://rs.internic.net**. More information on the Internet is included in Chapter 9 of this book.

TRADEMARKS

As your business builds goodwill, its name will become more valuable and you will want to protect it from others who may wish to copy it. To protect a name used to describe your goods or services, you can register it as a trademark (for goods) or a service mark (for services) with either the Secretary of State of the state of California or with the United States Patent and Trademark Office.

You cannot obtain a trademark for the name of your business, but you can trademark the name you use on your goods and services. In most cases, you use your company name on your goods as your trademark. In effect, it protects your company name. Another way to protect your company name is to incorporate. A particular corporate name can only be registered by one company in California.

STATE REGISTRATION

State registration would be useful if you only expect to use your trademark within the state of California. Federal registration would protect your mark anywhere in the country. The registration of a mark gives you exclusive use of the mark for the types of goods for which you register it. The only exception is persons who have already been using the mark. You cannot stop people who have been using the mark prior to your registration.

The procedure for state registration is simple and the filing fee is $70. Before a mark can be registered, it must be used in California. For goods, this means it must be used on the goods themselves, or on containers, tags, labels, or displays of the goods. For services, it must be used in the sale or advertising of the services. The use must be in an actual transaction with a customer. A sample mailed to a friend is not an acceptable use.

The $70 fee will register the mark in only one "class of goods." If the mark is used on more than one class of goods, a separate registration must be filed. The registration is good for ten years. Six months prior to its expiration, it must be renewed. The renewal fee is $30 for each class of goods. The Secretary of State provides the registration form with instructions.

FEDERAL
REGISTRATION

For federal registration the procedure is a little more complicated. There are two types of applications depending upon whether you have already made actual use of the mark or whether you merely have an intention to use the mark in the future. For a trademark which has been in use, you must file an application form along with specimens showing actual use, and a drawing of the mark which complies with all of the rules of the United States Patent and Trademark Office. For an *intent to use* application you must file two separate forms—one when you make the initial application, and the other after you have made actual use of the mark—as well as the specimens and drawing. Before a mark can be entitled to federal registration, the use of the mark must be in *interstate commerce* or in commerce with another country. The fee for registration is $245, but if you file an *intent to use* application, there is a second fee of $100 for the filing after actual use.

You can also register on the Internet at: **http://www.uspto.gov**. Click on all choices relating to Trademark registration, until you get to the application. A sample filled-in online application can be found at the end of this chapter on pages 37-38. For a blank worksheet of this same application, go to the appendix. (see form 3, p.233.)For explanation of the entire federal trademark registration procedure and the necessary application forms, see the references at the end of this book.

FICTITIOUS BUSINESS NAME STATEMENT

The following person (persons) is (are) doing business as

* __Joe's Diner__

at ** __1234 Main St. Anytown, CA 90000__ :

*** _____

_____

_____

_____

This business is conducted by **** __Joseph Frycook__

The registrant commenced to transact business under the fictitious business name or names listed above on ***** __1/1/01__

Signed   *Joseph Frycook*

Statement filed with the County Clerk of _____ Any _____ County on _____ 1/1/01 _____

NOTICE

THIS FICTITIOUS BUSINESS NAME STATEMENT EXPIRES FIVE YEARS FROM THE DATE IT WAS FILED IN THE OFFICE OF THE COUNTY CLERK. A NEW FICTITIOUS BUSINESS NAME STATEMENT MUST BE FILED BEFORE THAT TIME. THE FILING OF THIS STATEMENT DOES NOT OF ITSELF AUTHORIZE THE USE IN THIS STATE OF A FICTITIOUS BUSINESS NAME IN VIOLATION OF THE RIGHTS OF ANOTHER UNDER FEDERAL, STATE, OR COMMON LAW (SEE SECTION 14400 ET SEQ., BUSINESS AND PROFESSIONAL CODE).

Applicant Information

* Name	Rex Retailer

Entity Type: Click on the one appropriate circle to indicate the applicant's entity type and enter the corresponding information.

◉ Individual	Country of Citizenship	USA
○ Corporation	State or Country of Incorporation	
○ Partnership	State or Country Where Organized	
	Name and Citizenship of all General Partners	▲ ▼
○ Other	Specify Entity Type	▲ ▼
	State or Country Where Organized	
* Address	* Street Address	123 Main St. ▲ ▼
	* City	Anytown
	State	California ▼ If not listed above, please select 'OTHER' and specify here:
	* Country	USA ▼ If not listed above, please select 'OTHER' and specify here:
	Zip/Postal Code	
Phone Number	(123) 555-5555	
Fax Number	(123) 555-0000	
Internet E-Mail Address	www.rex.com ☒ Check here to authorize the USPTO to communicate with the applicant or its representative via e-mail. NOTE: While the application may list an e-mail address for the applicant, applicant's attorney, and/or applicant's domestic representative, only one e-mail address may be used for correspondence, in accordance with Office policy. The applicant must keep this address current in the Office's records.	

(pages 37-39 reproduced from http://www.uspto.gov. For a clear interface, go to this website and click all choices pertaining to Trademarks.)

Mark Information

Before the USPTO can register your mark, we must know exactly what it is. You can display a mark in one of two formats:

(1) typed; or (2) stylized or design. When you click on one of the two circles below, and follow the relevant instructions, the program will create a separate page that displays your mark once you validate the application (using the Validate Form button at the end of this form). You must print out and submit this separate page with the application form (even if you have listed the "mark" in the body of the application). If you have a stylized mark or design, but either you do NOT have a GIF or JPG image file or your browser does not permit this function, check the box to indicate you do NOT have the image in a GIF or JPG image file (and then see the special help instructions).

WARNING: AFTER SEARCHING THE USPTO DATABASE, EVEN IF YOU THINK THE RESULTS ARE "O.K.," DO NOT ASSUME THAT YOUR MARK CAN BE REGISTERED AT THE USPTO. AFTER YOU FILE AN APPLICATION, THE USPTO MUST DO ITS OWN SEARCH AND OTHER REVIEW, AND MIGHT REFUSE TO REGISTER YOUR MARK.

* Mark	● Typed Format	Click on this circle if you wish to register a word(s), letter(s), and/or number(s) in a format that can be reproduced using a typewriter. Also, only the following common punctuation marks and symbols are acceptable in a typed drawing (any other symbol, including a <u>foreign diacritical mark</u>, requires a stylized format): . ? " - ; ( ) % $ @ + , ! ' : / & # * = [ ] Enter the mark here: NOTE: The mark must be entered in ALL upper case letters, regardless of how you actually use the mark. E.g., MONEYWISE, not MoneyWise. MONEYWISE
	○ Stylized or Design Format	Click on this circle if you wish to register a stylized word(s), letter(s), number(s), and/or a design. Click on the 'Browse' button to select GIF or JPG image file from your local drive. ☐ Check this box if you do NOT have the image in a GIF or JPG image file, and click here for further instructions. For a stylized word(s) or letter(s), or a design that also includes a word(s), enter the LITERAL element only of the mark here:

BASIS FOR FILING AND GOODS AND/OR SERVICES INFORMATION

✔	Section 1(b). Intent to Use: Applicant has a bona fide intention to use or use through a related company the mark in commerce on or in connection with the goods and/or services identified below (15 U.S.C. §1051(b)).	
	International Class	If known, enter class number 001 - 042, A, B, or 200
	* Listing of Goods and/or Services	Financial Services

38

Fee Information

Number of Classes Paid   [1 ▼]

Note: The total fee is computed based on the Number of
Classes in which the goods and/or services associated with the $ [325] **= Number of Classes Paid x $325 (per class)**
mark are classified.

* Amount $ [325]

Declaration

The undersigned, being hereby warned that willful false statements and the like so made are punishable by fine or imprisonment, or both, under 18 U.S.C. §1001, and that such willful false statements may jeopardize the validity of the application or any resulting registration, declares that he/she is properly authorized to execute this application on behalf of the applicant; he/she believes the applicant to be the owner of the trademark/service mark sought to be registered, or, if the application is being filed under 15 U.S.C. §1051(b), he/she believes applicant to be entitled to use such mark in commerce; to the best of his/her knowledge and belief no other person, firm, corporation, or association has the right to use the mark in commerce, either in the identical form thereof or in such near resemblance thereto as to be likely, when used on or in connection with the goods/services of such other person, to cause confusion, or to cause mistake, or to deceive; and that all statements made of his/her own knowledge are true; and that all statements made on information and belief are believed to be true.

Signature   _____   Date Signed   _____

Signatory's Name   Rex Retailer

Signatory's Position   owner

Click on the desired action:

The "Validate Form" function allows you to run an automated check to ensure that all mandatory fields have been completed. You will receive an "error" message if you have not filled in one of the five (5) fields that are considered "minimum filing requirements" under the Trademark Law Treaty Implementation Act of 1998. For other fields that the USPTO believes are important, but not mandatory, you will receive a "warning" message if the field is left blank. This warning is a courtesy, if non-completion was merely an oversight. If you so choose, you may by-pass that "warning" message and validate the form (however, you cannot by-pass an "error" message).

[Validate Form]   [Reset Form]

Note: To print the completed application AND the separate sheet showing the representation of the mark, click on the Validate Form button, and follow the steps on the Validation Screen.

FINANCING YOUR BUSINESS 4

The way to finance your business is determined by how fast you want your business to grow and how much risk of failure you are able to handle. Letting the business grow with its own income is the slowest but safest way to grow. Taking out a personal loan against your house to expand quickly is the fastest but riskiest way to grow.

GROWING WITH PROFITS

Many successful businesses have started out with little money and used the profits to grow bigger and bigger. If you have another source of income to live on (such as a job or a spouse) you can plow all the income of your fledgling business into growth.

Some businesses start as hobbies or part time ventures on the weekend while the entrepreneur holds down a full time job. Many types of goods or service businesses can start this way. Even some multi-million dollar corporations, such as Apple Computer, started out this way.

This allows you to test your idea with little risk. If you find you're not good at running that type of business, or the time or location wasn't right for your idea, all you are out is the time you spent and your start-up capital.

However, a business can only grow so big from its own income. In many cases, as a business grows, it gets to a point where the orders are so big that money must be borrowed to produce the product to fill them. With this kind of order, there is the risk that if the customer cannot pay or goes bankrupt, the business will also go under. At such a point, a business owner should investigate the credit worthiness of the customer and weigh the risks. Some businesses have grown rapidly, some have gone under, and others have decided not to take the risk and stayed small. You can worry about that down the road.

Using Your Savings

If you have savings you can tap to get your business started, that is the best source. You won't have to pay high interest rates and you will not have to worry about reimbursing someone, such as relatives.

Home Equity
If you have owned your home for several years, it is possible that the equity has grown substantially and you can get a second mortgage to finance your business. If you have been in the home for many years and have a good record of paying your bills, some lenders will make second mortgages that exceed the equity. Just remember, if your business fails, you may lose your house.

Retirement Accounts
Be careful about borrowing from your retirement savings. There are tax penalties for borrowing from or against certain types of retirement accounts. Also, your future financial security may be lost if your business doesn't succeed.

Having Too Much Money
It probably does not seem possible to have too much money with which to start a business, but many businesses have failed for that reason. With plenty of start-up capital available, a business owner does not need to watch expenses and can become wasteful. Employees get used to lavish spending. Once the money runs out and the business must run on its own earnings, it fails.

Starting with the bare minimum forces a business to watch its expenses and be frugal. It necessitates finding the least expensive solutions to problems and creative ways to be productive.

BORROWING MONEY

It is extremely tempting to look to others to get the money to start a business. The risk of failure is less worrisome and the pressure is lower, but that is a problem with borrowing. If it is others' money, you do not have quite the same incentive to succeed as if everything you own is on the line.

Actually, you should be even more concerned when using the money of others. Your reputation should be more valuable than the money itself, which can always be replaced. Yet, that is not always the case. How many people borrow again and again from their parents for failed business ventures?

FAMILY   Depending on how much money your family can spare, it may be the most comfortable or most uncomfortable source of funds for you. If you have been assured a large inheritance, and your parents have more funds than they need to live on, you may be able to borrow against your inheritance without worry. It will be your money anyway and you need it much more now than you will ten, twenty, or more years from now. If you lose it all, it is your own loss.

However, if you are borrowing your widowed mother's source of income, asking her to cash in a CD she lives on to finance your get-rich-quick scheme, you should have second thoughts about it. Stop and consider all the real reasons your business might not take off and what your mother would do without the income.

FRIENDS   Borrowing from friends is like borrowing from family members. If you know they have the funds available and could survive a loss, you may want to risk it, but if they would be loaning you their only resources, do not chance it.

Financial problems can be the worst thing for a relationship, whether it is a casual friendship or a long term romantic involvement. Before you borrow from a friend, try to imagine what would happen if you could not pay it back, and how you would feel if it caused the end of your relationship.

The ideal situation is if your friend were a co-venturer in your business and the burden would not be totally on you to see how the funds were spent. Still, realize that such a venture will put extra strain on the relationship.

BANKS   In a way, a bank can be a more comfortable party from which to borrow because you do not have a personal relationship with them as you do with a friend or family member. If you fail, they will write your loan off rather than disown you. But a bank can also be the least comfortable party to borrow from because they will demand realistic projections and be on top of you to perform. If you do not meet their expectations, they may call in your loan just when you need it most.

The best thing about a bank loan is that they will require you to do your homework; you must have plans that make sense to a banker. If they approve your loan, you know that your plans are at least reasonable.

Bank loans are not cheap or easy. You will be paying a good interest rate, and you will have to put up collateral. If your business does not have equipment or receivables, they may require you to put up your house and other personal property to guarantee the loan.

Banks are a little easier to deal with when you get a Small Business Administration (SBA) loan. That is because the SBA guarantees that it will pay the bank if you default on the loan. SBA loans are obtained through local bank branches.

CREDIT CARDS   Borrowing against a credit card is one of the fastest growing ways of financing a business, but it can be one of the most expensive ways. The rates can go higher than twenty percent. Many cards, however, offer lower rates and some people are able to get numerous cards. Some successful businesses have used the partners' credit cards to get off the ground or to weather through a cash crunch, but if the business does not begin to generate the cash to make the payments, you could soon end up in bankruptcy. A good strategy is only to use credit cards for a long term asset like a computer or for something that will quickly generate cash, like buying inventory to fill an order. Do not use credit cards to pay expenses that are not generating revenue.

A RICH PARTNER

One of the best business combinations is a young entrepreneur with ideas and ambition and a retired investor with business experience and money. Together they can supply everything the business needs.

How do you find such a partner? Be creative. You should have investigated the business you are starting and know others who have been in such businesses. Have any of them had partners retire over the last few years? Are any of them planning to phase out of the business?

SELLING SHARES OF YOUR BUSINESS

Silent investors are the best source of capital for your business. You retain full control of the business and if it happens to fail, you have no obligation to them. Unfortunately, few silent investors are interested in a new business. It is only after you have proven your concept to be successful and built up a rather large enterprise, that you will be able to attract such investors.

The most common way to obtain money from investors is to issue stock to them. For this, the best type of business entity is the corporation. It gives you almost unlimited flexibility in the number and kinds of shares of stock you can issue.

The easiest way to find companies offering *venture capital*, the money at risk for starting a business that replaces or supplements the other business capital, is on the Internet. Type in "California venture capital" (don't forget the quotation marks) in a search engine, and you will find more than you need.

An additional source is **http://www.vfinance.com/calaw/htm**. This will lead you to a list of California law firms and accounting firms handling venture capital as well as where to find the money, business plans, and lots of other helpful information.

SECURITIES LAWS

There is one major problem with selling stock in your business, and that is all of the federal and state regulations with which you must comply. Both the state and federal governments have long and complicated laws dealing with the sales of *securities*. There are also hundreds of court cases attempting to explain what these laws mean. A thorough explanation of this area of law is obviously beyond the scope of this book.

Basically, securities have been held to exist in any case in which a person provides money to someone with the expectation that he will get a profit through the efforts of that person. This can apply to any situation where someone buys stock in, or makes a loan to your business. What the laws require is disclosure of the risks involved, and in some cases, registration of the securities with the government. There are some exemptions, such as for small amounts of money and for limited numbers of investors.

Penalties for violation of securities laws are severe, including triple damages and prison terms. You should consult a specialist in securities laws before issuing any security. You can often get an introductory consultation at a reasonable rate to learn your options.

For more information on securities laws, see the references at the end of this book.

USING THE INTERNET TO FIND CAPITAL

In 1995, the owners of Wit Beer made headlines in all the business magazines by successfully raising $1.6 million for their business on the Internet. It seemed so easy that every business wanted to try. What was not made clear in most of the stories was that the owner was a corporate securities lawyer and that he did all of the necessary legal work to prepare a prospectus and properly register the stock, something which would have cost anyone else over $100,000 in legal fees. Also, most of the interest in the stock came from the articles, not from the Internet promotion. Today, a similar effort would probably not be nearly as successful.

Before attempting to market your company's shares on the Internet, be sure to get an opinion from a securities lawyer or do some serious research into securities laws. The lawyer who marketed Wit Beer's shares on the Internet has started a business to advise others on raising capital. It is Wit Capital located at 826 Broadway, 6th Floor, New York, NY 10003.

The Internet does have many sources of capital listed. The following sites may be helpful:

http://www.businessfinance.com

http://www.sba.gov

http://www.nvst.com

LOCATING YOUR BUSINESS 5

The right location for your business will be determined by what type of business it is, and how fast you expect to grow. For some types of businesses, the location will not be important to your success or failure; in others it will be crucial.

WORKING OUT OF YOUR HOME

Many small businesses get started out of the home. Chapter 6 discusses the legalities of home businesses. This section discusses the practicalities.

Starting a business out of your home can save you the rent, electricity, insurance, and other costs of setting up at another location. For some people this is ideal, and they can combine their home and work duties easily and efficiently. For other people it is a disaster. A spouse, children, neighbors, television, and household chores can be so distracting that no other work gets done.

Since residential rates are usually lower than business lines, many people use their residential telephone line to conduct business, or they add a second residential line. However, if you wish to be listed in the yellow pages, you will need to have a business line in your home. If you are running two or more types of businesses, you can probably add their names as additional listings on the original number and avoid paying for another business line.

You should also consider whether the type of business you are starting is compatible with a home office. For example, if your business mostly consists of making phone calls or calling clients, then the home may be an ideal place to run it. If your clients need to visit you or you will need daily pickups and deliveries by truck, then the home may not be a good location. This is discussed in more detail in the next chapter.

If you need to do credit checks, contact your local credit bureau. They may have extra charges for home businesses to run credit reports.

CHOOSING A RETAIL SITE

For most types of retail stores the location is of prime importance. Such things to consider are how close it is to your potential customers, how visible it is to the public, and how easily accessible it is to both autos and pedestrians. You should also consider attractiveness and safety.

Location would be less important for a business that was the only one of its kind in the area. For example, if there was only one moped parts dealer, or Armenian restaurant in a metropolitan area, people would have to come to wherever you are if they want your products or services. However, even with such businesses, keep in mind that there is competition. People who want moped parts can order them by mail and restaurant customers can choose another type of cuisine.

You should look up all the businesses like the one you plan to open in the phone book and mark them on a map. For some businesses, like a cleaners, you would want to be far from the others. But for other businesses, like antique stores, you would want to be near the others. (Antique stores usually do not carry the same things, they do not compete, and people like to go to an "antique district" to visit all the shops.)

CHOOSING OFFICE, MANUFACTURING, OR WAREHOUSE SPACE

If your business will be the type where customers will not come to you, then locating it near customers is not as much of a concern and you can probably save money by locating away from the high-traffic, central business districts. However, you should consider the convenience for employees and not locate in an area that would be unattractive to them, or too far from where they would likely live.

For manufacturing or warehouse operations, you should consider your proximity to a post office, trucking company, or rail line. Where several sites are available, you might consider which one has the earliest or most convenient pick-up schedule for the carriers you plan to use.

LEASING A SITE

A lease of space can be one of the biggest expenses of a small business so you should do a lot of homework before signing one. There are a lot of terms in a commercial lease that can make or break your business. These are the most critical:

ZONING   Before signing a lease, you should be sure that everything that your business will need to do is allowed by the *zoning* of the property–those regulations that control the use of property and buildings.

RESTRICTIONS   In some shopping centers, existing tenants have guarantees that other tenants will not compete with them. For example, if you plan to open a restaurant and bakery, you may be forbidden to sell carry-out baked goods if the supermarket has a bakery and a noncompete clause.

SIGNS   Business signs are regulated by zoning laws, sign laws and property restrictions. If you rent a hidden location with no possibility for adequate signage, your business will have a lot smaller chance of success than with a more visible site or much larger sign.

ADA COMPLIANCE

The Americans with Disabilities Act (ADA) requires that reasonable accommodations be made to make businesses accessible to the handicapped. When a business is remodeled many more changes are required than if no remodeling is done. When renting space, you should be sure that it complies with the law, or that the landlord will be responsible for compliance, and that you are aware of the full costs you will bear.

EXPANSION

As your business grows, you may need to expand your space. The time to find out about your options is before you sign the lease. Perhaps you you can take over adjoining units when those leases expire.

RENEWAL

Location is a key to success for some businesses. If you spend five years building up a clientele, you do not want someone to take over your locale at the end of your lease. Therefore, you should have a renewal clause on your lease. This usually allows an increase in rent based on inflation.

GUARANTEE

Most landlords of commercial space will not rent to a small corporation without a personal guaranty of the lease. This is a very risky thing for a new business owner to do. The lifetime rent on a long term commercial lease can be hundreds of thousands of dollars and if your business fails, the last thing you want to do is be personally responsible for five years of rent. California requires the landlord to mitigate damages. This means that the landlord must try to rent the space you vacated. If the court decided that the landlord did not try hard enough, you do not owe the rent for that period. Do not count on this. Always try to avoid personal liability.

Where space is scarce or a location is hot, a landlord can get the guarantees he demands and there is nothing you can do about it (except perhaps set up an asset protection plan ahead of time). But where several units are vacant or the commercial rental market is soft, often you can negotiate out of the personal guaranty. If the lease is five years, maybe you can get away with a guaranty of just the first year. Give it a try. Also, consider the space you are going to rent. If there is nothing unusual about it, there should be no trouble re-renting it. However, if it is a *single-purpose building*, it may not be so easy to find another tenant.

Also remember that if the new tenant is paying less than you agreed to pay, you may be liable for the difference.

This brings up another possible problem. If you are going to sign a lease for several years, especially one that requires tenant improvements by the landlord, you may want to have someone examine it for you. There are clauses called *escalator* clauses that provide for periodic rent increases. Some of these clauses are based on formulas that are not easily understood. Find a lawyer, accountant, or real estate agent familiar with this type of lease and get some advice. You do not want any unexpected rent increases.

DUTY TO OPEN

Some shopping centers have rules requiring all shops to be open certain hours. If you can not afford to staff it the whole required time, or if you have religious or other reasons that make this a problem, you should negotiate it out of the lease or find another location.

SUBLEASE

At some point you may decide to sell your business, and in many cases the location is the most valuable aspect of it. For this reason you should be sure that you have the right to either assign your lease or to sublease the property. If this is impossible, one way around a prohibition is to incorporate your business before signing the lease. Then when you sell the business, sell the stock. But some lease clauses prohibit transfer of "any interest" in the business, so read the lease carefully.

The duty on the landlord to mitigate damages has weakened the prohibition of assignment. If you are going to move out (breach) and you supply the landlord with an acceptable tenant, the landlord must accept the tenant or you do not have to pay any more rent. Whether a tenant is acceptable would be a matter for a court to decide if the landlord refuses your tenant. If your business is not doing well or you want to relocate, finding a tenant to take your place could save you from paying rent after you move.

For more information about leasing you should see the references at the end of this book.

BUYING A SITE

If you are experienced with owning rental property, you will probably be more inclined to buy a site for your business. If you have no experience with real estate, you should probably rent and not take on the extra cost and responsibility of property ownership.

One reason to buy your site is that you can build up equity. Rather than pay rent to a landlord you can pay off a mortgage and eventually own the property.

SEPARATING THE OWNERSHIP
One risk in buying a business site is that if the business gets into financial trouble the creditors may go after the building as well. For this reason most people who buy a site for their business keep the ownership out of the business. For example, the business will be a corporation and the real estate will be owned personally by the owner or by a trust unrelated to the business.

EXPANSION
Before buying a site you should consider the growth potential of your business. If it grows quickly, will you be able to expand at that site or will you have to move? Might the property next door be available for sale in the future if you need it? Can you get an option on it? If the site is a good investment whether or not you have your business there, then by all means, buy it. But if its main use is for your business, think twice.

ZONING
Some of the concerns when buying a site are the same as when renting. You will want to make sure that the zoning permits the type of business you wish to start, or that you can get a variance without a large expense or delay. Be aware that just because a business is now using the site does not mean that you can expand or remodel the business at that site. Some zoning laws allow businesses to be grandfathered in, but not

expanded. Check with the zoning department and find out exactly what is allowed.

SIGNS

Signs are another concern. Some cities have regulated signs and do not allow new ones; or they require them to be smaller. Some businesses have used these laws to get publicity. A car dealer who was told to take down a large number of American flags on his lot filed a federal lawsuit and rallied the community behind him.

ADA
COMPLIANCE

ADA compliance is another concern when buying a commercial building. Find out from the building department if the building is in compliance or what needs to be done to put it in compliance. However, there may be stricter requirements if you remodel.

Note: When dealing with public officials always keep in mind they do not always know what the law is, or honestly tell you what it is. Some are overzealous and try to intimidate people into doing things that are not required by law. Read the requirements yourself and question the officials if they seem to be interpreting it wrong. Seek legal advice if they refuse to budge from a clearly erroneous position. But also consider that keeping them happy may be worth the price. If you are already getting away with something they have overlooked, do not make a big deal over a little thing they want changed or they may subject you to a full inspection or audit.

CHECK GOVERNMENTAL REGULATIONS

When looking for a site for your business, you should investigate the different governmental regulations in your area. For example, a location just outside the city or county limits might have a lower licensing fee, a lower sales tax rate, and less strict sign requirements.

LICENSING YOUR BUSINESS **6**

OCCUPATIONAL LICENSES AND ZONING

Some California counties and cities require you to obtain an occupational license. If you are in a city you may need both a city and a county license. Businesses which do work in several cities, such as builders, must obtain a license from each city in which they do work. This does not have to be done until you actually begin a job in a particular city.

Licensing requirements of county and city governments can be found by checking with your local city and county. An easy way to get this information is through the website at **http://www.Infospace.com**. This site will give you all city and county offices with appropriate telephone numbers and email addresses.

Be sure to find out if zoning allows your type of business before buying or leasing property. The licensing departments will check the zoning before issuing your license.

If you will be preparing or serving food, you will need to check with the local health department to be sure that the premises complies with their regulations. In some areas, if food has been served on the premises in the past, there is no problem getting a license. If food has never been served on the premises, then the property must comply with all the newest regulations. This can be very costly.

HOME
BUSINESSES

Problems occasionally arise when persons attempt to start a business in their home. Small new businesses cannot afford to pay rent for commercial space, and cities often try to forbid business in residential areas. Getting a county occupational license or advertising a fictitious name often gives notice to the city that a business is being conducted in a residential area.

Some people avoid the problem by starting their businesses without occupational licenses, figuring that the penalties for not having a license (if they are caught) are less expensive than the cost of office space. Others get the county license and ignore the city rules. If a person regularly parks commercial trucks and equipment on his property, or has delivery trucks coming and going, or employee cars parked along the street, there will probably be complaints from neighbors and the city will probably take legal action. But if a person's business consists merely of making phone calls out of the home and keeping supplies there, the problem may never become an issue.

If a problem does arise regarding a home business which does not disturb the neighbors, a good argument can be made that the zoning law which prohibits the business is unconstitutional. When zoning laws were first instituted, they were not meant to stop people from doing things in a residence that had historically been part of the life in a residence. Consider an artist. Should a zoning law prohibit a person from sitting in his home and painting pictures? Is there a difference if he sells them for a living? Can the government force him to rent commercial space just because he decides to sell the paintings he paints?

Similar arguments can be made for many home businesses. For hundreds of years people performed income-producing activities in their homes. But court battles with a city are expensive and probably not worth the effort for a small business. The best course of action is to keep a low profile. Using a post office box for the business is sometimes helpful in diverting attention away from the residence.

State-Regulated Professions

Many professionals require special state licenses. You will probably be called upon to produce such a license when applying for an occupational license.

If you are in a regulated profession, you should be aware of the laws which apply to your profession. The following pages contain a list of regulated professions and regulating agencies. You can make copies of these laws at your local public library or county law library. If you do not think your profession is regulated, you should read through the list anyway. Some of those included may surprise you.

California State Licensing

California Requires some type of license for almost every business. There is a list of the various boards that control the granting, monitoring, suspension, and revocation of licenses. (Cal. Bus. and Prof. Code, Section 101.)

The State Information Office can help you reach the proper one for your needs. The number to call is 916-322-9900. If the business you are starting is not on the list, check with the information office just to be sure that a state license is not required.

A list of regulated professions in California can be found in the *California License Handbook*. The book may be obtained from the California Trade and Commerce Agency, or you can contact any Small Business Administration office to get one. (See pages 7-12 of this book.) An easier way is to use the Internet. Type in "california license handbook" (do not forget quotation marks or other limiting designation required by the search engine you use). Or go to **http://commerce.ca.gov/business/small/management/pub/license/index.html**. By clicking on any business you can find the agency that regulates it, the requirements and cost of a license or permit, and where to make further contact.

FEDERAL LICENSES

So far there are few businesses that require federal registration. If you are in any of the types of businesses listed below, you should check with the federal agency listed with it.

Radio or television stations or manufacturers of equipment emitting radio waves:

> Federal Communications Commission
> 1919 M Street, NW
> Washington, DC 20550

Manufacturers of alcohol, tobacco or fire arms:

> Bureau of Alcohol, Tobacco and Firearms
> 650 Massachusetts Ave., NW
> Washington, DC 20226

Securities brokers and providers of investment advice:

> Small Business Ombudsman
> Securities and Exchange Commission
> 450 - 5th Street NW
> Mail Stop 3-4
> Washington, DC 20549

Manufacturers of drugs and processors of meat:

> Food and Drug Administration
> 5600 Fishers Lane
> Rockville, MD 28057

Interstate carriers:

Interstate Commerce Commission
12th St. & Constitution Ave.
Washington, DC 20423

Exporting:

Bureau of Export Administration
Department of Commerce
14th St. & Pennsylvania Ave., NW
Washington, DC 20230

Contract Laws 7

As a business owner, you will need to know the basics of forming a simple contract for your transactions with both customers and vendors. There is a lot of misunderstanding about what the law is and people may give you erroneous information. Relying on it can cost you money. This chapter will give you a quick overview of the principles that apply to your transactions and the pitfalls to avoid. If you face more complicated contract questions, you should consult a law library or an attorney familiar with small business law.

Traditional Contract Law

The simplest definition of a *contract* is: if you promise to do something and the law says that you can not change your mind and refuse to do it, you have made a contract. This is, obviously, not a technical definition and there are exceptions. However, the point is that you should not agree to do something unless you have given it some thought.

One of the first things taught in law school is that a contract is not legal unless three elements are present: offer, acceptance, and consideration. The rest of the semester dissects exactly what may be a valid offer, acceptance, and consideration. For your purposes, the important things to remember are:

☞ If you make an offer to someone, it may result in a binding contract, even if you change your mind or find out it was a bad deal for you.

☞ Unless an offer is accepted and both parties agree to the same terms, there is no contract.

☞ A contract does not always have to be in writing. Some laws require certain contracts to be in writing, but as a general rule an oral contract is legal. The problem is proving that the contract existed.

☞ Without *consideration* (the exchange of something of value or mutual promises) there is not a valid contract.

As mentioned above, an entire semester is spent analyzing each of the three elements of a contract. The most important rules for the business owner are:

☞ An advertisement is not an offer. Suppose you put an ad in the newspaper offering "New IBM computers only $1995!" but there is a typo in the ad and it says $19.95? Can people come in and say "I accept, here's my $19.95" creating a legal contract? Fortunately, no. Courts have ruled that the ad is not an offer that a person can accept. It is an invitation to come in and make offers, which the business can accept or reject.

☞ The same rule applies to the price tag on an item. If someone switches price tags on your merchandise, or if you accidentally put the wrong price on it, you are not required by law to sell it at that price. If you intentionally put the wrong price, you may be liable under the "bait and switch" law. Many merchants honor a mistaken price just because refusing to would constitute bad will and probably lose a customer.

☞ When a person makes an offer, several things may happen. It may be accepted, creating a legal contract. It may be rejected. It may expire before it has been accepted. Or, it may be withdrawn before acceptance. A contract may expire either by a date made in the offer ("This offer remains open until noon on January 29, 2001") or after a reasonable amount of time. What is reasonable is a factual question that a court must decide. If someone makes you an offer to sell goods, clearly you cannot come back five years later and accept. Can you accept a week or a month later and create a legal contract? That depends on the type of goods and the circumstances.

☛ A person accepting an offer cannot add any terms that materially change the offer to it. If you offer to sell a car for $1,000, and the other party says they accept as long as you put new tires on it, there is no contract. An acceptance with changed terms is considered a rejection and a counteroffer.

☛ When someone rejects your offer or makes a counteroffer, your offer is terminated and can no longer be accepted unless you make another offer. You may accept the counteroffer and form a contract.

These rules can affect your business on a daily basis. Suppose you offer to sell something to one customer over the phone and five minutes later another customer walks in and offers you more for it. To protect yourself, you should call the first customer and withdraw your offer before accepting the offer of the second customer. If the first customer accepts before you have withdrawn your offer, you may be sued if you have sold the item to the second customer. [Be sure to see the subsection on "Firm Offers" on page 69.]

There are a few exceptions to the basic rules of contracts, these are:

☛ Consent to a contract must be voluntary. If it is made under a threat, the contract is not valid. If a business refuses to give a person's car back unless they pay $200 for changing the oil, the customer could probably sue and get the $200 back.

☛ Contracts to do illegal acts or acts "against public policy" are not enforceable. If an electrician signs a contract to put some wiring in a house that is not legal, the customer could probably not force him to do it because the court would refuse to require an illegal act.

☛ If either party to an offer dies, then the offer terminates and cannot be accepted by the heirs. This is also true of personal contracts. If a painter is hired to paint a portrait and dies before completing it, his wife cannot finish it and require payment. However, a corporation does not die, even if its owners die. If a corporation is hired to build a house and the owner dies, his heirs may take over the corporation and finish the job and require payment.

☞ Contracts made under misrepresentation are not enforceable. For example, if someone tells you a car has 35,000 miles on it and you later discover it has 135,000 miles, you may be able to rescind the contract for fraud and misrepresentation.

☞ If there was a serious mutual mistake a contract may be rescinded. For example, if both you and the seller thought the car had 35,000 miles on it and both relied on that assumption, the contract could be rescinded if the car had 135,000 miles on it. However, if the seller knew the car has 135,000 miles on it, but you assumed it had 35,000 and did not ask, you probably could not rescind the contract.

Statutory Contract Law

The previous section discussed the basics of contract law. These are not usually stated in statutes, but are the legal principles decided by judges over the past hundreds of years. In recent times the legislatures have made numerous exceptions to these principles. In most cases, these laws have been passed when the legislature felt that traditional law was not fair. The important laws that affect contracts are the following:

Statute of
Frauds

All states have laws providing that certain types of contracts must be in writing in order to be enforceable in court. A law stating that a certain type of contract must be in writing is called a *statute of frauds*. California's statutes of frauds are set out in California Civil Code (Cal. Civ. Code), Section 1624 and California Commercial Code (Cal. Com. Code), Sections 2201 through 2210. According to California Civil Code, Section 1624(a),the following contracts will not be enforced by a court unless they are in writing:

(1) An agreement that by its terms is not to be performed within a year from the making thereof.

(2) A special promise to answer for the debt, default, or miscarriage of another, except in the cases provided for in Section 2794. [Section 2794 sets out six exceptions that are rather complicated. The general rule to remember is that if you agree to pay someone else's debt to benefit yourself rather than the debtor, you don't need a writing. Of course, a better thing to keep in mind is that agreeing to pay someone else's debt is usually a bad idea, whether you do it verbally or in writing.]

(3) An agreement to lease over a longer period than one year, or to sell real property, or to have an interest in these; such an agreement, if made by an agent of the party sought to be charged, is invalid, unless the authority of the agent is in writing, subscribed by the party sought to be charged.

(4) An agreement authorizing or employing an agent, broker, or any other person to purchase or sell real estate; or to lease real estate for a longer period than one year; or to procure, introduce, or find a purchaser or seller of real estate; or a lessee or lessor of real estate where the lease is for a longer period than one year, for compensation or commission.

(5) An agreement that, by its terms, is not to be performed during the lifetime of the promisor.

(6) An agreement by a purchaser of real property to pay an indebtedness by a mortgage or deed of trust upon the property purchased, unless assumption of the indebtedness by the purchaser is specifically provided for in the conveyance of the property.

(7) A contract, promise, undertaking, or commitment to loan money or to grant or extend credit, in an amount greater than one hundred thousand dollars ($100,000), not primarily for personal, family or household purposes, made by a person

engaged in the business of lending or arranging for the lending of money or extending credit.

Also, California Commercial Code, Section 2201 provides:

(1) Except as otherwise provided in this section, a contract for the sale of goods for the price of five hundred dollars ($500) or more is not enforceable by way of action or defense unless there is some writing sufficient to indicate that a contract for sale has been made between the parties and signed by the party against whom enforcement is sought or by his or her authorized agent or broker. A writing is not insufficient because it omits or incorrectly states a term agreed upon, but the contract is not enforceable under this paragraph beyond the quantity of goods shown in the writing.

In order for a contract to be written, it is not necessary that there be the type of document that most people think of when they use the word contract. All that is required is that there be some type of writing that shows the basic terms of the agreement, and that the writing be signed by the person being sued for not complying. Such a writing is frequently referred to as a *memorandum* of the agreement, which may be on a single sheet of paper, or on two or more pieces of paper (including a series of notes or letters between the two parties which outline the terms of the agreement).

The person who is to be forced to comply is called *the party to be charged*. Therefore, if you read legal texts about contracts you will usually see references to the requirement that there be "a memorandum of the agreement, signed by the party to be charged or by that party's agent." The writing does not need to be signed by the person who is trying to enforce the agreement, but only by the person the writing is being enforced against.

There are several exceptions to the statutes of frauds, some of which are fairly complicated. For example, there can be exceptions for those who are considered merchants. The easiest way to avoid problems is to use written contracts for all matters that you consider important. Also, do not make verbal agreements with the idea that you can always change your mind. These agreements may be enforceable, even those listed in the statutes of frauds.

FIRM OFFERS   The Uniform Commercial Code, commonly known as the UCC, creates exceptions to contract law for the sale of goods. One of these exceptions is the *merchant's firm offer*. If a merchant (one who deals regularly in a certain type of goods) makes an offer in writing that says that the offer will remain open, it must remain open for the stated time, or for a *reasonable* time if no time is stated. Regardless of what it says, it does not have to remain open for more than three months.

The point is that if you, as a merchant, write to someone and say that you will give them a month to decide whether they want to buy something from you, you can not accept another offer for the item or items offered until the month has passed.

CONSUMER
PROTECTION
LAW   Due to the alleged unfair practices by some types of businesses, laws have been passed controlling the types of contracts they may use. Most notable among these are health clubs and door-to-door solicitations. The laws covering these businesses usually give the consumer a certain time to cancel the contract. These laws are described in Chapter 12.

PREPARING YOUR CONTRACTS

Before you open your business, you should obtain or prepare the contracts or policies you will use in your business. In some businesses, such as a restaurant, you will not need much. Perhaps you will want a sign near the entrance stating "shirt and shoes required" or "diners must be seated by 10:30 P.M." However, if you are a building contractor or a similar business, you will need detailed contracts to use with your customers. If you do not clearly spell out your rights and obligations, you may end up in court. This will cost much more than some advice before making this contract.

Of course, the best way to have an effective contract is to have an attorney, who is experienced in the subject, prepare one to meet the needs of your business. However, since this may be too expensive for your new operation, you may want to go elsewhere. Three sources for the contracts you will need are other businesses like yours, trade associations, and legal forms books. You should obtain as many different contracts as possible, compare them, and decide which terms are most comfortable for you.

INSURANCE 8

There are few laws requiring you to have insurance. If you do not have insurance, you may face liability that could ruin your business. You should be aware of the types of insurance available and weigh the risks of a loss against the cost of a policy.

Be aware that there can be a wide range of price and coverage in insurance policies. You should get at least three quotes from different insurance agents and ask each one to explain the benefits of his or her policy.

Insurance is one of the few areas of starting a business that absolutely requires expert advice. You can keep your own books, do your own hiring, order your materials and do your own marketing. You can't write your own insurance policies.

Since you must consult with an insurance agent, find one who specializes in small business insurance and learn about all that is available. The most important things to remember are:

☛ Most agents are anxious to sell you insurance. Over-insuring can be very expensive, especially when you have not started deriving any income from your business. Always ask if the insurance is required.

☛ You can insure against almost anything. If the policy does not cover the particular situation you are concerned about, ask about a rider or endorsement. If the answer you get from the agent does not satisfy you, talk to another company.

☞ Shop wisely. The best places to start are industry trade groups. Insurance agents familiar with your industry know exactly what you need. Your trade association may have someone you may consult for advice. SCORE is another good source. (see Chapter 1, p.5.) Retired executives usually have the answers or know where to get them.

The types of insurance discussed in the rest of the chapter are either required or usually recommended.

WORKERS' COMPENSATION

California Labor Code (Cal. Lab. Code), Section 3700 requires every employer except the state to have Workers' Compensation insurance. For a private business this is done either through an insurance policy from one of the approximately 300 private insurers who write such policies or through self-insurance. If you plan to self-insure, you are far beyond the scope of this book.

The State Compensation Insurance Fund (SCIF), commonly known as State Fund, writes the most policies. Here is how they describe themselves:

> The California State Fund is a non-profit, public enterprise fund that operates like a mutual insurance carrier. Unused premium, in excess of operating expenses, claims costs and expenses, and necessary surplus are returned in the form of dividends to policyholders. State Fund has returned in excess of $4.8 billion to its policyholders since its founding—far and away the largest premium return among carriers.

For a list of local offices, go to the website:

http://www.scif.com/newscif2/aboutscif/locations.htm

Or, call the home office at: 415-565-1234 for a location nearest you.

CALIFORNIA
DIVISION OF
WORKERS'
COMPENSATION

The law is subject to frequent changes. The California Workers' Compensation Institute (CWCI) offers a sixteen-page booklet called *An Employer's Guide to California Workers' Compensation*, as well as many other informative publications. Write to them at 1111 Broadway #2350, Oakland, CA 94607, or order online at: **http://www.cwci.org**. Then click on their bookstore and catalogue.

The State of California Division of Workers' Compensation publishes changes in the law as well as other helpful information. They can be reached online at:

http://www.dir.ca.gov/dir/workers' compensation/dwc/dir2.htm

Headquarters is located at:

455 Golden Gate Ave., 9th Floor
San Francisco, CA 94102-3660
415-703-4600

LIABILITY INSURANCE

In most cases, you are not required to carry liability insurance. A notable exception is the limited liability partnership (LLP), which must have liability insurance. There are different amounts required, depending upon the purpose of the LLP (e.g., legal services, accountancy, architecture), which range from $500,000 to $10,000,000. If this applies to your business, see the California Corporations Code, beginning with Section 16956.

Liability insurance can be divided into two main areas: coverage for injuries on your premises and by your employees; and coverage for injuries caused by your products or services.

Coverage for the first type of injury is usually very reasonably priced. Injuries in your business or by your employees (such as in an auto accident) are covered by standard premises or auto policies. But coverage for injuries by products may be harder to find and more expensive. In the current liability crisis, juries have awarded ridiculously high judgments for accidents involving products that had little, if any, impact on the accident. The situation has become so bad that some entire industries have gone out of business or moved overseas.

ASSET
PROTECTION

Hopefully, laws will soon be passed to protect businesses from these unfair awards. For now, if insurance is unavailable or unaffordable, you can go without insurance. Use a corporation, and other asset protection devices to protect yourself from liability. For more information on this topic, see *Simple Ways to Protect Yourself from Lawsuits* listed at the back of this book.

The best way to find out if insurance is available for your type of business is to check with other businesses. If there is a trade group for your industry their newsletter or magazine may contain ads for insurers.

UMBRELLA
POLICY

As a business owner you will be a more visible target for lawsuits even if there is little merit to them. Lawyers know that a *nuisance suit* is often settled for thousands of dollars. Because of your greater exposure you should consider getting a *personal umbrella policy*. This is a policy that covers you for claims of up to one, two, or even five million dollars, and is very reasonably priced.

HAZARD INSURANCE

One of the worst things that can happen to your business is a fire, flood, or other disaster. With lost customer lists, inventory, and equipment, many businesses have been forced to close after such a disaster.

The premium for insurance protection from such disasters is usually reasonable, and could protect you from loss of your business. You can even get *business interruption* insurance, which will cover your loss of income while your business is getting back on its feet.

Home Business Insurance

There is a special insurance problem for home businesses. Most homeowner and tenant insurance policies do not cover business activities. In fact, under some policies you may be denied coverage if you used your home for a business.

If you merely use your home to make business phone calls and send letters, you will probably not have a problem and not need extra coverage. But if you own equipment, or have dedicated a portion of your home exclusively to the business, you could have a problem. Check with your insurance agent for the options that are available to you.

If your business is a sole proprietorship, and you have, say, a computer that you use both personally and for your business, it would probably be covered under your homeowners' policy. But if you incorporate your business and bought the computer in the name of the corporation, coverage might be denied. If a computer is your main business asset you could get a special insurance policy in the company name covering just the computer.

Automobile Insurance

If you or any of your employees will be using an automobile for business purposes, be sure that such use is covered. Sometimes a policy may include an exclusion for business use. Check to be sure your liability policy covers you if one of your employees causes an accident while running a business errand.

Health Insurance

While new businesses can rarely afford health insurance for their employees, the sooner they can obtain it, the better chance they will have to find and keep good employees. Those starting a business usually need insurance for themselves (unless they have a working spouse who can cover the family) and they can sometimes get a better rate if they get a small business package.

The Health Insurance Plan of California (known as Pacific Health Advantage or PacAdvantage) was established by the legislature in 1993 to provide affordable health coverage to small businesses. As of July 1, 1999, Pacific Business Group on Health (PBGH) will manage the program. Employers may contact them at 877-472-2238 or by mail at 221 Main Street, Suite 1500, San Francisco, CA 94105. Their website is:

http://www.pacadvantage.org

EMPLOYEE THEFT

If you fear that employees may be able to steal from your business, you may want to have them *bonded*. This can cover all existing and new employees.

Your Business and the Internet 9

The Internet has opened up a world of opportunities for businesses. A few years ago getting national visibility cost a fortune. Today a business can set up a Web page for a few hundred dollars and, with some clever publicity and a little luck, millions of people around the world will see it.

But this new world has new legal issues and new liabilities. Not all of them have been addressed by laws or by the courts. Before you begin doing business on the Internet, you should know the existing rules and the areas where legal issues exist.

Domain Names

A *domain name* is the address of your website. For example, www.apple.com is the domain name of Apple Computer Company. The last part of the domain name, the ".com" (or "dot com") is the *top level domain*, or TLD. Dot com is the most popular, but others are currently available in the United States, including .net and .org. Originally .net was only available to network service providers and .org only to nonprofit organizations, but regulations have eliminated those requirements.

It may seem like most words have been taken as a dot-com name, but if you combine two or three short words or abbreviations, a nearly unlimited number of possibilities are available. For example, if you have a business dealing with automobiles, most likely someone has already registered automobile.com and auto.com. But you can come up with all kinds of variations, using adjectives or your name, depending on your type of business:

autos4u.com	joesauto.com	autobob.com
myauto.com	yourauto.com	onlyautos.com
greatauto.com	autosfirst.com	usautos.com
greatautos.com	firstautoworld.com	4autos.com

When the Internet first began, some individuals realized that major corporations would soon want to register their names. Since the registration was easy and cheap, people registered names they thought would ultimately be used by someone else.

At first, some companies paid high fees to buy their names from the registrants. But one company, Intermatic, filed a lawsuit instead of paying. The owner of the mark they wanted had registered numerous trademarks, such as britishairways.com and ussteel.com. The court ruled that since Intermatic owned a trademark on the name, the registration of their name by someone else violated that trademark and that Intermatic was entitled to it.

Since then people have registered names that are not trademarks, such as CalRipkin.com, and have attempted to charge the individuals with those names to buy their domain. In 1998, Congress stepped in and passed the Anti-Cybersquatting Consumer Protection Act. This law makes it illegal to register a domain with no legitimate need to use it.

Registering a domain name for your own business is a simple process. There are many companies that offer registration services. For a list of those companies, visit the site of the Internet Corporation for Assigned Names and Numbers (ICANN) at **http://www.icann.org**. You can link directly to any member's site and compare the costs and registration procedures required for the different top-level domains.

WEB PAGES

There are many new companies eager to help you set up a website. Some offer turnkey sites for a low flat rate. Custom sites can cost tens of thousands of dollars. If you have plenty of capital you may want to have your site handled by one of these professionals. However, setting up a website is a fairly simple process, and once you learn the basics you can handle most of it in-house.

If you are new to the Web, you may want to look at the following sites, which will familiarize you with the Internet jargon and give you a basic introduction to the Web:

http://www.learnthenet.com   http://www.webopedia.com

SITE SETUP

There are seven steps to setting up a website: site purpose, design, content, structure, programming, testing, and publicity. Whether you do it yourself, hire a professional site designer, or use a college student, the steps toward creating an effective site are the same.

Before beginning your own site you should look at other sites, including those of major corporations and of small businesses. Look at the sites of all the companies that compete with you. Look at hundreds of sites and click through them to see how they work (or don't work!)

Site purpose. To know what to include on your site you must decide what its purpose will be. Do you want to take orders for your products or services, attract new employees, give away samples, or show off your company headquarters? You might want to do several of these things.

Site design. After looking at other sites you can see that there are numerous ways to design a site. It can be crowded, or open and airy; it can have several windows (frames) open at once or just one, and it can allow long scrolling or just click-throughs.

You will have to decide whether the site will have text only; text plus photographs and graphics; or text plus photos, graphics, and other design elements such as animation or Java script. Additionally, you will begin to make decisions about colors, fonts, and the basic graphic appearance of the site.

Site content. You must create the content for your site. For this, you can use your existing promotional materials, you can write new material just for the Web site, or you can use a combination of the two. Whatever you choose, remember that the written material should be concise, free of errors, and easy for your target audience to read. Any graphics, including photographs, and written materials not created by you require permission. You should obtain such permission from the lawful copyright holder in order to use any copyrighted material. Once you know your site's purpose, look, and content, you can begin to piece the site together.

Site structure. You must decide how the content (text plus photographs, graphics, animation, etc.) will be structured–what content will be on which page, and how a user will link from one part of the site to another. For example, your first page may have the business name and then choices to click on, such as "about us," "opportunities," "product catalog," etc. Have those choices connect to another page containing the detailed information so that a user will see the catalog when they click on "product catalog." Or your site could have a choice to click on a link to another website related to yours.

Site programming and setup. When you know nothing about setting up a website, it can seem like a daunting task that will require an expert. However, "programming" here means merely putting a site together. There are inexpensive computer programs available that make it very simple.

Commercial programs such as Microsoft FrontPage, Dreamweaver, Pagemaker, Photoshop, MS Publisher, and PageMill allow you to set up Web pages as easily as laying out a print publication. These programs will convert the text and graphics you create into HTML, the programming language of the Web. Before you choose Web design software and design your site, you should determine which Web hosting service you will use. Make sure that the design software you use is compatible with the host server's system. The Web host will be the provider who will give you space on their server and who may provide other services to you, such as secure order processing and analysis of your site to see who is visiting and linking to it.

If you have an America Online account, you can download design software and a tutorial for free. AOL has recently collaborated with a Web hosting service at **http://www.verioprimehost.com** and offers a number of different hosting packages for the consumer and e-business. You do not have to use AOL's design software in order to use this service. You are eligible to use this site whether you design your own pages, have someone else do the design work for you, or use AOL's templates. This service allows you to use your own domain name and choose the package that is appropriate for your business.

If you have used a page layout program, you can usually get a simple Web page up and running within a day or two. If you don't have much experience with a computer, you might consider hiring a college student to set up a Web page for you.

Site testing. Some of the website setup programs allow you to thoroughly check your new site to see if all the pictures are included and all the links are proper. There are also websites you can go to that will check out your site. Some even allow you to improve your site, such as by reducing the size of your graphics so they download faster. Use a major search engine listed on page 82 to look for companies that can test your site before you launch it on the Web.

Site publicity. Once you set up your website, you will want to get people to look at it. *Publicity* means getting your site noticed as much as possible by drawing people to it.

The first thing to do to get noticed is to be sure your site is registered with as many *search engines* as possible. These are pages that people use to find things on the Internet, such as Yahoo and Excite. They do not automatically know about you just because you created a website. You must tell them about your site, and they must examine and catalog it.

For a fee, there are services that will register your site with numerous search engines. If you are starting out on a shoestring, you can easily do it yourself. While there are hundreds of search engines, most people use a dozen or so of the bigger ones. If your site is in a niche area, such as geneology services, then you would want to be listed on any specific geneology search engines. Most businesses should be mainly concerned with getting on the biggest ones. The biggest search engines at this time are:

www.altavista.com	www.lycos.com
www.dejanews.com	www.magellan.com
www.excite.com	www.metacrawler.com
www.fastsearch.com	www.northernlight.com
www.goto.com	www.webcrawler.com
www.hotbot.com	www.yahoo.com
www.infoseek.com	

Most of these sites have a place to click to "add your site" to their system. There are sites that rate the search engines, help you list on the search engines, or check to see if you are listed. One site is:

http://www.searchiq.com

A *meta tag* is an invisible subject word added to your site that can be found by a search engine. For example, if you are a pest control company, you may want to list all of the scientific names of the pests you control and all of the treatments you have available; but you may not need them to be part of the visual design of your site. List these words as meta tags when you set up your page so people searching for those words will find your site.

Some companies thought that a clever way to get viewers would be to use commonly searched names, or names of major competitors, as meta tags to attract people looking for those big companies. For example, a small delivery service that has nothing to do with UPS or Federal

Express might use those company names as meta tags so people looking for them would find the smaller company. While it may sound like a good idea, it has been declared illegal trademark infringement. Today many companies have computer programs scanning the Internet for improper use of their trademarks.

Once you have made sure that your site is passively listed in all the search engines, you may want to actively promote your site. However, self-promotion is seen as a bad thing on the Internet, especially if its purpose is to make money.

Newsgroups are places on the Internet where people interested in a specific topic can exchange information. For example, expectant mothers have a group where they can trade advice and experiences. If you have a product that would be great for expectant mothers, that would be a good place for it to be discussed. However, if you log into the group and merely announce your product, suggesting people order it from your Web site, you will probably be *flamed* (sent a lot of hate mail).

If you join the group, however, and become a regular, and in answer to someone's problem, mention that you "saw this product that might help," your information will be better received. It may seem unethical to plug your product without disclosing your interest, but this is a procedure used by many large companies. They hire people to plug their product (or rock star) all over the Internet. So, perhaps it has become an acceptable marketing method and consumers know to take plugs with a grain of salt. Let your conscience be your guide.

Keep in mind that Internet publicity works both ways. If you have a great product and people love it, you will get a lot of business. If you sell a shoddy product, give poor service, and don't keep your customers happy, bad publicity on the Internet can kill your business. Besides being an equalizer between large and small companies, the Internet can be a filtering mechanism between good and bad products.

There is no worse breach of Internet etiquette ("netiquette") than to send advertising by e-mail to strangers. It is called *spamming*, and doing it can have serious consequences. There is anti-spamming legislation currently pending at the federal level. Many states, including California, Colorado, Connecticut, Delaware, Idaho, Illinois, Iowa, Louisiana, Missouri, Nevada, North Carolina, Oklahoma, Pennsylvania, Rhode Island, Tennessee, Virginia, Washington, and West Virginia, have enacted anti-spamming legislation. This legislation sets specific requirements for unsolicited bulk e-mail and makes certain practices illegal. You should check with an attorney to see if your business practices fall within the legal limits of these laws. Additionally, many Internet Service Providers (ISPs) have restrictions on unsolicited bulk e-mail (spam); you should check with your ISP to make sure you do not violate its policies.

ADVERTISING   *Banner ads* are the small rectangular ads on many Web pages which usually blink or move. Although most computer users seem to have become immune to them, there is still a big market in the sale and exchange of them.

If your site gets enough viewers, people may pay you to place their ads there. Another possibility is to trade ads with another site. In fact there are companies that broker ad trades among Web sites. Such trades used to be taxable transactions, but after January 5, 2000, such trades were no longer taxable under IRS Notice 2000-6.

LEGAL ISSUES

Before you set up a Web page, you should consider the legal issues described below.

JURISDICTION   Jurisdiction is the power of a court in a particular location to decide a particular case. Usually you have to have been physically present in a jurisdiction or have done business there before you can be sued there. Since the Internet extends your business's ability to reach people in far-away places, there may be instances when you could be subject to legal jurisdiction far from your own state (or country). There are a number of cases that have been decided in this country regarding the Internet and jurisdiction, but very few cases have been decided on this issue outside of the United States.

In most instances, U.S. courts use the pre-Internet test–whether you have been present in another jurisdiction or have had enough contact with someone in the other jurisdiction. The fact that the Internet itself is not a "place" will not shield you from being sued in another state when you have shipped you company's product there, have entered into a contract with a resident of that state, or have defamed a foreign resident with content on your website.

According to the Court, there is a spectrum of contact required between you, your website, and consumers, or audiences. (*Zippo Manufacturing Co. v. Zippo Dot Com, Inc.*, 952 F. Supp. 1119 (W.D. Pa 1997)) It is *clear* that the one end of the spectrum includes the shipping, contracting, and defamation mentioned above as sufficient to establish jurisdiction. The more interactive your site is with consumers, the more you target an audience for your goods in a particular location, and the farther you reach to send your goods out into the world, the more it becomes possible for someone to sue you outside of your own jurisdiction–possibly even in another country.

The law is not even remotely final on these issues. The American Bar Association, among other groups, is studying this topic in detail. At present, no final, global solution or agreement about jurisdictional issues exists.

One way to protect yourself from the possibility of being sued in a faraway jurisdiction would be to have a statement on your website stating that those using the site or doing business with you agree that "jurisdiction for any actions regarding this site" or your company will be in your home county.

For extra protection you can have a preliminary page that must be clicked before entering your website. However, this may be overkill for a small business with little risk of lawsuits. If you are in any business for which you could have serious liability, you should review some competitors' sites and see how they handle the liability issue. They often have a place to click for "legal notice" or "disclaimer" on their first page.

You may want to consult with an attorney to discuss the specific disclaimer you will use on your website, where it should appear, and whether you will have users of your site actively "agree" to this disclaimer or just "passively" read it. However, these disclaimers are not enforceable everywhere in the world. Until there is global agreement on jurisdictional issues, this may remain an area of uncertainty for some time to come.

LIBEL

Libel is any publication that injures the reputation of another. This can occur in print, writing, pictures, or signs. All that is required for *publication* is that you transmit the material to at least one other person. When putting together your website you must keep in mind that it is visible to millions of people all over the planet and that if you libel a person or company you may have to pay damages. Many countries do not have the freedom of speech that we do and a statement that is not libel in the United States may be libelous elsewhere.

Copyright infringement. It is so easy to copy and "borrow" information on the Internet that it is easy to infringe copyrights without even knowing it. A *copyright* exists for a work as soon as the creator creates it. There is no need to register the copyright or to put a copyright notice on it. So, practically everything on the Internet belongs to someone. Some people freely give their works away. For example, many people have created web artwork (*gifs* and *animated gifs)* that they freely allow people to copy. There are numerous sites that provide hundreds or thousands of free gifs that you can add to your Web pages. Some require you to acknowledge the source; some don't.

You should always be sure that the works are free for the taking before using them.

LINKING AND
FRAMING

One way to violate copyright laws is to improperly link other sites to yours either directly or with framing. *Linking* is when you provide a place on your site to click, which takes someone to another site. *Framing* occurs when you set up your site so that when you link to another site, your site is still viewable as a frame around the linked-to site.

While many sites are glad to be linked to others, some, especially providers of valuable information, object. Courts have ruled that linking and framing can be a copyright violation. One rule that has developed is that it is usually okay to link to the first page of a site, but not to link to some valuable information deeper within the site. The rationale for this is that the owner of the site wants visitors to go through the various levels of their site (viewing all the ads) before getting the information. By linking to the information you are giving away their product without the ads.

The problem with linking to the first page of a site is that it may be a tedious or difficult task to find the needed page from there. Many sites are poorly designed and make it nearly impossible to find anything.

The best solution, if you wish to link to another page, is to ask permission. Email the Webmaster or other person in charge of the site, if one is given, and explain what you want to do. If they grant permission, be sure to print out a copy of their e-mail for your records.

PRIVACY   Since the Internet is such an easy way to share information, there are many concerns that it will cause a loss of individual privacy. The two main concerns arise when you post information that others consider private, and when you gather information from customers and use it in a way that violates their privacy.

While public actions of politicians and celebrities are fair game, details about their private lives are sometimes protected by law, and details about persons who are not public figures are often protected. The laws in each state are different, and what might be allowable in one state could be illegal in another. If your site will provide any personal information about individuals, you should discuss the possibility of liability with an attorney.

Several well-known companies have been in the news lately for violations of their customers' privacy. They either shared what the customer was buying or downloading, or looked for additional information on the customer's computer. To let customers know that you do not violate certain standards of privacy, you can subscribe to one of the privacy codes that have been promulgated for the Internet. These allow you to put a symbol on your site guaranteeing to your customers that you follow the code.

The websites of three of the organizations that offer this service, and their fees at the time of this publication, are:

www.privacybot.com	$30
www.bbbonline.com	$150 to $3,000
www.trustee.com	$299 to $4,999

PROTECTING YOURSELF The easiest way to protect yourself personally from the various possible types of liability is to set up a corporation or limited liability company to own the website. This is not foolproof protection since, in some cases, you could be sued personally as well, but it is one level of protection.

COPPA If your website is aimed at children under the age of thirteen, or if it attracts children of that age, then you are covered by the federal Children Online Privacy Protection Act of 1998 (COPPA). This law requires such Web sites to:

☞ give notice on the site of what information is being collected;

☞ obtain verifiable parental consent to collect the information;

☞ allow the parent to review the information collected;

☞ allow the parent to delete the child's information or to refuse to allow the use of the information;

☞ limit the information collected to only that necessary to participate on the site; and

☞ protect the security and confidentiality of the information.

FINANCIAL TRANSACTIONS

In the future, there will be easy ways to exchange money on the Internet. Some companies have already been started that promote their own kinds of electronic money. Whether any of these become universal is yet to be seen.

For now, the easiest way to exchange money on the Internet is through traditional credit cards. Because of concerns that email can be abducted in transit and read by others, most companies use a "secure" site in which customers are guaranteed that their card data is encrypted before being sent.

When setting up your website, you should ask the provider if you can be set up with a secure site for transmitting credit card data. If they cannot provide it, you will need to contract with another software provider. Use a major search engine listed on page 82 to look for companies that provide credit card services to businesses on the web.

As a practical matter, there is very little to worry about when sending credit card data by email. If you do not have a secure site, another option is to allow purchasers to fax or phone in their credit card data. However, keep in mind that this extra step will lose some business unless your products are unique and your buyers are very motivated.

The least effective option is to provide an order form on the site, which can be printed out and mailed in with a check. Again, your customers must be really motivated or they will lose interest after finding out this extra work is involved.

FTC RULES

Because the Internet is an instrument of interstate commerce, it is a legitimate subject for federal regulation. The Federal Trade Commission (FTC) first said that all of its consumer protection rules applied to the

Internet, but lately it has been adding specific rules and issuing publications. The following publications are available from the FTC website at **http://www.ftc.gov/bcp/menu-internet.htm** or by mail from Consumer Response Center, Federal Trade Commission, 600 Pennsylvania, NW, Room H-130, Washington, DC 20580-0001.

☛ *Advertising and Marketing on the Internet: The Rules of the Road*

☛ *BBB-Online: Code of Online Business Practices*

☛ *Electronic Commerce: Selling Internationally. A Guide for Business Alert*

☛ *How to Comply With The Children's Online Privacy Protection Rule*

☛ *Internet Auctions: A Guide for Buyer and Sellers*

☛ *Selling on the Internet: Prompt Delivery Rules Alert*

☛ *Website Woes: Avoiding Web Service Scams Alert*

FRAUD

Because the Internet is somewhat anonymous, it is a tempting place for those with fraudulent schemes to look for victims. As a business consumer, you should exercise caution when dealing with unknown or anonymous parties on the Internet.

Recently, the U.S. Department of Justice, the FBI, and the National White Collar Crime Center launched the Internet Fraud Complaint Center (IFCC). If you suspect that you are the victim of fraud online, whether as a consumer or a business, you can report incidents to the IFCC on their website, **http://www.ifccfbi.gov**. The IFCC is currently staffed by FBI agents and representatives of the National White Collar Crime Center and will work with state and local law enforcement officials to prevent, investigate, and prosecute high-tech and economic crime online.

HEALTH AND SAFETY LAWS 10

FEDERAL LAWS

OSHA   The Occupational Safety and Health Administration (OSHA) is a good example of severe government regulation. Robert D. Moran, a former chairman of the committee that hears appeals from OSHA rulings once said that "there isn't a person on earth who can be certain he is in full compliance with the requirements of this standard at any point in time." The point of the law is to place the duty on the employer to keep the workplace free from recognized hazards that are likely to cause death or serious bodily injury to workers.

For example, OSHA decided to analyze repetitive-strain injuries, or "RSI," such as carpal tunnel syndrome. The Bureau of Labor Statistics estimated that seven percent of workplace illnesses are RSI and the National Safety Council estimated four percent. OSHA, however, determined that sixty percent is a more accurate figure and came out with a 600 page list of proposed regulations, guidelines, and suggestions. These regulations would have affected over one-half of all businesses in America and cost billions of dollars. Fortunately, these regulations were shot down by Congress in 1995, after an outcry from businesses. Shortly thereafter, OSHA officials ignored Congress' sentiment and promised to launch a new effort.

Fortunately, for small businesses the regulations are not as cumbersome as for larger enterprises. If you have ten or fewer employees or if you are in certain types of businesses, you do not have to keep a record of illnesses, injuries, and exposure to hazardous substances of employees. If you have eleven or more employees, you do have to keep this record, which is called *Log 200*. All employers are required to display a poster that you can get from OSHA.

Within forty-eight hours of an on-the-job death of an employee or injury of five or more employees on the job, the area director of OSHA must be contacted.

For more information, you should write or call an OSHA office:

> U.S. Department of Labor
> 200 Constitution Avenue, NW, Room N-3101
> Washington, DC 20210
>
> San Francisco: 415-703-5270

or visit their website at **http://www.osha-slc.gov** and obtain copies of their publications, *OSHA Handbook for Small Business* (OSHA 2209), and *OSHA Publications and Audiovisual Programs Catalog* (OSHA 2019). They also have a poster that is required to be posted in the workplace at:

> http://www.osha-slc.gov/OshDoc/Additional.html

HAZARD COMMUNICATION STANDARD

The Hazard Communication Standard requires that employees be made aware of the hazards in the workplace. Code of Federal Regulations, (C.F.R.) Title 29, Section 1910.1200. It is especially applicable to those working with chemicals, but this can include offices that use copy machines. Businesses using hazardous chemicals must have a comprehensive program for informing employees of the hazards and for protecting them from contamination.

For more information, you can contact OSHA at the previously-mentioned addresses, phone numbers, or websites. They can supply a copy of the regulation and a booklet called *OSHA 3084* which explains the law.

EPA The Worker Protection Standard for Agricultural Pesticides requires safety training, decontamination sites and, of course, posters. The Environmental Protection Agency will provide information on compliance with this law. They can be reached at their website at **http://www.epa.gov** or by mail at:

> U.S. Environmental Protection Agency
> 1200 Pennsylvania Ave., NW
> Washington, DC 20460

FDA The Pure Food and Drug Act of 1906 prohibits the misbranding or adulteration of food and drugs. It also created the Food and Drug Administration (FDA), which has promulgated tons of regulations and which must give permission before a new drug can be introduced into the market. If you will be dealing with any food or drugs you should keep abreast of their policies. Their website is: **http://www.fda.gov**, their small business site is: **http://www.fda.gov/opacom/morechoices/smallbusiness/toc.html** and their local small business representative is:

> FDA, Pacific Region
> 1301 Clay Street
> Oakland, CA 94512
> Phone 510-637-3960
> Fax 510-637-3976

HAZARDOUS MATERIALS TRANSPORTATION There are regulations that control the shipping and packing of hazardous materials. For more information contact the Office of Hazardous Materials Transportation at 400 Seventh St., S.W., Washington, DC 20590 or at 202-366-0656.

CPSC The Consumer Product Safety Commission has a set of rules that cover the safety of products. The commission feels that because its rules cover products, rather than people or companies, they apply to everyone producing such products. To determine how their rules apply to your business, contact the CPSC Ombudsman at 800-638-2772 (extension 234). The CPSC covers about 15,000 products. A few examples follow.

The CPSC rules are contained in C.F.R., Title 16 in the following parts. These can be found at most law libraries, some public libraries, and on the Internet at:

http://www.access.gpo.gov/nara/cfr/cfr-table-search.html

The CPSC's site is at:

http://cpsc.gov/index.html

PRODUCT	PART
Antennas, CB and TV	1402
Architectural Glazing Material	1201
Articles Hazardous to Children Under 3	1501
Baby Cribs-Full Size	1508
Baby Cribs-Non-Full Size	1509
Bicycle Helmets	1203
Bicycles	1512
Carpets and Rugs	1630, 1631
Cellulose Insulation	1209, 1404
Cigarette Lighters	1210
Citizens Band Base Station Antennas	1204
Coal and Wood Burning Appliances	1406
Consumer Products Containing Chlorofluorocarbons	1401
Electrically Operated Toys	1505
Emberizing Materials Containing Asbestos (banned)	1305
Extremely Flammable Contact Adhesives (banned)	1302
Fireworks	1507
Garage Door Openers	1211
Hazardous Lawn Darts (banned)	1306
Hazardous Substances	1500
Human Subjects	1028
Lawn Mowers, Walk-Behind	1205

Lead-Containing Paint (banned)	1303
Matchbooks	1202
Mattresses	1632
Pacifiers	1511
Patching Compounds Containing Asbestos (banned)	1304
Poisons	1700
Rattles	1510
Self-Pressurized Consumer Products	1401
Sleepwear-Childrens	1615, 1616
Swimming Pool Slides	1207
Toys, Electrical	1505
Unstable Refuse Bins (banned)	1301

ADDITIONAL REGULATIONS

Every day there are proposals for new laws and regulations. It would be impossible to include every conceivable one in this book. To be up to date on the laws that affect your type of business, you should belong to a trade association for your industry and subscribe to newsletters that cover your industry. Attending industry conventions is a good way to learn more and to discover new ways to increase your profits.

CALIFORNIA LAWS

HAZARDOUS OCCUPATIONS

California distinguishes between *high hazard employers*, *intermittent worker employers*, and *non-high hazard employers*, in determining what is necessary for the employer to do to minimize the risk to employees. The designation is sometimes established not by the type of industry, but by the tasks of the employees.

To find out what category your company fits into and what you must do to comply, publications such as *Injury and Illness Prevention Programs* and *Cal/OSHA for Workplace Security* are available. A publications order form is included in the appendix. (see form 9, p.253.) The publications are free. You can also order regulations. (see form 10, p.255.)

SMOKING   Smoking is not allowed in any enclosed "place of employment" in the state. (Cal. Lab. Code, Section 6404.5.) There are various exceptions, such as:

☛ In a hotel or motel, exceptions are made for certain permitted and designated smoking areas in a lobby; sixty-five percent of the guest rooms; and meeting and banquet rooms, except where food or beverage functions are taking place. When smoking is not permitted in a meeting or banquet room, it may be allowed in "areas adjacent to and serving the meeting or banquet room if no employee is stationed in that corridor or area on other than a passing basis."

☛ Retail or wholesale tobacco shops and private smokers' lounges.

☛ Cabs of motortrucks or truck tractors, if no nonsmoking employees are present. (California Vehicle Code (Cal. Veh. Code), Sections 410 and 655.)

☛ Warehouse facilities with more than 100,000 square feet of total floor space, and 20 or fewer full-time employees (this does not include any area that is utilized as office space).

☛ Gaming clubs (Cal. Bus. and Prof. Code, Section 19802), or bingo facilities (California Penal Code, Section 326.5), in which smoking is permitted by subdivision (f), and that restricts access to minors under 18 years of age.

☛ Bars and taverns, but only if smoking is permitted pursuant to standards of the Occupational Safety and Health Standards Board. A *bar* or *tavern* is a facility primarily devoted to serving alcoholic beverages for consumption by guests on the premises, in which the serving of food is incidental, including facilities located in a hotel or motel. When located in a building in conjunction with another use, including a restaurant, this exemption only applies to those areas used primarily for the sale and service of alcoholic beverages, and does not include the dining areas of a restaurant, regardless of whether alcoholic beverages are served there.

☛ Theatrical production sites, if smoking is an integral part of the story in the theatrical production.

☛ Medical research or treatment sites, if smoking is integral to the research and treatment being conducted.

☛ Private residences; except for private residences licensed as family day care homes, during the hours of operation as family day care homes and in areas where children are present.

☛ Patient smoking areas in long-term health care facilities. (California Health and Safety Code, Section 1418.)

☛ Breakrooms designed by employers for smoking, provided that all of the following conditions are met:

- Air from the smoking room must be exhausted directly to the outside by an exhaust fan, and not recirculated to other parts of the building.

- The employer must comply with any ventilation standard or other standard utilizing appropriate technology, adopted by Occupational Safety and Health Standards Board or the federal Environmental Protection Agency.

- The smoking room must be located in a nonwork area where no one, as part of his or her work responsibilities, is required to enter (this does not include custodial or maintenance work carried out in the breakroom when unoccupied).

- There must be sufficient nonsmoking breakrooms to accommodate nonsmokers.

☛ Employers with a total of five or fewer employees, either full-time or part-time, may permit smoking where all of the following conditions are met:

- The smoking area is not accessible to minors.

- All employees who enter the smoking area consent to permit smoking. An employer who is determined to have used coercion to obtain consent or who has required an employee to work in a smoking area is subject to the penalty provisions. (Cal. Lab. Code, Section 6427.)

- Air from the smoking area must be exhausted directly to the outside by an exhaust fan, and may not be recirculated to other parts of the building.

- The employer must comply with any ventilation standard or other standard utilizing appropriate technology, adopted by the Occupational Safety and Health Standards Board or the federal Environmental Protection Agency.

Employers are not required to provide accommodation to smokers, or to provide breakrooms for smokers or nonsmokers. Regardless of this law, an employer may prohibit smoking in an enclosed place of employment for any reason.

Any area not defined as a "place of employment" under this law, is subject to local regulation of smoking.

Under this law, the rules for bars, taverns, and gaming clubs seems more confusing, and more subject to change, than the rules for other types of businesses. Therefore, if you are planning to open a bar, tavern, or gaming club, be sure to take all measures possible to bring yourself up to date on the current law regarding smoking.

We have only presented a general summary of the smoking law. If you plan to prohibit smoking altogether in your workplace, or will have the type of business where you do not have any employees and do not have other people coming into your workplace (for example, you alone will be operating a mail order, or Internet-based business), you probably will not need to be concerned with the smoking laws. But if you will have employees or customers in your place of business, and plan to allow smoking on the premises, you should read California Labor Code, Section 6404 carefully and be sure you understand it.

EMPLOYMENT AND LABOR LAWS 11

HIRING AND FIRING LAWS

For small businesses, there are not many rules regarding who you may hire or fire. Fortunately, the ancient law that an employee can be fired at any time (or may quit at any time) still prevails for small businesses. But in certain situations, and as you grow, you will come under a number of laws that affect your hiring and firing practices.

One of the most important things to consider when hiring employees is that if you fire them, they may be entitled to *unemployment compensation*. If so, your unemployment compensation tax rate will go up and it can cost you a lot of money. Therefore, you should only hire people you are sure you will keep and you should avoid situations where your former employees can make claims against your company.

One way this can be done is by hiring only part-time employees. The drawback to this is that you may not be able to attract the best employees. When hiring dishwashers or busboys this may not be an issue, but when hiring someone to develop a software product, you do not want them to leave halfway through the development.

A better solution is to screen applicants to begin with and only hire those who you feel certain will work out. Of course this is easier said than done. Some people interview well but then turn out to be incompetent at the job.

The best record to look for is someone who has stayed a long time at each of their previous jobs. Next best is someone who has not stayed as long (for good reasons) but has always been employed. The worst type of hire would be someone who is or has been collecting unemployment compensation.

The reason those who have collected compensation are a bad risk is that if they collect in the future, even if it is not your fault, your employment of them could make you chargeable for their claim. For example, you hire someone who has been on unemployment compensation and they work out well for a year, but then they quit to take another job, and are fired after a few weeks. In this situation, you would be chargeable for most of their claim because their last five quarters of work are analyzed. Look for a steady job history.

In the author's experience, the intelligence of an employee is more important than his or her experience. An employee with years of typing experience may be fast, but unable to figure out how to use your new computer. Whereas an intelligent employee can learn the equipment quickly and eventually gain speed. Of course, common sense is important in all situations.

The bottom line is that you cannot know if an employee will be able to fill your needs from a resume and interview. Once you have found someone who you think will work out, offer them a job with a ninety-day probationary period. If you are not completely satisfied with them after the ninety days, offer to extend the probationary period for ninety additional days rather than end the relationship immediately. Of course, all of this should be in writing.

BACKGROUND CHECKS
Checking references is important, but beware that a former boss may be a good friend, or even a relative. It has always been considered acceptable to exaggerate on resumes, but in recent years, some applicants have been found to be completely fabricating sections of their education and experience.

POLYGRAPH
TESTS

Under the federal Employee Polygraph Protection Act you cannot require an employee or prospective employee to take a polygraph test unless you are in the armored car, guard, or pharmaceutical business.

DRUG TESTS

Under the Americans with Disabilities Act (ADA) drug testing can only be required of applicants who have been offered jobs conditioned upon passing the drug test. Random drug testing is no longer used in California. Companies with twenty-five or more employees must make a reasonable effort to accommodate an employee who wants to enter a drug rehabilitation program. Reasonable effort does not mean paying for the program or giving paid time off to the employee. However, if the employee does have accumulated sick time, the employer must allow the employee to use it.

FIRING

In most cases, unless you have a contract with an employee for a set time period, you can fire him or her at any time. This is only fair since the employee can quit at any time. The exceptions to this are: if you fired someone based on illegal discrimination, for filing some sort of health or safety complaint, or for refusing your sexual advances.

NEW HIRE REPORTING

In order to track down parents who do not pay child support, a federal law was passed in 1996 that requires the reporting of new hires. The Personal Responsibility and Work Opportunity Reconciliation Act of 1996 (PRWORA) provides that such information must be reported by employers to their state government.

Within twenty days of hiring a new employee, an employer must provide the state with information about the employee including the name, social security number, and address. This information can be submitted in several ways including mail, fax, magnetic tape or over the Internet. There is a special form that can be used for this reporting; however, an employer can use the W-4 form for this purpose. Since this form must be filled out for all employees anyway, it would be pointless to use a separate form for the new hire reporting. A copy of the W-4 form is included in the appendix. (see form 8, p.251.)

For more information about the program you can call the Employment Development Department at 888-745-3886.

EMPLOYMENT AGREEMENTS

To avoid misunderstanding with employees you should use an employment agreement or an employee handbook. These can spell out in detail the policies of your company and the rights of your employees. They can protect your trade secrets and spell out clearly that employment can be terminated at any time by either party.

While it may be difficult or awkward to ask an existing employee to sign such an agreement, an applicant hoping you will hire them will usually sign whatever is necessary to obtain the job. However, because of the unequal bargaining position, you should not use an agreement that would make you look bad if the matter ever went to court.

If having an employee sign an agreement is awkward, you can usually obtain the same rights by putting the company policies in an employee manual. Each existing and new employee should be given a copy along with a letter stating that the rules apply to all employees and that by accepting or continuing employment at your company they agree to abide by the rules. Having an employee sign a receipt for the letter and manual is proof that they received it.

One danger of an employment agreement or handbook is that it may be interpreted to create a long-term employment contract. To avoid this be sure that you clearly state in the agreement or handbook that the employment is *at will* and can be terminated at any time by either party.

Some other things to consider in an employment agreement or handbook are:

- ☞ what the salary and other compensation will be;
- ☞ what the hours of employment will be;
- ☞ what the probationary period will be;
- ☞ that the employee cannot sign any contracts binding the employer; and
- ☞ that the employee agrees to arbitration rather than filing a lawsuit.

An employment agreement, a confidentiality agreement, and a non-competition agreement are included in books referenced at the end of this book.

INDEPENDENT CONTRACTORS

One way to avoid problems with employees and taxes at the same time is to have all of your work done through independent contractors. This can relieve you of most of the burdens of employment laws and the obligation to pay social security and medicare taxes for the workers.

An independent contractor is, in effect, a separate business that you pay to do a job. You pay them just as you pay any company from which you buy products or services. If at the end of the year the amount paid exceeds $600, you will issue a 1099 form instead of a W-2.

This may seem too good to be true; and in some situations it is. The IRS does not like independent contractor arrangements because it is too easy for the independent contractors to cheat on their taxes. To limit the use of independent contractors, the IRS has strict regulations on who may and may not be classified as an independent contractor. Also, companies who do not appear to pay enough in wages for their field of business are audited.

The highest at-risk jobs are those that are not traditionally done by independent contractors. For example, you could not get away with hiring a secretary as an independent contractor. One of the most important factors considered in determining if a worker can be an independent contractor is the amount of control the company has over his or her work. If you need someone to paint your building and you agree to pay them a certain price to do it according to their own methods and schedule, you can pay them as an independent contractor. But if you tell them when to work, how to do the job and provide them with the tools and materials, they will be classified an employee.

If you just need some typing done and you take it to a typing service and pick it up when it is ready, you will be safe in treating them as independent contractors. But, if you need someone to come into your office to type on your machine at your schedule, you will probably be required to treat that person as an employee for tax purposes.

The IRS has a form you can use in determining if a person is an employee or an independent contractor. It is form SS-8 and is included in the appendix of this book. (see form 7, p.247.)

INDEPENDENT CONTRACTORS V. EMPLOYEES
In deciding whether to make use of independent contractors or employees, you should weigh the following advantages and disadvantages of using an independent contractor:

Advantages.

- ☛ Lower taxes. You do not have to pay social security, medicare, unemployment, or other employee taxes.

- ☛ Less paperwork. You do not have to handle federal withholding deposits or the monthly employer returns to the state or federal government.

- ☛ Less insurance. You do not have to pay workers' compensation insurance and since the workers are not your employees you do not have to insure against their possible liabilities.

- ☛ More flexibility. You can use independent contractors when you need them, and not pay them when business is slow.

Disadvantages.

☞ The IRS and state tax offices are strict about when workers may be qualified as independent contractors. They will audit companies whose use of independent contractors does not appear to be legitimate.

☞ If your use of independent contractors is found to be improper you may have to pay back taxes and penalties and have problems with your pension plan.

☞ While employees usually cannot sue you for their injuries (if you have covered them with workers' compensation) independent contractors can sue you if their injuries were your fault.

☞ If you are paying someone to produce a creative work (writing, photography, artwork) you receive fewer rights to the work of an independent contractor.

☞ You have less control over the work of an independent contractor and less flexibility in terminating them if you are not satisfied that the job is being done the way you require.

☞ You have less loyalty from an independent contractor who works sporadically for you and possibly others, than from your own full-time employees.

For some businesses, the advantages outweigh the disadvantages, but for others they do not. Consider your business plans and the consequences from each type of arrangement. Keep in mind that it will be easier to start with independent contractors and switch to employees than to hire employees and have to fire them to hire independent contractors.

TEMPORARY WORKERS

Another way to avoid the hassles of hiring employees is to get workers from a temporary agency. In this arrangement you may pay a higher amount per hour for the work, but the agency will take care of all of the tax and insurance requirements. Since these can be expensive and time-consuming, the extra cost may be well worth it.

Whether or not temporary workers will work for you depends upon the type of business you are in and tasks you need performed. For such jobs as sales management, you would probably want someone who will stay with you long-term and develop relationships with the buyers. For order fulfillment, temporary workers might work out well.

Another advantage of temporary workers is that you can easily stop using those who do not work out well for you. But if you find one who is ideal, you may be able to hire him or her on a full time basis.

In recent years a new wrinkle has developed in the temporary worker area. Many large companies are beginning to use them because they are so much cheaper than paying the benefits demanded by full time employees. For example, Microsoft Corp. has had as many as 6,000 temporary workers, some of whom worked for them for years. Some of the temporary workers recently won a lawsuit declaring that they are really employees and are entitled to the same benefits of other employees (such as pension plans).

The law is not yet settled in this area as to what arrangements will result in a temporary worker being declared an employee. That will take several more court cases, some of which have already been filed. A few things you can do to protect yourself are:

- ☛ Be sure that any of your benefit plans make it clear that they do not apply to workers obtained through temporary agencies.
- ☛ Do not keep the same temporary workers for longer than a year.
- ☛ Do not list temporary workers in any employee directories or hold them out to the public as your employees.
- ☛ Do not allow them to use your business cards or stationery.

DISCRIMINATION LAWS

FEDERAL LAW

There are numerous federal laws forbidding discrimination based upon race, sex, pregnancy, color, religion, national origin, age, or disability. The laws apply to both hiring and firing, and to employment practices such as salaries, promotions and benefits. Most of these laws only apply to an employer who has fifteen or more employees for twenty weeks of a calendar year or has federal contracts or subcontracts. Therefore, you most likely will not be required to comply with the law immediately upon opening your business. However, there are similar state laws that may apply to your business.

One exception is the Equal Pay Act, which applies to employers with two or more employees and requires that women be paid the same as men in the same type of job.

Employers with fifteen or more employees are required to display a poster regarding discrimination. This poster is available from the Equal Employment Opportunity Commission (EEOC), 1801 L Street N.W., Washington, DC 20507. Employers with 100 or more employees are required to file an annual report with the EEOC.

When hiring employees, some questions are illegal or inadvisable to ask. A sample employment application is in the appendix of this book. (see form 4, p.238.) The following questions should not be included on your employment application, or in your interviews, unless the information is somehow directly tied to the duties of the job:

☛ Do not ask about an applicant's citizenship or place of birth. But after hiring an employee you must ask about his or her right to work in this country.

☛ Do not ask a female applicant her maiden name. You can ask if she has been known by any other name in order to do a background check.

☛ Do not ask if applicants have children, plan to have them, or have child care. You can ask if an applicant will be able to work the required hours.

☛ Do not ask if the applicant has religious objections for working Saturday or Sunday. You can mention if the job requires such hours and ask whether the applicant can meet this job requirement.

☛ Do not ask an applicant's age. You can ask if an applicant is eighteen or over, or for a liquor-related job if they are twenty-one or over.

☛ Do not ask an applicant's weight.

☛ Do not ask if an applicant has AIDS or is HIV positive.

☛ Do not ask if the applicant has filed a workers' compensation claim.

☛ Do not ask about the applicant's previous health problems.

☛ Do not ask if the applicant is married or whether their spouse would object to the job, hours, or duties.

☛ Do not ask if the applicant owns a home, furniture, car, as it is considered racially-discriminatory.

☛ Do not ask if the applicant was ever arrested. You can ask if the applicant was ever convicted of a crime.

The most recent, and perhaps most onerous, law is the Americans with Disabilities Act of 1990 (ADA). Under this law employers who do not make "reasonable accommodations for disabled employees" will face fines of up to $100,000, as well as other civil penalties and civil damage awards.

While the goal of creating more opportunities for people with disabilities is a good one, the result of this law is to place all of the costs of achieving this goal on businesses that are faced with disabled applicants. For example, it has been suggested that the requirement of "reasonable accommodation" will require some companies to hire blind applicants for jobs that require reading and then to hire second employees to read to the blind employees. We will only know the extent to which this law can be applied after some unlucky employers have been taken to court.

A study released by two MIT economists in late 1998 indicated that since the ADA was passed, employers have hired less rather than more disabled people. It is theorized that this may be due to the expense of the "reasonable accommodations" or the fear of lawsuits by disabled employees.

The ADA currently applies to employers with fifteen or more employees. Employers who need more than fifteen employees might want to consider contracting with independent contractors to avoid problems with this law, particularly if the number of employees is only slightly larger than fifteen.

Tax benefits. There are three types of tax credits to help small businesses with the burden of these laws.

- ☞ Businesses can deduct up to $15,000 a year for making their premises accessible to the disabled and can depreciate the rest. (Internal Revenue Code (I.R.C.), Section 190.)

- ☞ Small businesses (under $1,000,000 in revenue and under thirty employees) can get a tax credit each year for 50% of the cost of making their premises accessible to the disabled, but this only applies to the amount between $250 and $10,500.

- ☞ Small businesses can get a credit of up to 40% of the first $6,000 of wages paid to certain new employees who qualify through IRS form 8850 and instructions. (see form 13, p.265.)

Records. To protect against potential claims of discrimination, all employers should keep detailed records showing reasons for hiring or not hiring applicants, and for firing employees.

CALIFORNIA
LAW

Discrimination. The California Government Code (Cal. Gov't. Code), Section 12940 (a) prohibits discrimination in employment based on race, religious creed, color, national origin, ancestry, physical disability, mental disability, medical condition, marital status, sex, or sexual orientation.

You may refuse to hire or may fire an employee whose physical, mental, or medical condition renders that person unable to perform the essential duties of the job, or would endanger the health and safety of others, even with reasonable accommodations. (Cal. Gov't. Code, Section 12940 (a) (1) and (2).)

You may cause spouses to work in different departments or facilities for reasons of supervision, safety, security, or morale. (Cal. Gov't. Code, Section 12940 (a) (3) (A).)

You may also favor Vietnam era veterans in hiring, even though it discriminates. Cal. Gov't. Code, Section 12940 (a) (4).

SEXUAL HARASSMENT

What began as protection for employees who were fired or not promoted for failing to succumb to sexual advances of their superiors has been expanded to outlaw nearly any sexual comments or references in the workplace. As an example of how far this has gone, one university was forced to take down a painting by Goya depicting a nude because a teacher felt sexually harassed by its presence.

FEDERAL LAW
In the 1980s, the EEOC interpreted the Title VII of the Civil Rights Act of 1964 to forbid sexual harassment. After that, the courts took over and reviewed all types of conduct in the workplace. The numerous lawsuits that followed began a trend toward expanding the definition of sexual harassment and favoring employees.

Some of the actions that have been considered harassment are:
- displaying sexually explicit posters in the workplace;
- requiring female employees to wear revealing uniforms;
- rating of sexual attractiveness of female employees as they passed male employees' desks; and
- continued sexual jokes and innuendos.

In 1993, the United States Supreme Court ruled that an employee can make a claim for sexual harassment even without proof of a specific injury. However, lower federal courts in more recent cases (such as the Paula Jones case against President Clinton) have dismissed cases where no specific injury was shown (although these cases may be overruled by a higher court). These new cases may indicate that the pendulum has stopped moving toward expanded rights for the employee.

On the other hand, another case ruled that an employer can be liable for the harassment of an employee by a supervisor, even if the employer was unaware of the supervisor's conduct, if the employer did not have a system in place to allow complaints against harassment. This area of law is still developing and to avoid a possible lawsuit you should be aware of the things that could potentially cause liability and avoid them.

Some things a business can do to protect against claims of sexual harassment are:

☛ Distribute a written policy against all kinds of sexual harassment to all employees;

☛ Encourage employees to report all incidents of sexual harassment; and

☛ Insure that there is no retaliation against those who complain.

CALIFORNIA LAW   California law prohibits sexual harassment. (Cal. Gov't. Code, Section 12940 (h and following).)

COMMON LAW   It is possible for an employee to sue for sexual harassment in civil court. However, this is difficult and expensive and would only be worthwhile where there were substantial *damages*, or money to be won.

WAGE AND HOUR LAWS

FEDERAL LAW   ***Businesses covered.*** The Fair Labor Standards Act (FLSA) applies to all employers who are engaged in *interstate commerce* or in the production of goods for interstate commerce (anything that will cross the state line) and all employees of hospitals, schools, residential facilities for the disabled or aged, or public agencies. It also applies to all employees of enterprises that gross $500,000 or more per year.

While many small businesses might not think they are engaged in interstate commerce, the laws have been interpreted so broadly that nearly any use of the mails, interstate telephone service, or other interstate services, however minor, is enough to bring a business under the law. The authors of our Constitution clearly intended for most rights to be reserved to the states, but the *commerce clause* has been used to expand federal control to many unintended areas.

Minimum wage. The federal wage and hour laws are contained in the FLSA. In 1996, Congress passed and President Clinton signed legislation raising the minimum wage to $5.15 an hour beginning September 1, 1997.

In certain circumstances a wage of $3.62 may be paid to employees under twenty years of age for a ninety day training period.

For employees who regularly receive more than $30 a month in tips, the minimum wage is $2.13 per hour. But if the employee's tips do not bring him up to the full $5.15 minimum wage, then the employer must make up the difference.

Overtime. Workers who work over forty hours in a week must be paid time-and-a-half for the time worked over forty hours.

Exempt employees. While nearly all businesses are covered, certain employees are exempt from the FLSA. Exempt employees include employees that are considered executives, administrative and managerial, professionals, computer professionals, and outside salespeople.

Whether or not one of these exceptions applies to a particular employee is a complicated legal question. Thousands of court cases have been decided on this issue but they have given no clear answers. In one case a person could be determined to be exempt because of his duties, but in another, a person with the same duties could be found not exempt.

One thing that is clear is that the determination is made on the employee's function, and not just the job title. You cannot make a secretary exempt by calling her a manager if most of her duties are clerical. For more information contact:

Wage and Hour Division
U. S. Department of Labor
200 Constitution Ave., N.W. Room S-3325
Washington, DC 20210

Or call a local office:
Glendale 818-240-5274
Sacramento 916-978-6120
San Diego 619-557-5606
San Francisco 415-744-5590
West Covina 818-966-0478

On the Internet you can obtain information on the Department of Labor's *Small Business Handbook* at:

http://www.dol.gov/dol/asp/public/programs/handbook/main.htm

CALIFORNIA LAW   The California Labor Code (Cal. Lab. Code), Sections 750-752 provides for overtime pay of one and one half times regular hourly pay for hours worked over eight in a twenty-four hour period or forty hours in a seven day period. Over twelve hours in a twenty-four hour period requires double pay.

If you hire an employee and make a contract in which the employee agrees not to require overtime pay, you will still have to pay the overtime pay if the employee later decided to file a complaint with the Labor Commission.

If you do hire someone who will be working extra hours and is willing to forgo overtime pay, you can form a contract that says that the employee's normal pay would be less if overtime were being paid. For example: The normal rate of pay is $2,500 per month. Because the employee will not receive overtime, the rate of pay is $3,000/month. Consult an attorney to draw the contract.

PENSION AND BENEFIT LAWS

There are no laws requiring small businesses to provide any types of special benefits to employees. Such benefits are given to attract and keep good employees. With pension plans the main concern is if you do start one it must comply with federal tax laws.

HOLIDAYS   There are no federal or California laws that require that employees be given holidays off, except for government employees or companies under government contract. You can require them to work Thanksgiving and Christmas and dock their pay or fire them for failing to show up. Of course you will not have much luck keeping employees with such a policy.

Most companies give full time employees a certain number of paid holidays, such as: New Year's Day (January 1); Memorial Day (last Monday in May); Fourth of July; Labor Day (first Monday in September); Thanksgiving (fourth Thursday in November) and Christmas (December 25). Some, but not many, employers include other holidays such as Martin Luther King, Jr.'s birthday (January 15); President's Day; and Columbus Day. If one of the holidays falls on a Saturday or Sunday, many employers give the preceding Friday or following Monday off.

California state employees get the following holidays off:

New Year's Day (January 1)

Martin Luther King, Jr. (Third Monday in January)

Abraham Lincoln's Birthday (February 12)

President's Day (Third Monday in February)

Memorial Day (last Monday in May)

July 4th

Labor Day (first Monday in September)

Columbus Day (second Monday in October)

Veterans' Day (November 11)

Friday following Thanksgiving

One personal holiday day

Every day appointed by Governor for a public fast, thanksgiving, or holiday

However, the fact that these are designated state holidays does not mean anything. In fact, not even the state government is closed on all of these days.

SICK DAYS

There is no federal or California law mandating that an employee be paid for time that he or she is home sick. The situation seems to be that the larger the company, the more paid sick leave is allowed. Part-time workers rarely get sick leave and small business sick leave is usually limited for the simple reason that they cannot afford to pay for time that employees do not work.

Some small companies have an official policy of no paid sick leave, but when an important employee misses a day because he or she is clearly sick, it is paid.

BREAKS

There are no federal or California laws requiring coffee breaks or lunch breaks. However, it is common sense that employees will be more productive if they have reasonable breaks for nourishment or to use the toilet facilities.

PENSION PLANS AND RETIREMENT ACCOUNTS

Few small new businesses can afford to provide pension plans for their employees. The first concern of a small business is usually how the owner can shelter income in a pension plan without having to set up a pension plan for an employee. Under most pension plans this is not allowed.

IRA. Anyone with $2,000 of earnings can put up to that amount in an Individual Retirement Account. Unless the person or his or her spouse are covered by a company pension plan and have income over a certain amount, the amount put into the account is fully tax deductible.

ROTH IRA. Contributions to a Roth IRA are not tax deductible but then when the money is taken out it is not taxable. People who expect to still have taxable income when they withdraw from their IRA can benefit from these.

SEP IRA, SAR-SEP IRA, SIMPLE IRA. With these types of retirement accounts, a person can put a much greater amount into a retirement plan and deduct it from their taxable income. Employees must also be covered by such plans, but certain employees are exempt so it is sometimes possible to use these for the owners alone. The best source for more information is a mutual fund company (such as Vanguard, Fidelity, Dreyfus, etc.) or a local bank, which can set up the plan and provide you with all of the rules. These have an advantage over qualified plans (discussed below) since they do not have the high annual fees.

Qualified Retirement Plans. Qualified retirement plans are 401(k) plans, Keough plans, and corporate retirement plans. These are covered by the Employee Retirement Income Security Act (ERISA), which is a complicated law meant to protect employee pension plans. Congress did not want employees who contributed to pension plans all their lives ending up with nothing when the plan goes bankrupt. The law is so complicated and the penalties so severe that some companies are cancelling their pension plans, and applications for new plans are a fraction of what they were previously. However, many banks and mutual funds have created "canned plans," which can be used instead of drafting one from scratch. Still the fees for administering them are steep. Check with a bank or mutual fund for details.

FAMILY AND MEDICAL LEAVE LAWS

FEDERAL LAW

To assist business owners in deciding what type of leave to offer their employees, Congress passed the Family and Medical Leave Act of 1993

(FMLA). This law requires an employee to be given up to twelve weeks of unpaid leave when:

☞ The employee or employee's spouse has a child;

☞ The employee adopts a child or takes in a foster child;

☞ The employee needs to care for an ill spouse, child, or parent; or

☞ The employee becomes seriously ill.

Fortunately, the law only applies to employers with fifty or more employees. Also, the top ten percent of an employer's salaried employees can be denied this leave because of the disruption in business their loss could cause.

CALIFORNIA
LAW

California also has a law concerning family and medical leave. (Cal. Gov't. Code, Section 12945.2.) Fortunately, the California law is similar to the federal law in many respects, including:

☞ Leave is available for the same reasons as the federal law.

☞ It only applies to employers with fifty or more employees within seventy-five miles of the worksite where the employee seeking the leave is employed.

☞ It provides that the top ten percent of salaried employees can be denied leave if it would disrupt business operations.

Most people reading this book will not be opening their business with fifty or more employees. However, if you are among those few who do plan to start with, or very rapidly grow to, fifty employees, you should obtain a copy of both the federal and California family and medical leave laws and become familiar with them.

If the California law applies, it basically provides that an employee "with more than 12 months of service with the employer, and who has at least 1,250 hours of service with the employer during the previous 12-month period [may] take up to a total of 12 workweeks in any 12-month period for family care and medical leave." Generally, this runs concurrent with the federal law.

Child Labor Laws

FEDERAL LAW

The FLSA also contains rules regarding the hiring of children. The basic rules are that children under sixteen years old may not be hired at all except in a few jobs such as acting and newspaper delivery, and those under eighteen may not be hired for dangerous jobs. Children may not work more than three hours a day/eighteen hours a week in a school week, or more than eight hours a day/forty hours a week in a non-school week. If you plan to hire children, you should check the FLSA, which is in United States Code (U.S.C.), Chapter 29 and also the related regulations, which are in Code of Federal Regulations (C.F.R.), Chapter 29.

CALIFORNIA LAW

California Child Labor Laws are discussed here a bit more extensively, not only because they may be helpful in your business (most likely to convince you that it is too much trouble to hire minors) but also because they are interesting. The laws regarding using babies in movies, fourteen year old professional baseball players, door-to-door begging, and candy selling are probably ones that you will not see in many other states. First, we will summarize the laws relating generally to various age groups. Second, we will discuss laws that apply to certain jobs or industries. Finally, we will mention a few general things about hiring minors. Unless otherwise indicated, all references are to sections of the California Labor Code (Cal. Lab. Code).

All Minors No minor may be employed or permitted to work in any occupation declared particularly hazardous for the employment of minors between sixteen and eighteen years of age, or declared detrimental to their health or well-being, in C.F.R., Title 29, Part 570, Subpart E, and Cal. Lab. Code, Section 1293.1(b).

There are special exceptions for minors with newspaper routes. Minors may enter a newspaper plant, except for areas where printing presses are located, if they are engaged in the processing and delivery of newspapers. (Cal. Lab. Code, Section 1294.1(c).) They are also allowed to make deliveries by foot, bicycle, public transportation, or by an automobile driven by a person sixteen years of age or older. (Cal. Lab. Code, Section 1294.4.) No minor under age twelve may be employed or permitted to work in or in connection with the occupation of selling or distributing newspapers, magazines, periodicals, or circulars. (Cal. Lab. Code, Section 1298(a).)

No minor under the age of eighteen may be employed or permitted to work as a messenger for any telegraph, telephone, or messenger company, or for the United States government or any of its departments while operating a telegraph, telephone, or messenger service, in the distribution, transmission, or delivery of goods or messages in cities of more than 15,000 inhabitants before 6:00 A.M. or after 9:00 P.M. (Cal. Lab. Code, Section 1297.)

No person under the age of sixteen may work in any of the following capacities, (Cal. Lab. Code, Section 1292(a), (b), and (c) and Section 1293):

☛ Adjusting any belt to any machinery;

☛ Sewing or lacing machine belts in any workshop or factory;

☛ Oiling, wiping, or cleaning machinery, or assisting therein;

☛ Operating or assisting in operating any of the following machines:

- Circular or band saws; wood shapers; wood-jointers; planers; sandpaper or wood-polishing machinery; wood turning or boring machinery;

- Picker machines or machines used in picking wool, cotton, hair, or other material; carding machines; leather-burnishing machines; laundry machinery;

- Printing-presses of all kinds; boring or drilling presses; stamping machines used in sheet-metal and tinware, in paper and leather manufacturing, or in washer and nut factories; metal or paper-cutting machines; paper-lace machines;

- Corner-staying machines in paper-box factories; corrugating rolls, such as are used in corrugated paper, roofing or wash-board factories;
- Dough brakes or cracker machinery of any description; and
- Wire or iron straightening or drawing machinery; rolling-mill machinery; power punches or shears; washing, grinding or mixing machinery; calendar rolls in paper and rubber manufacturing; steam-boilers; in proximity to any hazardous or unguarded belts, machinery or gearing.

☞ Upon any railroad, whether steam, electric, or hydraulic;

☞ Upon any vessel or boat engaged in navigation or commerce within the jurisdiction of the state;

☞ In, about, or in connection with any processes in which dangerous or poisonous acids are used, in the manufacture or packing of paints, colors, white or red lead, or in soldering;

☞ In occupations causing dust in injurious quantities, in the manufacture and use of dangerous or poisonous gases, or in the manufacture or preparation of compositions with dangerous or poisonous gases, or in the manufacture or use of compositions of lye in which the quantity is injurious to health;

☞ On scaffolding, in heavy work in the building trades, in any tunnel or excavation, or in, about, or in connection with any mine, coal breaker, coke oven, or quarry;

☞ In assorting, manufacturing, or packing tobacco;

☞ Operating any automobile, motorcar, or truck;

☞ In any occupation dangerous to the life or limb, or injurious to the health or morals of the minor;

☞ In any occupation declared particularly hazardous for the employment of minors below the age of 16 years in C.F.R., Title 29, Section 570.71 of Subpart E-1 of Part 570;

☛ In any occupation excluded from the application of C.F.R., Title 29, Section 570.33 of Subpart C of part 570 and paragraph (b) of Section 570.34;

☛ As a messenger for any telegraph, telephone, or messenger company, or for the United States government or any of its departments while operating a telegraph, telephone, or messenger service, in the distribution, transmission, or delivery of goods or messages in cities of more than 15,000 inhabitants; and

☛ Door-to-door sales of newspaper or magazine subscriptions, or of candy, cookies, flowers, or other merchandise or commodities, if those activities are more than fifty miles from the minor's place of residence.

Ages Fourteen and Fifteen. Some sections of the law state the type of jobs minors *may* hold. Minors who are fourteen and fifteen years of age may be employed in any occupation not otherwise prohibited by law, including, but not limited to, the following:

☛ Office and clerical work, including the operation of office machines;

☛ Cashiering, selling, modeling, art work, work in advertising departments, window trimming, and comparative shopping;

☛ Price marking and tagging by hand or by machine, assembling orders, patching and shelving;

☛ Bagging and carrying out customer's orders;

☛ Errand and delivery work by foot, bicycle, and public transportation;

☛ Cleanup work, including the use of vacuum cleaners and floor waxers, and maintenance of grounds, but not including the use of power-driven mowers and cutters;

☛ Kitchen work and other work involved in preparing and serving food and beverages, including the operation of machines and devices used in the performance of this work, such as dishwashers, toasters, dumbwaiters, popcorn poppers, milkshake blenders, and coffee grinders; and

☛ Cleaning vegetables and fruits, and wrapping, sealing, labeling, weighing, pricing, and stocking goods when performed in areas physically separate from areas where meat is prepared for sale and outside freezers or meat coolers.

Under Age Twelve. No minor under the age of twelve may be employed or permitted to work, or accompany or be permitted to accompany an employed parent or guardian, in any of the following capacities:

☛ In an agricultural zone of danger (defined as on or about moving equipment, in or about unprotected chemicals, on or about any unprotected water hazard, or any other hazards determined by the Department of Industrial Relations;

☛ In any of the occupations declared hazardous for employment of minors below age sixteen in C.F.R., Title 29, Section 570.71; or

☛ In or in connection with the occupation of selling or distributing newspapers, magazines, periodicals, or circulars. (Cal. Lab. Code, Section 1298.)

Under Age Six. No minor under the age of six may be permitted to engage in the door-to-door sales or street sales of candy, cookies, flowers, or any other merchandise or commodities. (Cal. Lab. Code, Section 1308.1(a).)

Now we will turn our attention to some laws that relate to the employment of minors in certain types of jobs or industries.

Gas Stations. Minors sixteen and seventeen years of age may work in gas service stations in the following activities. (Cal. Lab. Code, Section 1294.5):

☛ Dispensing gas or oil;

☛ Courtesy service;

☛ Car cleaning, washing, and polishing; or

☞ Activities specified in Cal. Lab. Code, Section 1294.3.

They may not perform work that involves the inflation of any tire mounted on a rim equipped with a removable retaining ring. Minors under the age of sixteen years may be employed in gas service stations to perform only those activities specified above under the heading "Ages Fourteen and Fifteen."

Entertainment Industry. As would be expected in California, there are special rules for children employed in the entertainment industry. The consent of the Labor Commissioner is required for any of the following (Cal. Lab. Code, Section 1308.5):

☞ The employment of any minor under the age of sixteen in the presentation of any drama or legitimate play, or in any radio broadcasting or television studio;

☞ The employment of any minor between the ages of twelve and fifteen in any other performance, concert, or entertainment;

☞ The appearance of any minor between the ages of eight and fifteen in any performance, concert, or entertainment during the public school vacation;

☞ Allowing any minor between the ages of eight and eighteen (who is permitted by California law to be employed as an actor, actress, or performer) in a theater, motion picture studio, radio broadcasting studio, or television studio, before 10:00 p.m., in the presentation of a performance, play, or drama continuing from an earlier hour until after 10:00 p.m., to continue his part in such presentation between the hours of 10:00 p.m. and midnight;

☞ The appearance of any minor under the age of sixteen in any entertainment which is noncommercial in nature;

☞ The employment of any minor artist under the age of sixteen in the making of phonograph recordings;

☞ The employment of any minor under the age of sixteen as an advertising or photographic model; or

☛ The employment or appearance of any minor under the age of sixteen pursuant to a contract approved by the superior court under the California Family Code (Cal. Fam. Code), beginning with Section 6750.

No minor may be employed in the entertainment industry more than eight hours in one day of twenty-four hours, or more than forty-eight hours in one week, or before 5:00 a.m., or after 10:00 p.m. on any day preceding a schoolday. However, a minor may work these hours during any evening preceding a non-school day until 12:30 a.m. of the non-school day. (Cal. Lab. Code, Section 1308.7.) (A "school day" is any day in which a minor is required to attend school for 240 minutes or more.)

No infant under the age of one month may be employed on any motion picture set or location unless a licensed physician and surgeon who is board-certified in pediatrics provides written certification that the infant is at least fifteen days old and, in his or her medical opinion, the infant was carried to full term, was of normal birth weight, is physically capable of handling the stress of filmmaking, and the infant's lungs, eyes, heart, and immune system are sufficiently developed to withstand potential risks. (Cal. Lab. Code, Section 1308.8.)

The law does not prohibit the appearance of a minor:

☛ in any radio or television broadcasting exhibition, where the minor receives no compensation directly or indirectly, where the engagement of the minor is limited to a single appearance lasting not more than one hour, and where no admission fee is charged for the radio broadcasting or television exhibition; or

☛ at any event during a calendar year, occurring on a day in which school attendance is not required or on the day preceding such a day, lasting four hours or less, where a parent or guardian of the minor is present, for which the minor does not directly or indirectly receive any compensation.

Professional Baseball Minors fourteen years of age and older may be employed during certain hours to perform *sports-attending services* in professional baseball. (C.F.R., Title 29, Section 570.35 (b).) The minor must obtain the written approval of either the school district, the school in which the minor is enrolled, or the county board of education of the county in which that school district is located. The hours are limited to outside of school hours until 12:30 a.m. during any evening preceding a non-school day, and until 10:00 p.m. during any evening preceding a school day. The child may not work more than five hours on any school day, more than eighteen hours in any week while school is in session, more than eight hours on a non-school day, or more than forty hours in any week that school is not in session. However, a sixteen or seventeen year old may be employed outside of school hours for up to five hours on any school day. (Cal. Lab. Code, Section 1295.5.)

Education and Training Exceptions Certain prohibitions for dangerous activities do not apply to any of the following (Cal. Lab. Code, Section 1295):

- ☛ Courses of training in vocational or manual training schools or in state institutions;

- ☛ Apprenticeship training programs, and work experience education programs, established pursuant to certain provisions of the Education Code;

- ☛ Student-learners in a bona fide vocational agriculture program; or

- ☛ Minors fourteen or fifteen years of age who hold certificates of completion of either a tractor operation or a machine operation program and who are working in the occupations for which they have been trained.

Permits, Inspections, and Penalties By hiring a minor, you open yourself up to additional permit requirements, inspections, and penalties. For example, permits of some type are required for the following:

- ☛ The employment of a minor as a musician at a concert or other musical entertainment, or as a performer in any form of entertainment. (Cal. Lab. Code, Section 1308.5.)

☞ Any person age eighteen or older who transports, or provides direction or supervision during transportation of, a minor under age sixteen to any location more than ten miles from the minor's residence (except for the minor's parent or guardian; a person solely providing transportation for hire, who is not otherwise subject to this requirement; and persons acting on behalf of a trustee, charitable corporation, or certain other entities defined in the California Government Code); or who directs or supervises a minor for the purpose of facilitating the minor's participation in door-to-door sales of any merchandise or commodity. This requires an initial registration fee of up to $100 and an annual renewal fee of up to $50. (Cal. Lab. Code, Section 1308.2.)

☞ Any individual, association, corporation, or other entity that employs or uses, either directly or indirectly through third persons, minors under sixteen years of age in door-to-door sales at any location more than ten miles from the minor's residence. This requires an initial registration fee of up to $350 and an annual renewal fee of up to $200. (Cal. Lab. Code, Section 1308.3.)

If you employ a minor, your business will be subject to inspections by the county attendance supervisor and probation officer according to the Labor Commissioner's office. (Cal. Lab. Code, Section 1302.) If you are required to have a permit, you may be required to show it at any time. You may also be required to maintain certain kinds of records for government inspectors, and may be required to give them access to your payroll records.

Penalties for violating the various child labor laws mentioned above range from fines of $1,000 to $10,000, or imprisonment for up to six months, or both.

The following child labor law provision will give you some idea of the type of laws you will encounter:

1308. (a) Any person is guilty of a misdemeanor and is punishable by a fine of not less than $1,000 and not more than $5,000, imprisonment for not exceeding six months, or both, who, as parent, relative, guardian, employer, or otherwise having the care, custody, or control of any minor under the age of 16 years, exhibits, uses, or employs, or in any manner or under any pretense, sells, apprentices, gives away, lets out, or disposes of the minor to any person, under any name, title, or pretense for, or who causes, procures, or encourages the minor to engage in any of the following:

(1) Any business, exhibition, or vocation injurious to the health or dangerous to the life or limb of the minor.

(2) The vocation, occupation, service, or purpose of singing, playing on musical instruments, rope or wire walking, dancing, begging, or peddling, or as a gymnast, acrobat, contortionist, or rider, in any place whatsoever.

(3) Any obscene, indecent, or immoral purposes, exhibition, or practice whatsoever. Notwithstanding any other provision of law, this paragraph shall apply to a person with respect to any minor under the age of 18 years.

(4) Any mendicant or wandering business.

(b) Nothing in this section applies to or affects any of the following:

(1) The employment or use of any minor as a singer or musician in any church, school, or academy, or the teaching or learning of the science or practice of music.

(2) The employment of any minor as a musician at any concert or other musical entertainment, or as a performer in any form of entertainment, on the written consent of the Labor Commissioner pursuant to Section 1308.5.

(3) The participation by any minor of any age, whether or not the minor receives payment for his or her services or receives money prizes, in any horseback riding exhibition, contest, or event other than a rough stock rodeo event, circus, or race. As used in this paragraph, "rough stock rodeo event" means any rodeo event operated for profit or operated by other than a nonprofit organization in which unbroken, little-trained, or imperfectly trained animals are ridden or handled by the participant, and shall include, but not be limited to, saddle bronc riding, bareback riding, and bull riding. As used in this paragraph, "race" means any speed contest between two or more animals that are on a course at the same time and that is operated for profit or operated other than by a nonprofit organization.

(4) The leading of livestock by a minor in nonprofit fairs, stock parades, livestock shows and exhibitions.

IMMIGRATION LAWS

FEDERAL LAW

In 1986, a law was passed by Congress, which imposes stiff penalties for any business that hires aliens who are not eligible to work. Under this law you must verify both the identity and the employment eligibility of anyone you hire by using form I-9. Both you and the employee must fill out the form and you must check an employee's identification cards or papers. Fines for hiring illegal aliens range from $250 to $2,000 for the first offense and up to $10,000 for the third offense. Failure to maintain the proper paperwork may result in a fine of up to $1,000. The law does not apply to independent contractors with whom you may contract, and it does not penalize you if the employee used fake identification.

There are also penalties that apply to employers of four or more persons for discriminating against eligible applicants because they appear foreign or because of their national origin or citizenship status.

A sample filled-in Form I-9 can be found at the end of this chapter. A blank form with instructions is in the appendix. (See form 5, p.240.) The blank form can also be downloaded from the following website:

http://www.ins.usdoj.gov/

For more information, contact:

U. S. Department of Justice
Immigration and Naturalization Service
425 I Street, NW
Washington, DC 20536

The Illegal Immigration Reform and Immigrant Responsibility Act of 1996 (IIRIRA) required changes in the rules, but as of early 1999 the INS had not yet promulgated final versions of the rules. The interim rule made the following changes to the requirements:

☞ Remove documents 2, 3, 8 and 9 from column A;

☛ Allow document 4 only for aliens authorized to work for a specific employer; and

☛ New rules for employees who do not have their original documents.

CALIFORNIA
LAW

California law requires that any contract made with a foreign worker (i.e., one who is not a U.S. citizen but is legally entitled to work) must be written in the language of the worker and must contain all the material terms of employment, including pay, housing, transportation, and any other benefits the worker will receive.

HIRING "OFF THE BOOKS"

Because of the taxes, insurance, and red tape involved with hiring employees, some new businesses hire people "off the books." They pay them in cash and never admit they are employees. While the cash paid in wages would not be deductible, they consider this a smaller cost than compliance. Some even use "off the books" receipts to cover it.

Except when your spouse or child is giving you some temporary help this is a terrible idea. Hiring people off the books can result in civil fines, loss of insurance coverage, and even criminal penalties. When engaged in dangerous work like roofing or using power tools, you are risking millions of dollars in potential liability if a worker is killed or seriously injured.

It may be more costly and time consuming to comply with the employment laws, but if you are concerned with long term growth with less risk, it is the wiser way to go.

FEDERAL CONTRACTS

Companies that do work for the federal government are subject to several laws.

The *Davis-Bacon Act* requires contractors engaged in U.S. government construction projects to pay wages and benefits that are equal to or better than the prevailing wages in the area.

The *McNamara-O'Hara Service Contract Act* sets wages and other labor standards for contractors furnishing services to agencies of the U.S. government.

The *Walsh-Healey Public Contracts Act* requires the Department of Labor to settle disputes regarding manufacturers supplying products to the U.S. government.

MISCELLANEOUS LAWS

FEDERAL LAWS

Affirmative action. In most cases, the federal government does not yet tell employers who they must hire. This would be especially true for small new businesses. The only situation where a small business would need to comply with affirmative action requirements would be if it accepted federal contracts or subcontracts. These requirements could include the hiring of minorities or of Vietnam veterans.

Layoffs. Companies with 100 or more full-time employees at one location are subject to the Worker Adjustment and Retraining Notification Act. This law requires a sixty-day notification prior to certain lay-offs and has other strict provisions.

Unions. The National Labor Relations Act of 1935, gives employees the right to organize a union or to join one. (U.S.C., Title 29, beginning with Section 151.) There are things employers can do to protect themselves, but you should consult a labor attorney or a book on the subject before taking action that might be illegal and result in fines.

Poster laws. Yes, there are laws regarding what posters you may or may not display in the workplace. For example, a federal judge in 1991, ruled that Playboy posters in a workplace were sexual harassment. This ruling is being appealed by the American Civil Liberties Union (ACLU).

However, there are other poster laws that require certain posters to be displayed to inform employees of their rights. Not all businesses are required to display all posters, but the following list should be of help.

☞ All employers must display the wage and hour poster, which is available from:

  http://www.dol.gov/dol/osbp/public/sbrefa/poster/main.htm

☞ Employers with fifteen or more employees for twenty weeks of the year must display the sex, race, religion, and ethnic discrimination poster and the age discrimination poster available from the above website.

☞ Employers with federal contracts or subcontracts of $10,000 or more must display the sex, race, etc. discrimination poster mentioned above plus a poster regarding Vietnam Era Veterans available from the local federal contracting office.

☞ Employers with government contracts subject to the Service Contract Act or the Public Contracts Act must display a notice to employees working on government contracts available from the above website.

U.S. Department of Justice
Immigration and Naturalization Service

OMB No. 1115-0136

Employment Eligibility Verification

Please read instructions carefully before completing this form. The instructions must be available during completion of this form. ANTI-DISCRIMINATION NOTICE: It is illegal to discriminate against work eligible individuals. Employers CANNOT specify which document(s) they will accept from an employee. The refusal to hire an individual because of a future expiration date may also constitute illegal discrimination.

Section 1. Employee Information and Verification. To be completed and signed by employee at the time employment begins.

Print Name: Last	First	Middle Initial	Maiden Name
REDDENBACHER	MARY	J.	HASSENFUSS

Address (Street Name and Number)	Apt. #	Date of Birth (month/day/year)
1234 LIBERTY LANE		1/26/69

City	State	Zip Code	Social Security #
SAN DIEGO	CA	94564	123-45-6789

I am aware that federal law provides for imprisonment and/or fines for false statements or use of false documents in connection with the completion of this form.

I attest, under penalty of perjury, that I am (check one of the following):

[X] A citizen or national of the United States
[ ] A Lawful Permanent Resident (Alien # A_____)
[ ] An alien authorized to work until ___/___/___
(Alien # or Admission #) _____

Employee's Signature *Mary Reddenbacher*	Date (month/day/year) 1/29/01

Preparer and/or Translator Certification. *(To be completed and signed if Section 1 is prepared by a person other than the employee.) I attest, under penalty of perjury, that I have assisted in the completion of this form and that to the best of my knowledge the information is true and correct.*

Preparer's/Translator's Signature	Print Name

Address (Street Name and Number, City, State, Zip Code)	Date (month/day/year)

Section 2. Employer Review and Verification. To be completed and signed by employer. Examine one document from List A OR examine one document from List B and one from List C, as listed on the reverse of this form, and record the title, number and expiration date, if any, of the document(s)

	List A	OR	List B	AND	List C
Document title:	PASSPORT				
Issuing authority:	PASSPORT AGENCY SNDG				
Document #:	123456789				
Expiration Date (if any):	10/5/06		___/___/___		___/___/___
Document #:					
Expiration Date (if any):	___/___/___				

CERTIFICATION - I attest, under penalty of perjury, that I have examined the document(s) presented by the above-named employee, that the above-listed document(s) appear to be genuine and to relate to the employee named, that the employee began employment on (month/day/year) 02/02/02 and that to the best of my knowledge the employee is eligible to work in the United States. (State employment agencies may omit the date the employee began employment.)

Signature of Employer or Authorized Representative *Darron Krebbs*	Print Name Darron Krebbs	Title owner

Business or Organization Name Address (Street Name and Number, City, State, Zip Code)	Date (month/day/year)
Krebbs Company 100 Maynard Dr., San Diego, CA 92456	2/2/02

Section 3. Updating and Reverification. To be completed and signed by employer.

A. New Name (if applicable)	B. Date of rehire (month/day/year) (if applicable)

C. If employee's previous grant of work authorization has expired, provide the information below for the document that establishes current employment eligibility.

Document Title:_____	Document #:_____	Expiration Date (if any):___/___/___

I attest, under penalty of perjury, that to the best of my knowledge, this employee is eligible to work in the United States, and if the employee presented document(s), the document(s) I have examined appear to be genuine and to relate to the individual.

Signature of Employer or Authorized Representative	Date (month/day/year)

Form I-9 (Rev. 11-21-91)N

ADVERTISING AND PROMOTION LAWS 12

ADVERTISING LAWS AND RULES

FEDERAL LAWS   The federal government regulates advertising through the Federal Trade Commission (FTC). The rules are contained in the Code of Federal Regulations (C.F.R.). You can find these rules in most law libraries and many public libraries. If you plan any advertising that you think may be questionable, you might want to check the rules. If you question it, most likely the Washington bureaucrats have forbidden it. As you read the rules below, you will probably think of many violations you see every day.

Federal rules do not apply to every business; and small businesses that operate only within the state, and do not use the postal service, may be exempt. However, many of the federal rules have been adopted into law by the state of California. Therefore, a violation could be prosecuted by the state rather than the federal government.

Some of the important rules are summarized below. If you wish to learn more details about the rules you should obtain copies from your library.

Deceptive pricing. (C.F.R., Title 16, Chapter I, Part 233.) When prices are being compared, it is required that actual and not inflated prices are used. For example, if an object would usually be sold for $7, you should not first offer it for $10 and then start offering it at thirty percent off. It is considered misleading to suggest that a discount from list price is a bargain if the item is seldom actually sold at list price. If most surrounding stores sell an item for $7 it is considered misleading to say it has a "retail value of $10" even if there are some stores elsewhere selling it at that price.

Bait advertising. (C.F.R., Title 16, Chapter I, Part 238.) *Bait advertising* is placing an ad when you do not really want the respondents to buy the product offered, but to switch to another item.

Use of "free," "half-off," and similar words. (C.F.R., Title 16, Chapter I, Part 251.) Use of words such as "free," "1¢ sale" and the like must not be misleading. This means that the "regular price" must not include a mark-up to cover the "free" item. The seller must expect to sell the product without the free item at some time in the future.

Substantiation of claims. (C.F.R., Title 16, Section 3.40 and Federal Regulation (Fed. Reg.) Volume 48, Page 10,471 (1983).) The FTC requires that advertisers be able to substantiate their claims. Some information on this policy is contained on the Internet at:

http://www.ftc.gov/bcp/guides/ad3subst.htm.

Endorsements. (C.F.R., Title 16, Chapter I, Part 255.) This rule forbids endorsements that are misleading. An example is a quote from a film review that is used in such a way as to change the substance of the review. It is not necessary to use the exact words of the person endorsing the product as long as the opinion is not distorted. If a product is changed, an endorsement that does not apply to the new version cannot be used. For some items, such as drugs, claims cannot be used without scientific proof. Endorsements by organizations cannot be used unless one is sure that the membership holds the same opinion.

Unfairness. (U.S.C., Title 15, Section 45.) Any advertising practices that can be deemed to be "unfair" are forbidden by the FTC. An explanation of this policy is located on the Internet at:

http://www.ftc.gov/bcp/policy stmt/ad-unfair.htm

Negative option plans. (C.F.R., Title 16, Chapter I, Part 425.) When a seller uses a sales system in which the buyer must notify the seller if he does not want the goods, the seller must provide the buyer with a form to decline the sale and at least ten days in which to decline. Bonus merchandise must be shipped promptly and the seller must promptly terminate any request after completion of the contract.

Laser eye surgery. (U.S.C., Title 15, Sections 45, 52,-57.) Under the laws governing deceptive advertising, the FTC and the FDA are regulating the advertising of laser eye surgery. Anyone involved in this area should obtain a copy of these rules. They are located on the Internet at:

http://www.ftc.gov/bcp/guides/eyecare2.htm

Food and dietary supplements. (U.S.C., Title 21, Section 343.) Under the Nutritional Labeling and Education Act of 1990, the FTC and the FDA regulate the packaging and advertising of food and dietary products. Anyone involved in this area should obtain a copy of these rules. For the FDA food code, as well as information on dietary supplements, go to the FDA website at:

http://www.fda.gov

Jewelry and precious metals. (Fed. Reg., Volume 61, Page 27,212.) The FTC has numerous rules governing the sale and advertising of jewelry and precious metals. Anyone in this business should obtain a copy of these rules. The are located on the Internet at:

http://www.ftc.gov/bcp/guides/jewel-gd.htm.

CALIFORNIA LAWS

California law regulating advertising is contained in several different codes, especially the Civil Code and the Business and Professional Code. The gist of these laws is that you can advertise almost anything if you tell the truth, fully inform the public of the nature of the product or service, and inform the public about the risks or costs involved.

Under the California Civil Code (Cal. Civ. Code), Section 1770, it is forbidden to make any misrepresentations of goods or services to the public including the following:

- ☞ Passing off goods or services as those of another;

- ☞ Misrepresenting the source, sponsorship, approval, or certification by, another;

- ☞ Misrepresenting the affiliation, connection, or association with, or certification by, another;

- ☞ Using deceptive representations or designations of geographic origin in connection with goods or services;

- ☞ Representing that goods or services have sponsorship, approval, characteristics, ingredients, uses, benefits, or quantities, which they do not have or that a person has a sponsorship, approval, status, affiliation, or connection which he or she does not have;

- ☞ Representing that goods are original or new if they have deteriorated unreasonably or are altered, reconditioned, reclaimed, used, or secondhand;

- ☞ Representing that goods or services are of a particular standard, quality, or grade, or that goods are of a particular style or model, if they are of another;

- ☞ Disparaging the goods, services, or business of another by false or misleading representation of fact;

- ☞ Advertising goods or services with intent not to sell them as advertised;

- ☞ Advertising goods or services with intent not to supply reasonably expected demand, unless the advertisement discloses a limitation of quantity;

- ☞ Advertising furniture without clearly indicating that it is unassembled if that is the case;

☛ Advertising the price of unassembled furniture without clearly indicating the assembled price of that furniture if the same furniture is available assembled from the seller;

☛ Making false or misleading statements of fact concerning reasons for, existence of, or amounts of price reductions;

☛ Representing that a transaction confers or involves rights, remedies, or obligations that it does not have or involve, or that are prohibited by law;

☛ Representing that a part, replacement, or repair service is needed when it is not;

☛ Representing that the subject of a transaction has been supplied in accordance with a previous representation when it is not;

☛ Representing that the consumer will receive a rebate, discount, or other economic benefit, if the earning of the benefit is contingent on an event to occur subsequent to the consummation of the transaction;

☛ Misrepresenting the authority of a salesperson, representative, or agent to negotiate the final terms of a transaction with a consumer;

☛ Inserting an unconscionable provision in the contract; or

☛ Advertising that a product is being offered at a specific price plus a specific percentage of that price unless (1) the total price is set forth in the advertisement, which may include, but is not limited to, shelf tags, displays, and media advertising, in a size larger than any other price in that advertisement, and (2) the specific price plus a specific percentage of that price represents a markup from the seller's costs or from the wholesale price of the product. This does not apply to in-store advertising by businesses open only to members or cooperative organizations organized pursuant to the California Corporations Code (Cal. Corp. Code), beginning with Section 12000, where more than fifty percent of purchases are made at the specific price set forth in the advertisement.

The California Business and Professions Code (Cal. Bus. and Prof. Code), Sections 17530 through 17539.6, cover a wide range of advertising and sales prohibitions and requirements applying to specific professions or products, including:

☞ Retail sale of caskets, alternative containers, or outer burial containers by someone other than a funeral director. (Cal. Bus. and Prof. Code, Section 17530.7);

☞ Secondhand, used, defective, or blemished merchandise; merchandise known as "seconds"; or merchandise that has been rejected by its manufacturer as not first class. (Cal. Bus. and Prof. Code, Section 17531);

☞ The sale of surplus materials, as defined in the federal Surplus Property Act of 1944. U.S.C., Title 50, Section 1622 and California Business and Professions Code, Section 17531.5; and the use of words such as "Army," "Navy," "United States," "Federal," "treasury," "procurement," "G.I.," or others, which have a tendency to lead the public to believe, contrary to fact, that there is some official relationship to the United States Government; or that all of the articles are such surplus materials; or that the articles are of higher quality and lower prices than those elsewhere obtainable. (Cal. Bus. and Prof. Code, Section 17.533.5);

☞ Mailed solicitation materials that contain a seal, insignia, trade or brand name, or any other term or symbol that reasonably could be interpreted or construed as implying any state or local government connection, approval, or endorsement. (Cal. Bus. and Prof. Code, Section 17533.7);

☞ The use of the words "Made in the U.S.A.," "Made in America,: "U.S.A.," or similar words when the merchandise or any article, unit, or part thereof, has been entirely or substantially made, manufactured, or produced outside of the United States. (Cal. Bus. and Prof. Code, Section 17533.7);

☞ Advertisements for a prize or gift, with the intent to offer a sales presentation. (Cal. Bus. and Prof. Code, Section 17533.8);

- Advertisements for the sale of tear gas, tear gas devices, and tear gas weapons. (Cal. Bus. and Prof. Code, Section 17533.9); and

- Advertisements for the sale of anabolic steroids. (Cal. Bus. and Prof. Code, Section 17533.10.)

INTERNET SALES LAWS

There are not yet specific laws governing Internet transactions that are different from laws governing other transactions. The FTC feels that its current rules regarding deceptive advertising, substantiation, disclaimers, refunds, and related matters must be followed by Internet businesses and that consumers are adequately protected by them. See the first three pages of this chapter for that information.

For some specific guidelines on Internet advertising, see the FTC's site at:

http://www.ftc.gov/bcp/conline/pubs/buspubs/ruleroad.htm

Most California code sections regarding advertising simply include the Internet in the list of advertising media.

HOME SOLICITATION LAWS

FEDERAL LAW   The Federal Trade Commission has rules governing door-to-door sales. In any such sale it is a deceptive trade practice to fail to furnish a receipt explaining the sale (in the language of the presentation) and giving notice that there is a right to back out of the contract within three days, known as a right of rescission. The notice must be supplied in duplicate, must be in at least ten-point type and must be captioned either "Notice of Right to Cancel" or "Notice of Cancellation."

The notice on the following page, which is in ten-point type, contains the required wording.

NOTICE OF CANCELLATION

_____

Date

YOU MAY CANCEL THIS TRANSACTION, WITHOUT ANY PENALTY OR OBLIGATION, WITHIN THREE BUSINESS DAYS FROM THE ABOVE DATE.

IF YOU CANCEL, ANY PROPERTY TRADED IN, ANY PAYMENTS MADE BY YOU UNDER THE CONTRACT OR SALE, AND ANY NEGOTIABLE INSTRUMENT EXECUTED BY YOU WILL BE RETURNED TO YOU WITHIN 10 BUSINESS DAYS FOLLOWING RECEIPT BY THE SELLER OF YOUR CANCELLATION NOTICE, AND ANY SECURITY INTEREST ARISING OUT OF THE TRANSACTION WILL BE CANCELLED.

IF YOU CANCEL, YOU MUST MAKE AVAILABLE TO THE SELLER AT YOUR RESIDENCE, IN SUBSTANTIALLY AS GOOD CONDITION AS WHEN RECEIVED, ANY GOODS DELIVERED TO YOU UNDER THIS CONTRACT OR SALE; OR YOU MAY IF YOU WISH, COMPLY WITH THE INSTRUCTIONS OF THE SELLER REGARDING THE RETURN SHIPMENT OF THE GOODS AT THE SELLER'S EXPENSE AND RISK.

IF YOU DO MAKE THE GOODS AVAILABLE TO THE SELLER AND THE SELLER DOES NOT PICK THEM UP WITHIN 20 DAYS OF THE DATE OF YOUR NOTICE OF CANCELLATION, YOU MAY RETAIN OR DISPOSE OF THE GOODS WITHOUT ANY FURTHER OBLIGATION. IF YOU FAIL TO MAKE THE GOODS AVAILABLE TO THE SELLER, OR IF YOU AGREE TO RETURN THE GOODS AND FAIL TO DO SO, THEN YOU REMAIN LIABLE FOR PERFORMANCE OF ALL OBLIGATIONS UNDER THE CONTRACT.

TO CANCEL THIS TRANSACTION, MAIL OR DELIVER A SIGNED AND DATED COPY OF THIS CANCELLATION NOTICE OR ANY OTHER WRITTEN NOTICE, OR SEND A TELEGRAM, TO _____ [name of seller], AT _____ [address of seller's place of business] NOT LATER THAN MIDNIGHT OF _____ (date).

I HEREBY CANCEL THIS TRANSACTION.

_____   _____

(Buyer's signature)   (Date)

The seller must complete the notice and orally inform the buyer of the right to cancel. He cannot misrepresent the right to cancel, assign the contract until the fifth business day, nor include a confession of judgment in the contract. For more specific details see the rules contained in C.F.R., Title 16, Chapter I, Part 429.

CALIFORNIA LAW

California Civil Code, Sections 1689.5 through 1693 cover a "home solicitation contract or offer." These sections cover all transactions that:

☞ are for the sale, rental, or lease of goods, services, or both; and

☞ involve an amount of at least $25 (including all charges, interest, etc.); and

☞ are made other than at the seller's regular place of business.

The law specifically does not apply to:

☞ any contract under which the buyer has the right to rescind under the Federal Consumer Credit Protection Act, Title 1, Chapter 2, Section 125; or

☞ any contract for repair services with a licensed contractor if the contract price is less than $100, the negotiation was initiated by the buyer, and "the contract contains a written and dated statement signed by the prospective buyer stating that the negotiation between the parties was initiated by the prospective buyer."

Written Agreement. According to California Civil Code, Section 1689.7, the contract or offer must:

☞ be written in the same language as principally used in the oral sales presentation;

☞ be dated and signed by the buyer; and

☞ contain in immediate proximity to the space reserved for the buyer's signature a conspicuous statement in a size equal to at least ten-point bold type, as follows: "You, the buyer, may cancel this transaction at any time prior to midnight of the third business day after the date of this transaction. See the attached notice of cancellation form for an explanation of this right."

Right to cancel. Any such sale described above may be cancelled by the buyer by written notice, in any form, deposited in the mail any time before midnight of the "third business day" after the sales day. Business days do not include Sunday, New Year's Day, Washington's Birthday, Memorial Day, Independence Day, Labor Day, Columbus Day, Veterans Day, Thanksgiving Day, and Christmas Day.

The code specifically provides for a seven-day right to cancel for sales of a *personal emergency response unit*. (Cal. Civ. Code, Section 1689.6.) The code also provides for repairs made after a *disaster*, unless the repairs are necessary for the safety of the buyer or the buyer's property. (Cal. Civ. Code, Section 1689.14.)

The code also provides for a three-day right to cancel after a sale made at a "seminar". The importance of this law is that these sales may be cancelled even if made at the seller's place of business. (Cal. Civ. Code, Section 1689.20.)

The agreement or offer to purchase must be accompanied by a completed form, in duplicate, captioned "Notice of Cancellation" which must be attached to the agreement or offer to purchase and be easily detachable, and which must contain in at least ten point type the statement on the following page, written in the same language used in the contract (the statement on page 140 is an example):

Seller's Duty Upon Cancellation. Within ten days after cancellation, the seller must return any payments made by the buyer and any note or other evidence of indebtedness. If the down payment included goods traded in, the goods must be returned to the buyer in substantially as good condition as when received. Until the seller has complied with the above obligations, the buyer may retain possession of goods delivered to him by the seller and has a lien on the goods for any recovery to which he is entitled. (Cal. Civ. Code, Section 1689.10.)

If the seller has performed any services prior to cancellation, the seller is not entitled to compensation. If the seller's services result in the alteration of property of the buyer, the seller must restore the property to substantially as good condition as it was at the time the services were rendered. (Cal. Civ. Code, Section 1689.11(c).)

Buyer's Duty Upon Cancellation. Within twenty days after cancellation, the buyer, upon demand of the seller, must tender to the seller any goods delivered by the seller pursuant to the sale or offer, but the buyer is not obligated to tender the goods at any place other than his own address. If the seller fails to demand possession of goods within twenty days after cancellation, the goods become the property of the buyer without obligation to pay for them. (Cal. Civ. Code, Section 1689.11(a).)

The buyer has a duty to take reasonable care of the goods in his possession both prior to cancellation and during the twenty-day period following. During the twenty-day period, except for the buyer's duty of care, the goods are at the seller's risk. (Cal. Civ. Code, Section 1689.11(b).)

TELEPHONE SOLICITATION LAWS

FEDERAL LAWS

Phone calls. Telephone solicitations are governed by the Telephone Consumer Protection Act (U.S.C., Title 47, Section 227), and the Federal Communications Commission (FCC) rules implement the act. (C.F.R., Title 47, Section 64.1200.) Violators of the act can be sued for $500 damages by consumers and can be fined $10,000 by the FCC. Some of the requirements under the law are:

☛ Calls can only be made between 8 A.M. and 9 P.M.

☛ Solicitors must keep a "do not call" list and honor requests to not call.

☛ There must be a written policy that the parties called is told the name of the caller, the callers business name and phone number or address, that the call is a sales call and the nature of the goods or services.

☛ Personnel must be trained in the policies.

☛ Recorded messages cannot be used to call residences.

Faxes. It is illegal under the act to send advertising faxes to anyone who has not consented to receiving such faxes or is an existing customer.

CALIFORNIA
LAW

The California Business and Professions Code, Sections 17511 through 17513 cover telephone solicitations. These sections apply both to unsolicited calls and those made in response to a mailing. The typical mailing is one that tells the person receiving the mail that she should call the buyer for a free prize of some sort. An exception to the mailing law would be the normal catalogue we all receive from time to time. Even these must be at least twenty-four pages and distributed in more than one state to qualify.

The exceptions to the law are too numerous to discuss. Some important ones involve potential purchasers you are already dealing with and calling to try and set up an appointment. If you plan to solicit by phone, you must register with the Department of Justice, Consumer Law Section. A form giving information about yourself and your company must be filled out, and a fee of $50 paid. At that time, you can determine if you qualify for an exemption.

Telephone sales falling under the law require written notice of the three-day right to cancel. The following is the form that must be furnished to the purchaser. No information may be added to the form and it must be in the same language in which the solicitation was made.

NOTICE OF BUYER'S RIGHT OF CANCELLATION

You may cancel this transaction, without any penalty or obligation, within three business days following your receipt of this notice of cancellation and the receipt of any products, or in the case of services, within three business days following receipt of the attached notice of confirmation.

If you cancel, any payments made by you or authorized by you, pursuant to any telephonic solicitation and purchase agreement shall be returned to you within 10 days following receipt by the seller of your cancellation notice.

If you cancel, you must make available to the seller at your residence, in substantially as good condition as when received, any goods delivered to you under this contract, agreement, or sale, or you may, if you wish, comply with the instructions of the seller regarding the return shipment of the goods at the seller's expense and risk.

If you do make the goods available to the seller and the seller does not pick them up within 20 days of the date of your notice of cancellation, you may retain or dispose of the goods without any further obligation. If you fail to make the goods available to the seller, or if you agree to return the goods to the seller and fail to do so, then you remain liable for the performance of all obligations under the contract.

To cancel this transaction, mail or deliver a signed and dated copy of this cancellation notice, or any other written notice, or send a telegram to _____ (name of seller), at _____ _____ (address of seller's place of business) not later than midnight of the third business day after receipt of the products and this notice of cancellation.

I HEREBY CANCEL THIS TRANSACTION.

_____
DATE

_____
BUYER'S SIGNATURE

PRICING, WEIGHTS, AND LABELING

FEDERAL LAW

Food products. Beginning in 1994, all food products were required to have labels with information on the product's nutritional values such as calories, fat, and protein. For most products, the label must be in the required format so that consumers can easily compare products. However, if such a format will not fit on the product label, the information may be in another format that is easily readable.

Metric measures. In 1994, federal rules requiring metric measurement of products took effect. Some federal agencies, such as the federal highway department, indefinitely postponed implementation of the rules, but the Federal Trade Commission (FTC) and the Food and Drug Administration (FDA) intend to enforce the rules against businesses.

Under these rules, metric measures do not have to be the first measurement on the container, but they must be included. Food items that are packaged as they are sold (such as delicatessen items), do not have to contain metric labels.

CALIFORNIA LAW

The California Business and Professions Code, Section 12655, describes the legislature's intent to have unit pricing by labeling products by their price per ounce, per pound, per gallon, or their metric equivalent, or by per one hundred square feet or per hundred count.

Sections 7100 through 7106 of the California Civil Code require item pricing for grocery items in stores using an automatic checkout system on at least eighty-five percent of the items. There are many exceptions and the law does not apply to stores where there are not more than two permanent employees other than the owner or the owner's parents or children.

The Business and Professions Code contains numerous provisions on labelling, including:

☛ Sections 22900-22927, deal specifically with agriculture, utility, and industrial equipment sold by retailers under agreements with manufacturers and distributors. If this applies to you, check with the manufacturer or distributor as well as reading the code sections.

☛ Sections 12500-12517, require a certificate of approval for all designs of weighing and measuring devices used for a commercial purpose.

☛ Sections 12200-12214, describe the office of the *county sealer* who is appointed by each county's board of supervisors. The more common name for the county sealer is the *weights and measures inspector*.

☛ Sections 12300-12314, provide the standards (metric) for anyone contracting with the state.

☛ Sections 12100-12108, give the general authority for weights and measures to the Department of Agriculture. The Department oversees, instructs, and makes suggestions to the county sealers. The department may make inspections or accept the inspections of county sealers.

Sections 12601 through 12615.5 of the California Business and Professions Code describe how packaged commodities must be labeled. The gist of the law is to require labeling so that the consumer knows both what and how much is in the package. The law applies to "any person engaged in the packaging or labeling of any commodity for distribution or sale, or for any person (other than a common carrier for hire, a contract carrier for hire, or a freight forwarder for hire) engaged in the distribution of any packaged or labeled commodity." The law does not apply to wholesale or retail distributors, unless they "(1) are engaged in the packaging or labeling, (2) specify the manner of packaging or labeling, or (3) have knowledge of the violation of any labeling law requirements. (Cal. Bus. and Prof. Code, Section 12602.)

According to California Business and Professions Code, Section 12603, the packaging must:

- Bear a label specifying the identity of the commodity and the name and place of business of the manufacturer, packer, or distributor; and

- Separately and accurately state the net quantity of the contents (in terms of weight or mass, measure, numerical count, or time), in a uniform location on the principal display panel of the label, using the most appropriate units of both the customary inch-pound system of measure, and the metric system;

  However, on a random package labeled in terms of pounds and decimal fractions of the pound, the statement may be carried out to not more than three decimal places and is not required to include a metric system. Also, the requirements of concerning the metric system do not apply to nonconsumer packages, or foods that are packaged at the retail store level.

The label may not use any qualifying words or phrases in conjunction with the statement of net quantity; or use the words "minimum," or "when packaged," or words of similar import; or qualify any unit of weight, measure, or count by any term that tends to exaggerate the amount (such as "jumbo," "giant," or "full"). Cal. Bus. and Prof. Code, Section 12605.

California Business and Professions Code, Section 12606 applies to the labeling of packaging and containers that are not subject to Section 403(d) of the Federal Food, Drug and Cosmetic Act. (U.S.C., Title 21, Section 343(d), and C.F.R., Title 21, Section 100.100.) No container may have a false bottom, false sidewalls, false lid or covering, or be in any way constructed or filled so as to facilitate the perpetration of deception or fraud. (Cal. Bus. and Prof. Code, Section 12606(a).)

No container or packaging may be made, formed, or filled so as to be misleading. (Cal. Bus. and Prof. Code, Section 12606(b).) A container that does not allow the consumer to fully view its contents is considered to be filled so as to be misleading if it contains nonfunctional *slack fill* (the difference between the actual capacity of a container and the volume of product it contains). The law gives fifteen situations in which slack fill is acceptable, such as:

- ☛ Where necessary to protect the contents;

- ☛ Where there is unavoidable product settling during shipping and handling;

- ☛ Where necessary to provide space for mandatory and necessary labeling information;

- ☛ Where the product is packaged in a decorative or presentational container that has value independent of its function to hold the product (such as a gift combined with a container intended for use after the product is consumed), or a durable commemorative or promotional package, or along with a free gift;

- ☛ Where the package size is necessary to discourage pilfering, facilitate handling, or accommodate tamper-resistant devices;

- ☛ Where space is necessary for mixing, adding, shaking, or dispensing liquids or powders;

- ☞ Where the packaging contains a product delivery or dosing device; if the device is readily apparent to the consumer; and

- ☞ Where the "exterior packaging or immediate product container encloses computer hardware or software designed to serve a particular computer function, if the particular computer function to be performed is clearly and conspicuously disclosed on the exterior packaging."

California Business and Professions Code, Section 12606.2 has similar provisions that apply to food containers that are subject to Section 403 (d) of the Federal Food, Drug and Cosmetic Act. (U.S.C., Title 21, Section 343(d), and C.F.R., Title 21, Section 100.100.)

Every manufacturer, wholesaler, jobber, distributor, or other person, who packages children's toys for sale to a retailer, must clearly state on the outside of the package that the toy is unassembled if that is the case. If toys are packaged in another state, such labelling is the responsibility of the first wholesaler, jobber, distributor, or other person who has possession or control of the toys in California. (Cal. Bus. and Prof. Code, Section 17531.1.)

We have only presented a brief summary of these laws. If you will be involved in packaging your product, you should obtain a copy of these laws and become familiar with them.

PAYMENT AND COLLECTION 13

Depending on the business you are in, you may be paid by cash, checks, credit cards, or some sort of financing arrangement such as a promissory note and mortgage. Both state and federal laws affect the type of payments you collect, and failure to follow the laws can cost you considerably.

CASH

Cash is probably the easiest form of payment and it is subject to few restrictions. The most important one is that you keep an accurate accounting of your cash transactions and that you report all of your cash income on your tax return. Recent efforts to stop the drug trade have resulted in some serious penalties for failing to report cash transactions and for money laundering. The laws are so sweeping that even if you deal in cash in an ordinary business you may violate the law and face huge fines and imprisonment.

The most important law to be concerned with is the one requiring the filing of IRS Form 8300 for cash transactions of $10,000 or more. (see form 12, p.261.) A transaction does not have to happen in one day. If a person brings you smaller amounts of cash that add up to $10,000 and the government can construe them as one transaction, then the form must be filed. Under this law, *cash* also includes travelers' checks, and money orders, but not cashier's checks or bank checks.

CHECKS

ACCEPTING
CHECKS

It is important to accept checks in your business. While there is a small percentage that will be bad, most checks will be good, and you will be able to accommodate more customers. To avoid having problems with checks, you should follow the following rules.

☛ Accept only preprinted checks.

☛ Accept only checks drawn on local banks.

☛ Have the checks signed in your presence.

☛ Verify the sufficient funds with the bank on checks over a certain amount. If you are not selling "big ticket" items, you may want to set a maximum amount that you will accept.

☛ Do not accept third party checks. The person who gives you the check should be the drawer.

☛ Ask to see a picture identification such as a driver's license, California identification card, or military identification card.

Common sense always applies. Once you get to know your customers, you may want to relax your procedures a little.

You are not required by law to accept checks. (Cal. Civ. Code, Section 1725(d).) However, if you do accept checks, California Civil Code, Section 1725, forbids a business from:

☛ Requiring a customer to provide a credit card as a condition of acceptance of the check, or recording the number of the credit card;

☛ Requiring a customer to sign a statement agreeing to allow his or her credit card to be charged to cover the check if it is returned as no good;

☛ Recording a credit card number; and

☛ Contacting a credit card issuer to determine if the amount of any credit available to the person paying with a check will cover the amount of the check.

The penalty for an intentional violation is a fine of $250 for the first violation and $1,000 for each subsequent violation. However, no fine may be assessed if the business shows that the violation was not intentional and resulted from a bona fide error. If you are unsure about something regarding this law, contact an attorney.

However, a business may:

☛ Require the production of reasonable forms of identification, other than a credit card, which may include a driver's license or a California state identification card, or where one of these is not available, another form of photo identification, as a condition of acceptance of a negotiable instrument.

☛ Request, but not require, a purchaser to voluntarily display a credit card as an indication of creditworthiness or financial responsibility, or as an additional identification, provided that the only information recorded is the type of card, the issuer of the card, and the expiration date of the card. If you request the display of a credit card, you must inform the customer, by either of the following methods, that displaying the credit card is not a requirement for check writing:

- By posting the following notice in a conspicuous location in the unobstructed view of the public within the premises where the check is being written, clearly and legibly: "Check writing ID: credit card may be requested but not required for purchases."

- By training and requiring sales clerks or retail employees requesting the credit card to inform all check-writing customers that they are not required to display a credit card to write a check.

☛ Request production of, or recording, a credit card number as a condition for cashing a check that is being used solely to receive cash back.

☛ Request, receive, or record a credit card account.

BAD CHECKS

A payee of a check passed on insufficient funds can collect a service charge of not more that $25 on the first check passed and not more than $35 on each subsequent check. (Cal. Civ. Code, Section 1719.)

In addition, the payee can send a certified letter to the person who passed the check demanding payment for the amount of the check, the service charge, and the cost of the certified mailing. The letter must contain the provisions of the California Civil Code, Section 1719, the amount of the check, and the amount of the service charge. If payment is not made within thirty days from the date the written demand was mailed, the payee may collect three times the amount of the check (called *treble damages*), subject to a minimum of $100 and a maximum of $1,500. If the payee collects treble damages, no service charge or mailing charge may be added. See California Civil Code, Section 1719 for forms and more details about what is required to bring the payee to court and win.

Insufficient funds can be lack of funds in the account, not having an open account, or stopping payment on the check. However, stop payments do not constitute insufficient funds if there is a good faith dispute as to the transaction. Similarly, it would not constitute insufficient funds if there is written confirmation of an error or delay caused by the bank; or a delay in the regularly scheduled transfer or posting of a direct deposit of a social security or government benefit assistance payment.

REFUNDS AFTER ACCEPTING A CHECK

A popular scam is for a person to purchase something by using a check and then come back the next day demanding a refund. After making the refund the business discovers the initial payment check bounced. Do not make refunds until checks clear.

REFUNDS

If you do not have a full refund or exchange policy for at least seven days after purchase, you must conspicuously display your policy. The California Civil Code, Section 1723, reproduced below, gives the exact details. The rule is a common sense one. If you mark an item "as is" or "no return accepted," you are okay. Foods or any items that could cause a health problem if resold are not subject to the rule. The customer must provide proof of purchase and return the item in the original package.

1723. (a) Every retail seller which sells goods to the public in this state that has a policy as to any of those goods of not giving full cash or credit refunds, or of not allowing equal exchanges, or any combination thereof, for at least seven days following purchase of the goods if they are returned and proof of their purchase is presented, shall conspicuously display that policy either on signs posted at each cash register and sales counter, at each public entrance, on tags attached to each item sold under that policy, or on the retail seller's order forms, if any. This display shall state the store's policy, including, but not limited to, whether cash refund, store credit, or exchanges will be given for the full amount of the purchase price; the applicable time period; the types of merchandise which are covered by the policy; and any other conditions which govern the refund, credit, or exchange of merchandise.

(b) This section does not apply to food, plants, flowers. perishable goods, goods marked "as is," "no returns accepted," "all sales final," or with similar language, goods used or damaged after purchase, customized goods received as ordered, goods not returned with their original package, and goods which cannot be resold due to health considerations.

A retailer violating this law is liable to the buyer for the amount of the purchase if the buyer returns, or attempts to return, the goods on or before the thirtieth day after purchase. However, even if you post a strict policy, you may want to balance potential loss of taking back an item against the loss of a customer.

CREDIT CARDS

In our buy-now, pay-later society, charge cards can add greatly to your sales potential, especially with large, discretionary purchases. For MasterCard, Visa, and Discover, the fees are about two percent, and this amount is easily paid for by the extra purchases that the cards allow. American Express charges four to five percent, and you may decide this is not worth paying, since almost everyone who has an American Express card also has another card. You will find that affluent purchasers prefer to use American Express.

For businesses that have a retail outlet, there is usually no problem getting *merchant status*, which allows you to process credit card payments. Most commercial banks can handle it. Discover can also set you up to accept their card as well as MasterCard and Visa, and they will wire the money into your bank account daily.

MAIL ORDER BUSINESSES

For mail order businesses, especially those operating out of the home, it is much harder to get merchant status. This is because of the number of scams in which large amounts are charged, no products are shipped and the company folds. At one point, even a business offering to post a large cash bond and let the bank hold the charges for six months was refused.

Today things are a little better. Some companies are even soliciting merchants. But beware of those that charge exorbitant fees (such as $5 or $10 per order for "processing"). One good thing about American Express is that they will accept mail order companies operating out of the home. However, not as many people have their cards as others.

Some companies open a small storefront (or share one) to get merchant status, then process mostly mail orders. The processors usually do not want to accept you if you will do more than fifty percent mail order; but if you do not have many complaints, you may be allowed to process mostly mail orders. Whatever you do, keep your charge customers happy so that they do not complain.

California's credit card statutes are found in the "Song-Beverly Credit Card Act of 1971." (Cal. Civ. Code, Sections 1747 through 1748.7.) You may want to put in an hour or two reading this if you plan to offer sales by credit card. The major points of this law that relate to offering credit through a major credit card company are summarized below. If you plan to offer your own credit, as opposed to merely using one or more of the major credit card companies, you will need to know and understand the entire Act.

RUNNING CHARGES THROUGH ANOTHER BUSINESS

You might be tempted to try to run your charges through the account of another business. This may be okay if you actually sell your products through them, but if not, both you and the other business may be breaking the law. Also, the other business may lose its merchant status. For example, if you sell books and use the account of your friend's florist shop, people who bought a book by mail from you and then have a charge on their statement from the florist shop will probably call the credit card company saying that they never bought anything from the florist shop. Too many of these complaints and your friend's account will be closed.

No person may, and no retailer may permit any person to, "process, deposit, negotiate, or obtain payment of a credit card charge through a retailer's account with a financial institution or through a retailer's agreement with a financial institution, card issuer, or organization of financial institutions or card issuers if that retailer did not furnish or agree to furnish the goods or services that are the subject of the charge." (Cal. Civ. Code, Section 1748.7.) There are a few exceptions, including:

☞ Where a person furnishes goods or services on the business premises of a general merchandise retailer (defined as "any person or entity, regardless of the form of organization, that has continuously offered for sale or lease more than 100 different types of goods or services to the public in this state throughout a period which includes the immediately preceding five years");

☞ Where there is a franchisee/franchisor relationship; or

☞ Where less than $500 of credit card charges in any one year period are processed through a retailer's account.

Violation is a misdemeanor, with each occurrence as a separate offense. Also, any person injured by a violation may bring an action for the recovery of damages, equitable relief, reasonable attorney's fees, and costs.

SURCHARGES AND DISCOUNTS

The California Civil Code forbids charging a surcharge to a customer for using a credit card. (Cal. Civ. Code, Section 1748.1(a).) This does not apply if a retailer only accepts credit cards for payment of telephone orders and only accepts cash at a public store or other facility of the same retailer. (Cal. Civ. Code, Section 1748.1(b).) The law does allow you to sell items at a discount for cash, but the discount must be the same for all customers. (Cal. Civ. Code, Section 1748.1(a).) Charges for third-party credit card guarantee services, if added to the price charged if cash were paid, are considered prohibited surcharges even if they are payable directly to the third party or are charged separately. (Cal. Civ. Code, Section 1748.1(d).) Furthermore, a credit card issuer cannot prevent a retailer from offering a discount for cash. (Cal. Civ. Code, Section 1748.)

IDENTIFICATION AND PERSONAL INFORMATION

Under California Civil Code, Section 1747.8, if you accept a credit card, you may not do any of the following:

☞ Request or require the cardholder to write any personal identification information (defined as "information concerning the cardholder, other than information set forth on the credit card, and including, but not limited to, the cardholder's address and telephone number") on the credit card transaction form or otherwise.

☞ Request or require the cardholder to provide personal identification information, which you or your employee writes, causes to be written, or otherwise records on the credit card transaction form or otherwise.

☞ Utilize a credit card form that contains preprinted spaces specifically designated for filling in personal identification information of the cardholder.

However, you may request or require personal identification information for:

☛ When the credit card is being used as a deposit to secure payment in the event of default, loss, damage, or other similar occurrence;

☛ Cash advance transactions;

☛ When you are contractually obligated to provide personal identification information in order to complete the credit card transaction or are obligated to collect and record the personal identification information by federal law or regulation;

☛ When personal identification information is required for a special purpose incidental but related to the individual credit card transaction, including, but not limited to, information relating to shipping, delivery, servicing, or installation of the purchased merchandise, or for special orders;

☛ When this section does not prohibit any person, firm, partnership, association, or corporation from requiring the cardholder, as a condition to accepting the credit card as payment in full or in part for goods or services, to provide reasonable forms of positive identification, which may include a driver's license or a California state identification card, or where one of these is not available, another form of photo identification, provided that none of the information contained thereon is written or recorded on the credit card transaction form or otherwise. If the cardholder pays for the transaction with a credit card number and does not make the credit card available upon request to verify the number, the cardholder's driver's license number or identification card number may be recorded on the credit card transaction form or otherwise.

Violations are punishable by a fine of up to $250 for the first violation and $1,000 for subsequent violations. However, no fine may be assessed if the defendant shows that the violation was not intentional and resulted from a bona fide error. Check with an attorney if you are in this situation.

RECEIPTS FOR CREDIT CARD PURCHASES	In California, you may not print more than the last five digits of the credit card account number or the expiration date on any receipt provided to the cardholder. (Cal. Civ. Code, Section 1747.9.) This requirement applies to receipts that are electronically printed and not to transactions in which the sole means of recording the person's credit card number is by handwriting or by an imprint or copy of the credit card. This law goes into effect on January 1, 2004, with respect to any cash register, other machine or device that electronically prints receipts for credit card transactions that is in use before January 1, 2001; and goes into effect on January 1, 2001, with respect to any cash register, other machine or device that electronically prints receipts for credit card transactions that is first put into use on or after January 1, 2001.
BILLING ERRORS	Any billing error made by the retailer must be corrected within sixty days from the date on which an inquiry concerning a billing error was mailed by the cardholder. (Cal. Civ. Code, Section 1747.60.) Failure to correct the billing error within this period makes the retailer liable to the cardholder for the amount by which the outstanding balance of the cardholder's account is greater than the correct balance, plus any interest, finance charges, service charges, or other charges on the obligation giving rise to the billing error. Also, any cardholder injured by a willful violation may sue for damages, and judgment may be entered for three times the amount of actual damages, plus attorney's fees and costs. A card issuer is not liable for a billing error made by a retailer, and a retailer is not liable for a billing error made by a card issuer. (Cal. Civ. Code, Section 1747.65.)

FINANCING LAWS

Some businesses can more easily make sales if they finance the purchases themselves. If the business has enough capital to do this, it can earn extra profits on the financing terms. Nonetheless, because of abuses, many consumer protection laws have been passed by both the federal and state governments.

FEDERAL LAW   ***Reg. Z.*** Two important federal laws regarding financing are called the *Truth in Lending Act* and the *Fair Credit Billing Act*. These are implemented by what is called *Regulation Z* (commonly known as *Reg. Z*), issued by the Board of Governors of the Federal Reserve System. (C.F.R., Volume 12, page 226.) This is a very complicated law and some have said that no business can be sure to be in compliance with it.

The regulation covers all transactions in which four conditions are met:

1. credit is offered;

2   the offering of credit is regularly done;

3. there is a finance charge for the credit or there is a written agreement with more than four payments; and

4. the credit is for personal, family, or household purposes.

It also covers credit card transactions where only the first two conditions are met. It applies to leases if the consumer ends up paying the full value and keeping the item leased. It does not apply to the following transactions:

☛ transactions with businesses or agricultural purposes;

☛ transactions with organizations such as corporations or the government;

☛ transactions of over $25,000 that are not secured by the consumer's dwelling;

☛ credit involving public utilities;

☛ credit involving securities or commodities; and

☛ home fuel budget plans.

The way for a small business to avoid Reg. Z violations is to avoid transactions that meet the conditions, or to make sure all transactions fall under the exceptions. For many businesses this is easy. Instead of extending credit to customers, accept credit cards and let the credit card company extend the credit. However, if your customers usually do not have credit cards or if you are in a business, such as used car sales, which often extends credit, you should consult a lawyer knowledgeable about Reg. Z or, get a copy for yourself.

CALIFORNIA
LAW

California also has laws regarding financing arrangements. (Cal. Civ. Code, Sections 1810 through 1810.12.) These laws cover disclosure to the consumer of finance charges in an installment sales agreement, what constitutes a finance charge and other guidelines. Anyone engaged in installment sales in California should carefully review the latest versions of these sections of the Civil Code. There are several other code sections that apply to specific business, such as home improvements, automotive repair, and real estate. Check with your industry association to see if any such special financing laws apply to you.

The California Commercial Code covers debt secured by collateral. If you are going to hold the goods until the debt is paid, or be able to repossess the goods for nonpayment, you will need to use a security agreement and financing statement. This will be covered in the next chapter.

USURY

Usury is the charging of an illegally high rate of interest. California's usury law in contained in Article 15 of the state constitution. The legal rate of interest is seven percent, but parties may agree in writing to a rate up to ten percent for those things used primarily for "personal, family, or household purposes." Real estate is not included.

For other purposes, the maximum rate is the higher of ten percent or five percent above the prevailing rate of the Federal Reserve Bank of San Francisco's loan rate as of the 25th of the month preceding the loan.

There are many businesses exempt from usury laws, such as banks, savings and loans, finance companies, pawn brokers, and mortgage brokers. Check your industry association for your status.

The penalty for charging interest in excess of the legal rate is that the borrower does not have to pay **any** interest and the lender has to repay double the amounts received. Charging or receiving interest at a rate of over 25% but less than 45% is a misdemeanor; and charging or receiving interest of 45% or greater is a felony. The borrower may also sue for damages, costs, punitive damages, and attorney's fees.

COLLECTIONS

FEDERAL LAW   The Fair Debt Collection Practices Act of 1977 bans the use of deception, harassment, and other unreasonable acts in the collection of debts. It has strict requirements whenever someone is collecting a debt for someone else. If you are in the collection business, you must get a copy of this law.

The Federal Trade Commission has issued some rules that prohibit deceptive representations such as pretending to be in the motion picture industry, the government, or a credit bureau; or using questionnaires that do not say that they are for the purpose of collecting a debt. (C.F.R., Title 16, Chapter I, Part 237.)

CALIFORNIA LAW   The Rosenthal Fair Debt Collection Practices Act, specifies prohibited methods of collecting debts. (Cal. Civ. Code, beginning with Section 1788.) These prohibited practices are summarized below. The general idea is that you cannot use force or threat of force; lie by pretending to be someone you are not, such as a police officer, government official, or attorney; or tell others of the debt, such as employers or relatives of the debtor, unless there is a reason to tell them, such as trying to locate the debtor or to enforce a garnishment after a judgment.

Under the Rosenthal Fair Debt Collection Practices Act a debt collector may not:

☞ Use, or threaten to use, physical force or violence, or any criminal means, to cause harm to anyone's person, reputation, or property;

- ☞ Threaten to (falsely) accuse the debtor of committing a crime;

- ☞ Communicate, or threaten to communicate, to any person the fact that a debtor has engaged in conduct, other than the failure to pay a consumer debt, which will defame the debtor;

- ☞ Threaten to to sell or assign a consumer debt to another person, with an accompanying false representation that sale or assignment would result in the debtor losing any defense to the debt;

- ☞ Threaten any person that nonpayment of the consumer debt may result in the arrest of the debtor or the seizure, garnishment, attachment, or sale of any property; or the garnishment or attachment of wages of the debtor; unless such action is in fact contemplated by the debt collector and permitted by the law;

- ☞ Threaten to take any action against the debtor that is prohibited by law;

- ☞ Use obscene or profane language;

- ☞ Place telephone calls without disclosing the caller's identity, provided that an employee of a licensed collection agency may identify himself by using his registered alias name as long as he correctly identifies the agency he represents;

- ☞ Cause expense to any person for long distance telephone calls, telegram fees, or charges for other similar communications, by misrepresenting to such person the purpose of such telephone call, telegram, or similar communication;

- ☞ Cause a telephone to ring repeatedly or continuously to annoy the person called;

- ☞ Communicate, by telephone or in person, with the debtor with such frequency as to be unreasonable and to constitute harassment of the debtor under the circumstances.;

- ☞ Communicate with the debtor's employer regarding a consumer debt, unless necessary to the collection of the debt, or unless the debtor or his attorney consented in writing to such communication. A communication is necessary to the collection of the debt only if it is made for the purposes of verifying the debtor's employment, locating the debtor, or effecting garnishment of wages after judgment; or, in the case of a medical debt, to discover the existence of medical insurance. Any such communication, other than in the case of a medical debt by a health care provider or its agent for the purpose of discovering the existence of medical insurance, must be in writing unless such written communication receives no response within fifteen days and may be made only as many times as is necessary to the collection of the debt. Communications to a debtor's employer regarding a debt may not contain language that would be improper if the communication were made to the debtor. One communication solely for the purpose of verifying employment may be oral without prior written contact;

☞ Communicate information regarding a consumer debt to any member of the debtor's family, other than the debtor's spouse or the parents or guardians of the debtor who is either a minor or who resides in the same household with such parent or guardian, prior to obtaining a judgment against the debtor, except where the purpose of the communication is to locate the debtor, or where the debtor or his attorney has consented in writing to such communication;

☞ Communicate to any person any list of debtors that discloses the nature or existence of a consumer debt, commonly known as "deadbeat lists," or advertising any consumer debt for sale, by naming the debtor;

☞ Communicate with the debtor by means of a written communication that displays or conveys any information about the consumer debt or the debtor other than the name, address, and telephone number of the debtor and the debt collector; and which is intended both to be seen by another person and to embarrass the debtor. However, information may be provided to a consumer reporting agency or to any other person reasonably believed to have a legitimate business need for such information;

☞ Communicate with the debtor other than in the name of the debt collector or the person on whose behalf the debt collector is acting;

☞ Make any false representation that any person is an attorney or counselor at law;

☞ Communicate with a debtor in the name of an attorney or counselor at law or upon stationery or like written instruments bearing the name of the attorney or counselor at law, unless such communication is by an attorney or counselor at law or has been approved or authorized by such attorney or counselor at law;

☞ Represent that any debt collector is vouched for, bonded by, affiliated with, or is an instrumentality, agent, or official of any federal, state, or local government, or any agency of federal, state, or local government, unless the collector is actually employed by the particular governmental agency in question and is acting on behalf of such agency in the debt collection matter;

☞ Falsely represent that the consumer debt may be increased by the addition of attorney's fees, investigation fees, service fees, finance charges, or other charges if such fees or charges may not legally be added to the existing obligation;

☞ Falsely represent that information concerning a debtor's failure or alleged failure to pay a consumer debt has been or is about to be referred to a consumer reporting agency;

☞ Falsely represent that a debt collector is a consumer reporting agency;

☞ Falsely represent that collection letters, notices, or other printed forms are being sent by or on behalf of a claim, credit, audit, or legal department;

☞ Falsely represent the true nature of the business or services being rendered by the debt collector;

☞ Falsely represent that a legal proceeding has been, is about to be, or will be instituted unless payment of a consumer debt is made;

☞ Falsely represent that a consumer debt has been, is about to be, or will be sold, assigned, or referred to a debt collector for collection;

☞ Obtain an affirmation of a consumer debt that has been discharged in bankruptcy, without clearly and conspicuously disclosing to the debtor, in writing, at the time such affirmation is sought, the fact that the debtor is not legally obligated to make an affirmation;

☞ Collect or attempt to collect from the debtor the whole or any part of the debt collector's fee or charge for services rendered, or other expense incurred by the debt collector in the collection of the consumer debt, except as permitted by law;

☞ Initiate communications, other than statements of account, with the debtor with regard to the consumer debt, when the debt collector has been notified in writing by the debtor's attorney that the debtor is represented by the attorney with respect to the consumer debt, and such notice includes the attorney's name and address, and a request that all communications regarding the consumer debt be addressed to the attorney; unless the attorney fails to answer correspondence, return telephone calls, or discuss the obligation in question. This does not apply where prior approval has been obtained from the debtor's attorney, or where the communication is a response in the ordinary course of business to the debtor's inquiry;

☞ Collect or attempt to collect a consumer debt by means of judicial proceedings when the debt collector knows that service of process, where essential to jurisdiction over the debtor or his property, has not been legally effected;

☞ Collect or attempt to collect a consumer debt, other than one already reduced to judgment, by means of judicial proceedings in a county other than the county in which the debtor has incurred the debt or the county in which the debtor resides at the time such proceedings are instituted, or resided at the time the debt was incurred; or

☞ Send a communication that simulates legal or judicial process or which gives the appearance of being authorized, issued, or approved by a governmental agency or attorney when it is not.

(Any violation of the provisions of this is a misdemeanor, punishable by imprisonment for up to six months, or by a fine of up to $2,500, or both.)

Also, a licensed collection agency may not send any communication to a debtor demanding money, unless the claim is actually assigned to the collection agency.

BUSINESS RELATIONS LAWS 14

THE UNIFORM COMMERCIAL CODE

The Uniform Commercial Code (UCC) is a set of laws regulating numerous aspects of doing business. A national group drafted this set of uniform laws to avoid having a patchwork of different laws around the fifty states. Although some states modified some sections of the laws, the UCC is basically the same in most of the states. California's version is simply called the Commercial Code (Cal. Com. Code), and is fairly easy to understand. It is a good idea to obtain a copy (you can download it over the Internet). The purpose of the UCC is to make it easier for people to do business. The UCC takes contract law and changes those areas that would be difficult to use in millions of transactions taking place daily.

For example, a buyer sends an order (an offer). The seller sends back a confirmation that the order has been received and will be filled (an acceptance). Under contract law, the acceptance must exactly match the offer for a contract to be formed. Suppose the printed portion of the seller's confirmation does not exactly match the buyer's printed portion of the order. The UCC looks at whether the difference is minor or important. If it is not a "material" change, the UCC says it becomes part of the contract if there is no objection. There are other rules, but this gives you the general idea of what the UCC is trying to accomplish.

The UCC applies to everyone. If you buy something at your neighbor's yard sale, the Code applies. However, the code applies higher standards to those in business. The Code calls these people (or companies) merchants. A *merchant* is someone who deals regularly in the goods involved or has special knowledge of them (expertise). For example, a sawmill sold a saw to another sawmill. In a lawsuit that followed, the question arose as to whether the seller was a merchant. The answer was no because sawmills do not regularly sell saws.

The UCC covers transactions in goods. *Goods* are usually defined as moveable items. Some are obvious. A car or pencil would be a good. However, there are times when you may not be sure if the item is covered by the Code. Those things covered by other laws are real estate, services, and what are called "paper rights," such as stocks and bonds.

You hire a roofer to install a new roof on your building. There is a combination of product and service involved. Also, once the roof is installed, it is real estate. This type of situation will not come up often, but if it does, see a lawyer.

Other sections of the UCC that you should know concern warranties, negotiable instruments (like checks and notes), letters of credit, secured transactions, shipping terms, sale on approval, and sale or return. We will discuss some of the things that you should know, but cannot cover the entire UCC.

BANKING

If you are starting a business, you should pick a bank to use. Sit down with whomever is going to handle your account and go over negotiable instruments. Ask what you should know about both the law and the bank's policy. If you are selling items that you will repossess if payments are not made, ask them about that too. A good banker knows the UCC and can be a valuable asset to your business.

USAGE OF TRADE

One area that may be of even greater importance is called *usage of trade*. This means that you can be responsible for contract language that may not mean what you think it means. There was a case where a biscuit company contracted to buy 100,000 sacks of potatoes. When the time for performance came, the buyer only took about 60,000 sacks. The seller sued. The court held that in this industry the promise to buy a certain amount is only an approximation of the amount that the buyer will need and the buyer did not breach the contract by taking the smaller amount. The moral of the story is that you must know your industry and how contracts are interpreted. If you are not sure, put right in your contract that it will be controlled by the plain meaning of the words and that usage of trade shall not be used to interpret the contract.

SHIPPING TERMS

If you are going to ship goods, it is important that you are familiar with shipping terms. Abbreviations such as F.O.B. (free on board), F.A.S. (free alongside), C.I.F. (cost, insurance, and freight), CandF and CF (cost and freight), and Ex-Ship mean different things as to when the title and risk of loss will pass from the seller to the buyer. (Cal. Com. Code, Sections 2319 through 2322.) Even if insurance is involved, it is important to know which party has to deal with the insurance company.

SALE ON APPROVAL

A *sale on approval* is one where the buyer is going to use the goods for a certain period to decide whether to keep them. If you're going to sell products on approval, there are a few things you should know. We have all seen the ads "Try it for ten days. If you're not satisfied, return it and owe nothing." Suppose during those ten days the goods are destroyed, stolen, or the buyer declares bankruptcy. What are the rights of the seller? (Cal. Com. Code, Section 2326.) If you sell on approval, you retain title and risk of loss until the goods are accepted and paid for. This is good if the buyer declares bankruptcy. You still own the goods and the buyer's creditors cannot get them. However, if the goods are stolen or damaged through no fault of the buyer, it is you who must bear the loss. Talk to your insurance agent about this possibility.

SALE OR RETURN

Sale or return (also called *sale and return*) is a sale to someone who will resell the goods. Example: You manufacture bathing suits. You sell to stores with the agreement that they may return any unsold suits at the end of the season. This encourages them to buy more suits.

In a sale or return, the buyer has title and risk of loss. If the buyer declares bankruptcy, you lose the goods and become a general creditor for any unpaid balance. If they are stolen or damaged, it's the buyer's problem. You are still entitled to payment in full. (Cal. Com. Code, Section 2327.)

Warranties

CALIFORNIA
COMMERCIAL
CODE
WARRANTIES

There are several types of warranties, some of which we usually think of when buying or selling a product; some of which we do not. Let's look at each briefly. (Cal. Com. Code, Sections 2311 through 2317; Cal. Civ. Code, Sections 1792 through 1795.7.) These are summarized below.

Warranty of Title. When you sell (or lease) goods, you warrant that you have the right to do so. In other words, if you sell goods, you warrant that you own the goods or are acting as an agent for the owner. You also warrant that there is no one who is owed money for the goods or has any other claim to them.

Suppose you find something and decide to sell it. You know there is an owner somewhere. You cannot warrant that you are the owner. You must let the buyer know that you are not giving this warranty. Simply saying that the goods are sold "as is" will not do it. You must specifically disclaim the warranty. You can do this by letting the buyer know that you found the goods or by saying (writing) that there is no warranty of title given.

Express Warranties. These are warranties given with words (oral or written). The words must first pertain to the goods themselves. A promise about delivery terms would not be a warranty. A description ("when it arrives, it will be painted green"), sample or model ("it's going to look just like this model"), or promise ("if it breaks, I'll fix it") is a warranty. What is not a warranty is a non-factual opinion ("I think you're going to like it").

Implied Warranties. These are automatic warranties. You give them just by selling (or leasing) the goods.

Warranty of Merchantability. This is a warranty given only by a merchant. The main idea of the warranty is that the goods are what the ordinary buyer would think they are. If you sell a camera, you warrant that it has a lens, a shutter, a place to put the film, and that under normal circumstances, it will take pictures. If you sell a toaster, you warrant that it will make toast. The product must also be adequately labeled and packaged. When you disclaim the warranty of merchantability, you are really saying that you do not know if the product will work. Merchants do not usually do this.

Warranty of Fitness for a Particular Purpose. This is a warranty of which you should be careful. If a seller knows or has reason to know of the buyer's use of the product, and buyer is relying on the seller's recommendation, the seller gives a warranty that the product is fit for the buyer's purpose. The seller can either tell the buyer that the product will do what the buyer wants or simply hands the buyer the product.

☞ ***Example***: A buyer walks into your camera shop and asks to buy a lens that will take a picture of a small animal at one hundred yards. You take a lens off the shelf and hand it to the buyer. You are giving the buyer the warranty. There may be nothing wrong with the lens. It is fit for its ordinary use. However, if it will not take a picture of a small animal at one hundred yards, you have breached your warranty.

☞ ***Example***: A buyer comes into your paint store and tells you that she has run out of paint in the middle of painting a room. The buyer hands you a sample of the paint she has been using. You know that you not only have to sell her paint that is fit for its ordinary use (warranty of merchantability) but paint that will match exactly the paint she has been using (warranty of fitness for a particular purpose).

Implied warranties may be disclaimed by selling the product "as is" or "with all faults." You may also specifically state that there is no warranty of merchantability (conspicuously *if* in writing) or no warranty of fitness for a particular purpose (conspicuously ***and only*** in writing).

We have all heard of *limited warranties*. You may limit your warranties instead of disclaiming them. They may be limited to time, such as a thirty day warranty, or to part of the product, such as the drive train of a car. Always limit your warranty in some way, even if you want to give a complete warranty.

FEDERAL
WARRANTIES

In 1975, the federal government got involved in warranties with the Magnuson-Moss Warranty Act. Two things you must know about the act. First, the act provides for attorney's fees to be paid by the seller for breach of warranty. This means that the buyer could afford to sue for the toaster that would not make toast. This means that no matter how small an amount is involved, pay attention. You could end up paying thousands in lawyer's fees over the toaster.

The next thing the act did was to define a *full* warranty. To this day, no one is quite sure what a full warranty is. This is why even warranties that seem to cover everything are called limited.

There are many other features to the Magnuson-Moss Act. If someone is threatening to sue for breach of warranty, and you do not want to give in, see a lawyer.

LIMITATION OF REMEDIES

You may limit remedies of the buyer. You could, for example, say that the buyer may exchange the item sold, but not get a refund. Limitations of remedies are generally upheld if reasonable. For example, you give the buyer a new item five times and each one is defective. The court would probably say that your remedy has failed and allow the buyer a refund or other remedy. You may not limit remedies when the product has caused physical injury.

COMMERCIAL DISCRIMINATION

FEDERAL LAW

The Robinson-Patman Act of 1936 prohibits businesses from injuring competition by offering the same goods at different prices to different buyers. This means that the large chain stores should not be getting a better price than your small shop. It also requires that promotional allowances must be made on proportionally the same terms to all buyers. As a small business, you may be a victim of Robinson-Patman Act violations. A good place to look for information on the act is the following website:

http://www.lawmall.com/rpa/

CALIFORNIA LAW

Although there is no specific California law on this subject, the California Supreme Court, in *ABC International Traders, Inc. v. Matsushita Electric Corporation of America*, ruled that Section 17045 of the California Business and Professional Code extends to price discrimination.

RESTRAINING TRADE

FEDERAL LAW

One of the earliest federal laws affecting business is the Sherman Antitrust Act of 1890. The purpose of the law was to protect competition in the marketplace by prohibiting monopolies. For example, one large company might buy out all of its competitors and then raise prices to astronomical levels. In recent years, this law was used to break up AT&T.

Examples of some things that are prohibited are:

☞ agreements between competitors to sell at the same prices;

☛ agreements between competitors on how much will be sold or produced;

☛ agreements between competitors to divide up a market;

☛ refusing to sell one product without a second product; and

☛ exchanging information among competitors that results in similarity of prices.

As a new business you probably will not be in a position to violate the act, but you should be aware of it in case a larger competitor tries to put you out of business. A good place to find information on the act is the following Internet site:

http://www.lawmall.com/sherman.act/index.html

CALIFORNIA
LAW

California's Business and Professions Code contains several provisions relating to restraint of trade, including the following:

☛ Section 16720 prohibits trusts. A *trust*, as defined in this section, is closer to what the average person would call a *conspiracy*. When two or more persons combine capital, skill, or acts to restrict trade or create unfair competition, it is a trust. This includes price fixing and limiting production to keep prices high.

☛ Section 16721 makes it unlawful to exclude anyone from a business transaction "on the basis of a policy expressed in any document or writing which requires discrimination against such other person on the basis of the person's sex, race, color, religion, ancestry or national origin or on the basis that the person conducts or has conducted business in a particular location." However, to confuse things, the law then states: "Nothing in this section shall be construed to prohibit any person, on this basis of his or her individual ideology or preferences, from doing business or refusing to do business with any other person consistent with law."

☛ Section 16725 makes it clear that industry associations that try to improve industry standards and promote trade are allowed.

☞ Section 16727 prohibits the setting of a price, or giving rebates or discounts to a buyer in exchange for the buyer's agreement not to buy elsewhere.

☞ Section 16728 gives an exemption to *motor carriers of property* (as defined in the California Vehicle Code, Section 34601), which "may voluntarily elect to participate in uniform cargo liability rules, uniform bills of lading or receipts for property being transported, uniform cargo credit rules, joint line rates or routes, classifications, mileage guides, and pooling." This is to comply with federal law. (U.S.C., Title 49, Section 14501(c).) The election may be made by either participating in an agreement pursuant to U.S.C., Title 49 Section 13703; or by filing a notice and certain documents with the Department of Motor Vehicles.

INTELLECTUAL PROPERTY PROTECTION

As a business owner you should know enough about intellectual property law to protect your own creations and to keep from violating the rights of others. Intellectual property is that which is the product of human creativity, such as writings, designs, inventions, melodies and processes. They are things that can be stolen without being physically taken. For example, if you write a book, someone can steal the words from your book without stealing a physical copy of it.

As the Internet grows, intellectual property is becoming more valuable. Smart business owners are those who will take the action necessary to protect their company's intellectual property. Additionally, business owners should know intellectual property law to be sure that they do not violate the rights of others. Even an unknowing violation of the law can result in stiff fines and penalties.

The following are the types of intellectual property and the ways to protect them.

A *patent* is protection given to new and useful inventions, discoveries and designs. To be entitled to a patent, a work must be completely new and "unobvious." A patent is granted to the first inventor who files for the patent. Once an invention is patented, no one else can make use of that invention, even if they discover it independently after a lifetime of research. A patent protects an invention for 17 years; for designs it is 3-1/2, 7 or 14 years. Patents cannot be renewed. The patent application must clearly explain how to make the invention so that when the patent expires, others will be able to freely make and use the invention. Patents are registered with the United States Patent and Trademark Office (PTO). Examples of things that would be patentable would be mechanical devices or new drug formulas.

A *copyright* is protection given to "original works of authorship," such as written works, musical works, visual works, performance works, or computer software programs. A copyright exists from the moment of creation, but one cannot register a copyright until it has been fixed in tangible form. Also, one cannot copyright titles, names, or slogans. A copyright currently gives the author and his heirs exclusive right to his work for the life of the author plus seventy years. Copyrights first registered before 1978 last for ninety-five years. This was previously seventy-five years but was extended twenty years to match the European system. Copyrights are registered with the Register of Copyrights at the Library of Congress. Examples of works that would be copyrightable are books, paintings, songs, poems, plays, drawings, and films.

A *trademark* is protection given to a name or symbol that is used to distinguish one person's goods or services from those of others. It can consist of letters, numerals, packaging, labeling, musical notes, colors, or a combination of these. If the name or symbol is used in connection with services, as opposed to goods, it is called a *service mark*. A trademark lasts indefinitely if it is used continuously and renewed properly. Trademarks are registered with the United States Patent and Trademark Office and with individual states. This is explained further in Chapter 3. Examples of trademarks are the "Chrysler" name on automobiles, the red border on TIME magazine and the shape of the Coca-Cola bottle.

A *trade secret* is some information or process that provides a commercial advantage that is protected by keeping it a secret. Examples of trade secrets may be a list of successful distributors, the formula for Coca-Cola, or some unique source code in a computer program. Trade secrets are not registered anywhere, they are protected by the fact that they are not disclosed. They are protected only for as long as they are kept secret. If you independently discover the formula for Coca-Cola tomorrow, you can freely market it. (But you cannot use the trademark "Coca-Cola" on your product to market it.)

Some things are just not protectable. Such things as ideas, systems and discoveries are not allowed any protection under any law. If you have a great idea, such as selling packets of hangover medicine in bars, you cannot stop others from doing the same thing. If you invent a new medicine, you can patent it; if you pick a distinctive name for it, you can register it as a trademark; if you create a unique picture or instructions for the package, you can copyright them. But you cannot stop others from using your basic business idea of marketing hangover medicine in bars.

Notice the subtle differences between the protective systems available. If you invent something two days after someone else does, you cannot even use it yourself if the other person has patented it. But if you write the same poem as someone else and neither of you copied the other, both of you can copyright the poem. If you patent something, you can have the exclusive rights to it for the term of the patent, but you must disclose how others can make it after the patent expires. However, if you keep it a trade secret, you have exclusive rights as long as no one learns the secret.

We are in a time of transition of the law of intellectual property. Every year new changes are made in the laws and new forms of creativity win protection. For more information, you should consult a new edition of a book on these types of property. Some are listed in the section of this book "for further reference."

ENDLESS LAWS 15

The state of California and the federal government have numerous laws and rules that apply to every aspect of every type of business. There are laws governing even such things as fence posts, hosiery, rabbit raising, refund policies, frozen desserts, and advertising. Every business is affected by one or another of these laws.

Some activities are covered by both state and federal laws. In such cases, you must obey the stricter of the rules. In addition, more than one agency of the state or federal government may have rules governing your business. Each of these may have the power to investigate violations and impose fines or other penalties.

Penalties for violations of these laws can range from a warning to a criminal fine and even jail time. In some cases, employees can sue for damages. Recently, employees have been given awards of millions of dollars from employers who violated the law. Since "ignorance of the law is no excuse," it is your duty to learn which laws apply to your business, or to risk these penalties.

Very few people in business know the laws that apply to their businesses. If you take the time to learn them, you can become an expert in your field, and avoid problems with regulators. You can also fight back if one of your competitors uses some illegal method to compete with you.

The laws and rules that affect the most businesses are explained in this section. Following that is a list of more specialized laws. You should read through this list and see which ones may apply to your business. Then go to your public library or law library and read them. Some may not apply to your phase of the business, but if any of them do apply, you should make copies to keep on hand.

No one could possibly know all the rules that affect business, much less comply with them all. The Interstate Commerce Commission alone has 40 trillion (that is 40 million million or 40,000,000,000,000) rates on its books telling the transportation industry what it should charge! But if you keep up with the important rules you will stay out of trouble and have more chance of success.

FEDERAL LAWS

The federal laws that are most likely to affect small businesses are rules of the Federal Trade Commission (FTC). The FTC has some rules that affect many businesses such as the rules about labeling, warranties, and mail order sales. Other rules affect only certain industries.

If you sell goods by mail you should send for their booklet, *A Business Guide to the Federal Trade Commission's Mail Order Rule*. If you are going to be involved in a certain industry such as those listed below, or using warranties or your own labeling, you should ask for their latest information on the subject. The address is:

Federal Trade Commission
Washington, DC 20580

The rules of the FTC are contained in the Code of Federal Regulations (C.F.R.) in Chapter 16. Some of the industries covered are:

INDUSTRY	PART
Adhesive Compositions	235
Aerosol Products Used for Frosting Cocktail Glasses	417

INDUSTRY	PART
Automobiles (New car fuel economy advertising)	259
Barber Equipment and Supplies	248
Binoculars	402
Business Opportunities and Franchises	436
Cigarettes	408
Decorative Wall Paneling	243
Dog and Cat Food	241
Dry Cell Batteries	403
Extension Ladders	418
Fallout Shelters	229
Feather and Down Products	253
Fiber Glass Curtains	413
Food (Games of Chance)	419
Funerals	453
Gasoline (Octane posting)	306
Gasoline	419
Greeting Cards	244
Home Entertainment Amplifiers	432
Home Insulation	460
Hosiery	22
Household Furniture	250
Jewelry	23
Ladies' Handbags	247
Law Books	256
Light Bulbs	409
Luggage and Related Products	24
Mail Order Insurance	234
Mail Order Merchandise	435
Men's and Boys' Tailored Clothing	412
Metallic Watch Band	19

INDUSTRY	PART
Mirrors	21
Nursery	18
Ophthalmic Practices	456
Photographic Film and Film Processing	242
Private Vocational and Home Study Schools	254
Radiation Monitoring Instruments	232
Retail Food Stores (Advertising)	424
Shell Homes	230
Shoes	231
Sleeping Bags	400
Tablecloths and Related Products	404
Television Sets	410
Textile Wearing Apparel	423
Textiles	236
Tires	228
Used Automobile Parts	20
Used Lubricating Oil	406
Used Motor Vehicles	455
Waist Belts	405
Watches	245
Wigs and Hairpieces	252

Some other federal laws that affect businesses are as follows:

☛ Alcohol Administration Act (U.S.C., Title 29, beginning with Section 201.)

☛ Child Protection and Toy Safety Act (1969)

☛ Clean Water Act (U.S.C., Title 33)

☛ Comprehensive Smokeless Tobacco Health Education Act (1986). See also C.F.R., Title 16, Chapter I, Part 307 for rules.

☛ Consumer Credit Protection Act (1968)

- Consumer Product Safety Act (1972)
- Energy Policy and Conservation Act. See also C.F.R., Title 16, Chapter I, Part 305 for rules about energy cost labeling.
- Environmental Pesticide Control Act of 1972
- Fair Credit Reporting Act (1970)
- Fair Packaging and Labeling Act (1966). See also C.F.R., Title 16, Chapter I, Parts 500-503 for rules.
- Flammable Fabrics Act (1953). See also C.F.R., Title 16, Chapter II, Parts 1602-1632 for rules.
- Food, Drug, and Cosmetic Act (U.S.C., Title 21, beginning with Section 301.)
- Fur Products Labeling Act (1951). See also C.F.R., Title 16, Chapter I, Part 301 for rules.
- Hazardous Substances Act (1960)
- Hobby Protection Act. See also C.F.R., Title 16, Chapter I, Part 304 for rules.
- Insecticide, Fungicide, and Rodenticide Act (U.S.C., Title 7, beginning with Section 136.)
- Magnuson-Moss Warranty Act. See also C.F.R., Title 16, Chapter I, Part 239 for rules.
- Poison Prevention Packaging Act of 1970. See also C.F.R., Title 16, Chapter II, Parts 1700-1702 for rules.
- Solid Waste Disposal Act (U.S.C., Title 42, beginning with Section 6901.)
- Textile Fiber Products Identification Act. See also C.F.R., Title 16, Chapter I, Part 303 for rules.
- Toxic Substance Control Act (U.S.C., Title 15.)
- Wool Products Labeling Act (1939). See also C.F.R., Title 16, Chapter I, Part 300 for rules.

☛ Nutrition Labeling and Education Act of 1990. See also C.F.R., Title 21, Chapter 1, Subchapter B

☛ Food Safety Enforcement Enhancement Act of 1997.

CALIFORNIA LAWS

California laws are too numerous to try and cover them all in this book. For example, if you look up adoption agencies by using the "key words" feature, there are fifteen different references covering over two hundred sections of six different codes. Unless you are a lawyer who is willing to spend a lot of time on research, you are not going to know all of the law for your new business.

This is why industry associations and programs like SCORE are so important. Some advice from a person who is familiar with your type of business is worth more than reading endless laws. Also, see the listing of regulated professions and businesses in Chapter 6.

BOOKKEEPING AND ACCOUNTING 16

It is beyond the scope of this book to explain all the intricacies of setting up a business's bookkeeping and accounting systems. But the important thing is to realize that if you do not set up an understandable bookkeeping system your business will undoubtedly fail.

Without accurate records of where your income is coming from and where it is going, you will be unable to increase profits, lower expenses, obtain needed financing or make the right decisions in all areas of your business. The time to decide how you will handle your bookkeeping is when you open your business, not a year later when it is tax time.

INITIAL BOOKKEEPING

If you do not understand business taxation you should pick up a good book on the subject, as well as the IRS tax guide for your type of business (proprietorship, partnership, or corporation). A few good books on the subject are listed in the back of this book.

The IRS tax book for small businesses is Publication 334, *Tax Guide for Small Businesses*. There are also instruction booklets for each type of business form: Schedule C for proprietorships, Form 1120 or 1120S for

C corporations and S corporations, and 1165 for partnerships and businesses, which are taxed like partnerships (LLCs, LLPs).

Keep in mind that the IRS does not give you the best advice for saving on taxes and does not give you the other side of contested issues. For that you need a private tax guide or advisor.

The most important thing to do is to set up your bookkeeping so that you can easily fill out your monthly, quarterly, and annual tax returns.

The best way to do this is to get copies of the returns, note the categories that you will need to supply, and set up your bookkeeping system to arrive at those totals.

For example, for a sole proprietorship you will use "Schedule C" to report business income and expenses to the IRS at the end of the year. Use the categories on that form to sort your expenses. To make your job especially easy, every time you pay a bill, put the category number on the check.

ACCOUNTANTS

Most likely your new business will not be able to afford hiring an accountant to handle your books. But that is good. Doing them yourself will force you to learn about business accounting and taxation. The worst way to run a business is to know nothing about the tax laws and turn everything over to an accountant at the end of the year to find out what is due.

You should know the basics of tax law before making basic decisions, such as whether to buy or rent equipment or premises. You should understand accounting so you can time your financial affairs appropriately. If you were a boxer who only needed to win fights, you could turn everything over to an accountant. If your business needs to buy supplies, inventory, or equipment and provides goods or services throughout the year, you need to at least have a basic understanding of the system within which you are working.

Once you can afford an accountant you should weigh the cost against your time and the risk that you will make an error. Even if you think you know enough to do your own corporate tax return, you should at least take it to an accountant the first year to see if you have been missing any deductions. You might decide that the money saved is worth the cost of the accountant's services.

COMPUTER PROGRAMS

Today every business should keep its books by computer. There are inexpensive programs, such as Quicken, which can instantly provide you with reports of your income and expenses and the right figures to plug into your tax returns.

Most programs even offer a tax program each year that will take all of your information and print it out on the current year's tax forms.

TAX TIPS

A tax timetable is provided in the appendix. (see form 1, p.230.) However, here are a few tax tips for small businesses that will help you save money:

☞ Usually when you buy equipment for a business, you must amortize the cost over several years. That is, you do not deduct it all when you buy it, you take, say, twenty-five percent of the cost off your taxes each year for four years. (The time is determined by the theoretical usefulness of the item.) However, small businesses are allowed to write off the entire cost of a limited amount of items (Internal Revenue Code (I.R.C.), Section 179.) If you have income to shelter, use it.

- Owners of S corporations do not have to pay social security or medicare taxes on the part of their profits that is not considered salary. As long as you pay yourself a reasonable salary, other money you take out is not subject to these taxes.

- You should not neglect to deposit withholding taxes for your own salary or profits. Besides being a large sum to come up with at once in April, there are penalties that must be paid for failure to do so.

- Do not fail to keep track of and remit your employees' withholding. You will be personally liable for them even if you are a corporation.

- If you keep track of the use of your car for business you can deduct 31.5¢ per mile (this may go up or down each year). If you use your car for business a considerable amount of time you may be able to depreciate it.

- If your business is a corporation and if you designate the stock as "section 1244 stock," then if the business fails you are able to get a much better deduction for the loss.

- By setting up a retirement plan you can exempt up to twenty percent of your salary from income tax. See Chapter 11. But do not use money you might need later. There are penalties for taking it out of the retirement plan.

- When you buy things that will be resold or made into products that will be resold, you do not have to pay sales taxes on those purchases. See Chapter 18.

Paying Federal Taxes 17

Federal Income Tax

The manner in which each type of business pays taxes is as follows:

SOLE PROPRIETORSHIP
A sole proprietor reports profits and expenses on Schedule C attached to the usual Form 1040 and pays tax on all of the net income of the business. Each quarter Form ES-1040 must be filed along with payment of one-quarter of the amount of income tax and social security taxes estimated to be due for the year.

PARTNERSHIP
The partnership files a return showing the income and expenses but pays no tax. Each partner is given a form showing his share of the profits or losses and reports these on Schedule E of Form 1040. Each quarter, Form ES-1040 must be filed by each partner along with payment of one-quarter of the amount of income tax and social security taxes estimated to be due for the year.

C CORPORATION
A regular corporation is a separate taxpayer, and pays tax on its profits after deducting all expenses, including officers' salaries. If dividends are distributed, they are paid out of after-tax dollars, and the shareholders pay tax a second time when they receive the dividends. If a corporation needs to accumulate money for investment, it may be able to do so at lower tax rates than the shareholders. But if all profits will be

distributed to shareholders, the double-taxation may be excessive unless all income is paid as salaries. A C corporation files Form 1120.

S CORPORATION

A small corporation has the option of being taxed like a partnership. If Form 2553 is filed by the corporation and accepted by the Internal Revenue Service, the S corporation will only file an informational return listing profits and expenses. Then each shareholder will be taxed on a proportional share of the profits (or be able to deduct a proportional share of the losses). Unless a corporation will make a large profit that will not be distributed, S-status is usually best in the beginning. An S corporation files Form 1120S and distributes Form K-1 to each shareholder. If any money is taken out by a shareholder that is not listed as wages subject to withholding, then the shareholder will usually have to file form ES-1040 each quarter along with payment of the estimated withholding on the withdrawals.

LIMITED LIABILITY COMPANIES AND PARTNERSHIPS

Limited liability companies and limited liability partnerships are allowed by the IRS to elect to be taxed either as a partnership or a corporation. To make this election you file Form 8832, Entity Classification Election with the IRS.

TAX INFORMATION

The IRS now offers tax help for small businesses. The Small Business Resource Guide-CD-ROM 2000 can be ordered by calling 800-829-3676. Ask for "Publication 3207." The first copy is free. This can also be ordered online at **http://www.irs.gov**, by clicking "small business publications."

FEDERAL WITHHOLDING, SOCIAL SECURITY, AND MEDICARE TAXES

If you need basic information on business tax returns, the IRS publishes a rather large booklet that answers most questions and is available free of charge. Call or write them and ask for "Publication No. 334." If you have any questions, call 800-829-3676. If you want more creative answers and tax saving information, you should find a good local accountant. But to get started you will need the following:

EMPLOYER IDENTIFICATION NUMBER

If you are a sole proprietor with no employees, you can use your social security number for your business. If you are a corporation, a partnership or a proprietorship with employees, you must obtain an "Employer Identification Number." This is done by filing form SS-4. (see form 6, p.243.) It usually takes a week or two to receive. You will need this number to open bank accounts for the business, so you should file this form a soon as you decide to go into business. A sample filled-in form and instructions are at the end of this chapter.

EMPLOYEE'S WITHHOLDING ALLOWANCE CERTIFICATE

You must have each employee fill out a W-4 form to calculate the amount of federal taxes to be deducted and to obtain their social security numbers. (see form 8, p.251.) (The number of allowances on this form is used with IRS Circular E, Publication 15, to figure out the exact deductions.) A sample filled-in form is at the end of this chapter.

FEDERAL TAX DEPOSIT COUPONS

After taking withholdings from employees' wages, you must deposit them at a bank that is authorized to accept such funds. If at the end of any month you have over $1,000 in withheld taxes (including your contribution to FICA) you must make a deposit prior to the 15th of the following month. If on the 3rd, 7th, 11th, 15th, 19th, 22nd, or 25th of any month you have over $3,000 in withheld taxes, you must make a deposit within three banking days. The deposit is made using the coupons in the Form 8109 booklet. A sample 8109-B coupon, which you will use to order your booklet, is shown at the end of this chapter.

ELECTRONIC FILING

Businesses that make $50,000 or more a year in federal tax deposits are required to begin electronic filing by June 30, 1999. However, this deadline has been extended in the past and may be again. (It was originally scheduled for July 1, 1997, but faced strong business opposition.)

ESTIMATED TAX PAYMENT VOUCHER

Sole proprietors and partners usually take draws from their businesses without the formality of withholding. However, they are still required to make deposits of income and FICA taxes each quarter. If more than $500 is due in April on a person's 1040 form, then not enough money was withheld each quarter and a penalty is assessed unless the person falls into an exception. The quarterly withholding is submitted on Form 1040-ES on April 15th, June 15th, September 15th, and January 15th each year. If these days fall on a weekend then the due date is the following Monday. The worksheet with Form 1040-ES can be used to determine the amount to pay. ***Important Note***: One of the exceptions to the rule is that if you withhold the same amount as last year's tax bill, then you do not have to pay a penalty. This is usually a lot easier than filling out the 1040-ES worksheet.

EMPLOYER'S QUARTERLY TAX RETURN

Each quarter you must file Form 941 reporting your federal withholding and FICA taxes. If you owe more than $1,000 at the end of a quarter, you are required to make a deposit at the end of any month that you have $1,000 in withholding. The deposits are made to the Federal Reserve Bank or an authorized financial institution on Form 501. Most banks are authorized to accept deposits. If you owe more than $3,000 for any month, you must make a deposit at any point in the month in which you owe $3,000. After you file form SS-4, the 941 forms will be sent to you automatically if you checked the box saying that you expect to have employees.

WAGE AND TAX STATEMENT

At the end of each year, you are required to issue a W-2 Form to each employee. This form shows the amount of wages paid to the employee during the year as well as the amounts withheld for taxes, social security, medicare, and other purposes. A sample W-2 is at the end of this chapter.

MISCELLANEOUS

If you pay at least $600 to a person other than an employee (such as independent contractors) you are required to file a Form 1099 for that person. Along with the 1099s, you must file a form 1096, which is a summary sheet.

Many people are not aware of this law and fail to file these forms, but they are required for such things as services, royalties, rents, awards and prizes that you pay to individuals (but not corporations). The rules for this are quite complicated so you should either obtain "Package 1099" from the IRS or consult your accountant. Sample forms 1099 and 1096 are at the end of this chapter.

Persons who are not liable to pay income tax may have the right to a check from the government because of the "Earned Income Credit." You are required to notify your employees of this. You can satisfy this requirement with one of the following:

☛ A W-2 Form with the notice on the back;

☛ A substitute for the W-2 Form with the notice on it;

☛ A copy of Notice 797; or

☛ A written statement with the wording from Notice 797.

A Notice 797 can be obtained by calling 800-829-3676.

FEDERAL EXCISE TAXES

Excise taxes are taxes on certain activities or items. Most federal excise taxes have been eliminated since World War II, but a few remain.

Some of the things that are subject to federal excise taxes are tobacco, alcohol, gasoline, tires and inner tubes, some trucks and trailers, firearms, ammunition, bows, arrows, fishing equipment, the use of highway vehicles of over 55,000 pounds, aircraft, wagering, telephone and teletype services, coal, hazardous wastes, and vaccines. If you are involved with any of these, you should obtain from the IRS publication No. 510, *Information on Excise Taxes*.

UNEMPLOYMENT COMPENSATION TAXES

You must pay federal unemployment taxes if you paid wages of $1,500 in any quarter, or if you had at least one employee for twenty calendar weeks. The federal tax amount is 0.8% of the first $7,000 of wages paid each employee. If more than $100 is due by the end of any quarter (if you paid $12,500 in wages for the quarter), then Form 508 must be filed with an authorized financial institution or the Federal Reserve Bank in your area. You will receive Form 508 when you obtain your employer identification number.

At the end of each year, you must file Form 940 or Form 940EZ. This is your annual report of federal unemployment taxes. You will receive an original form from the IRS.

Form **SS-4**

(Rev. April 2000)

Department of the Treasury
Internal Revenue Service

Application for Employer Identification Number

(For use by employers, corporations, partnerships, trusts, estates, churches, government agencies, certain individuals, and others. See instructions.)

▶ Keep a copy for your records.

EIN

OMB No. 1545-0003

Please type or print clearly.

1 Name of applicant (legal name) (see instructions)

John Doe and James Doe

2 Trade name of business (if different from name on line 1) Doe Company	**3** Executor, trustee, "care of" name
4a Mailing address (street address) (room, apt., or suite no.) 123 Main Street	**5a** Business address (if different from address on lines 4a and 4b)
4b City, state, and ZIP code Libertyville, CA 95202	**5b** City, state, and ZIP code

6 County and state where principal business is located

Libertyville, CA

7 Name of principal officer, general partner, grantor, owner, or trustor—SSN or ITIN may be required (see instructions) ▶ 123-45-6789

John Doe

8a Type of entity (Check only one box.) (see instructions)

Caution: *If applicant is a limited liability company, see the instructions for line 8a.*

☐ Sole proprietor (SSN) _____

☒ Partnership   ☐ Personal service corp.

☐ REMIC   ☐ National Guard

☐ State/local government   ☐ Farmers' cooperative

☐ Church or church-controlled organization

☐ Other nonprofit organization (specify) ▶ _____

☐ Other (specify) ▶

☐ Estate (SSN of decedent) _____

☐ Plan administrator (SSN) _____

☐ Other corporation (specify) ▶ _____

☐ Trust

☐ Federal government/military

_____ (enter GEN if applicable) _____

8b If a corporation, name the state or foreign country (if applicable) where incorporated

State	Foreign country

9 Reason for applying (Check only one box.) (see instructions)

☒ Started new business (specify type) ▶_____
    clothing manufacturer

☐ Hired employees (Check the box and see line 12.)

☐ Created a pension plan (specify type) ▶

☐ Banking purpose (specify purpose) ▶ _____

☐ Changed type of organization (specify new type) ▶ _____

☐ Purchased going business

☐ Created a trust (specify type) ▶ _____

☐ Other (specify) ▶

10 Date business started or acquired (month, day, year) (see instructions) 10-15-2001	**11** Closing month of accounting year (see instructions) December

12 First date wages or annuities were paid or will be paid (month, day, year). **Note:** *If applicant is a withholding agent, enter date income will first be paid to nonresident alien. (month, day, year)* . . . . ▶ 10-22-2001

13 Highest number of employees expected in the next 12 months. **Note:** *If the applicant does not expect to have any employees during the period, enter -0-. (see instructions)* . . . . ▶	Nonagricultural	Agricultural	Household

14 Principal activity (see instructions) ▶ clothing manufacturing

15 Is the principal business activity manufacturing? . . . . ☒ Yes   ☐ No

If "Yes," principal product and raw material used ▶   fabric

16 To whom are most of the products or services sold? Please check one box.   ☒ Business (wholesale)

☐ Public (retail)   ☐ Other (specify) ▶   ☐ N/A

17a Has the applicant ever applied for an employer identification number for this or any other business? . . . . ☐ Yes   ☒ No

Note: *If "Yes," please complete lines 17b and 17c.*

17b If you checked "Yes" on line 17a, give applicant's legal name and trade name shown on prior application, if different from line 1 or 2 above.

Legal name ▶   Trade name ▶

17c Approximate date when and city and state where the application was filed. Enter previous employer identification number if known.

Approximate date when filed (mo., day, year)	City and state where filed	Previous EIN

Under penalties of perjury, I declare that I have examined this application, and to the best of my knowledge and belief, it is true, correct, and complete.

Name and title (Please type or print clearly.) ▶   John Doe, Partner

Business telephone number (include area code)

(760) 555-0000

Fax telephone number (include area code)

( )

Signature ▶ *John Doe*   Date ▶ *10/15/01*

Note: *Do not write below this line. For official use only.*

Please leave blank ▶	Geo.	Ind.	Class	Size	Reason for applying

For Privacy Act and Paperwork Reduction Act Notice, see page 4.   Cat. No. 16055N   Form **SS-4** (Rev. 4-2000)

Form W-4 (2001)

Purpose. Complete Form W-4 so your employer can withhold the correct Federal income tax from your pay. Because your tax situation may change, you may want to refigure your withholding each year.

Exemption from withholding. If you are exempt, complete only lines 1, 2, 3, 4, and 7, and sign the form to validate it. Your exemption for 2001 expires February 18, 2002.

Note: *You cannot claim exemption from withholding if (1) your income exceeds $750 and includes more than $250 of unearned income (e.g., interest and dividends) and (2) another person can claim you as a dependent on their tax return.*

Basic instructions. If you are not exempt, complete the **Personal Allowances Worksheet** below. The worksheets on page 2 adjust your withholding allowances based on itemized deductions, certain credits, adjustments to

income, or two-earner/two-job situations. Complete all worksheets that apply. They will help you figure the number of withholding allowances you are entitled to claim. **However, you may claim fewer (or zero) allowances.**

Head of household. Generally, you may claim head of household filing status on your tax return only if you are unmarried and pay more than 50% of the costs of keeping up a home for yourself and your dependent(s) or other qualifying individuals. See line E below.

Tax credits. You can take projected tax credits into account in figuring your allowable number of withholding allowances. Credits for child or dependent care expenses and the child tax credit may be claimed using the **Personal Allowances Worksheet** below. See **Pub. 919,** How Do I Adjust My Tax Withholding? for information on converting your other credits into withholding allowances.

Nonwage income. If you have a large amount of nonwage income, such as interest or dividends,

consider making estimated tax payments using **Form 1040-ES,** Estimated Tax for Individuals. Otherwise, you may owe additional tax.

Two earners/two jobs. If you have a working spouse or more than one job, figure the total number of allowances you are entitled to claim on all jobs using worksheets from only one Form W-4. Your withholding usually will be most accurate when all allowances are claimed on the Form W-4 for the highest paying job and zero allowances are claimed on the others.

Check your withholding. After your Form W-4 takes effect, use Pub. 919 to see how the dollar amount you are having withheld compares to your projected total tax for 2001. Get Pub. 919 especially if you used the **Two-Earner/Two-Job Worksheet** on page 2 and your earnings exceed $150,000 (Single) or $200,000 (Married).

Recent name change? If your name on line 1 differs from that shown on your social security card, call 1-800-772-1213 for a new social security card.

Personal Allowances Worksheet (Keep for your records.)

A Enter "1" for **yourself** if no one else can claim you as a dependent . . . . **A** _____

B Enter "1" if:
- You are single and have only one job; or
- You are married, have only one job, and your spouse does not work; or
- Your wages from a second job or your spouse's wages (or the total of both) are $1,000 or less.

B 1

C Enter "1" for your **spouse.** But, you may choose to enter -0- if you are married and have either a working spouse or more than one job. (Entering -0- may help you avoid having too little tax withheld.) . . . . **C** _____

D Enter number of **dependents** (other than your spouse or yourself) you will claim on your tax return . . . . . . **D** _____

E Enter "1" if you will file as **head of household** on your tax return (see conditions under **Head of household** above) . **E** _____

F Enter "1" if you have at least $1,500 of **child or dependent care expenses** for which you plan to claim a credit . . **F** _____

(**Note:** *Do not include child support payments. See* **Pub. 503,** *Child and Dependent Care Expenses, for details.*)

G **Child Tax Credit** (including additional child tax credit).
- If your total income will be between $18,000 and $50,000 ($23,000 and $63,000 if married), enter "1" for each eligible child.
- If your total income will be between $50,000 and $80,000 ($63,000 and $115,000 if married), enter "1" if you have two eligible children, enter "2" if you have three or four eligible children, or enter "3" if you have five or more eligible children. **G** 1

H Add lines A through G and enter total here. (**Note:** *This may be different from the number of exemptions you claim on your tax return.*) ▶ **H** _____

For accuracy, complete all worksheets that apply.
- If you plan to **itemize or claim adjustments to income** and want to reduce your withholding, see the **Deductions and Adjustments Worksheet** on page 2.
- If you are **single,** have **more than one job** and your combined earnings from all jobs exceed $35,000, **or** if you are **married** and have a **working spouse or more than one job** and the combined earnings from all jobs exceed $60,000, see the **Two-Earner/Two-Job Worksheet** on page 2 to avoid having too little tax withheld.
- If **neither** of the above situations applies, **stop here** and enter the number from line H on line 5 of Form W-4 below.

- - - - - - - - - - - - - - - - **Cut here and give Form W-4 to your employer. Keep the top part for your records.** - - - - - - - - - - - - - - - -

Form **W-4**
Department of the Treasury
Internal Revenue Service

Employee's Withholding Allowance Certificate

▶ **For Privacy Act and Paperwork Reduction Act Notice, see page 2.**

OMB No. 1545-0010

2001

1 Type or print your first name and middle initial	Last name	**2** Your social security number
John A.	Smith	123 45 6789

Home address (number and street or rural route)
567 Wharf Blvd.

3 ☒ Single ☐ Married ☐ Married, but withhold at higher Single rate.
Note: *If married, but legally separated, or spouse is a nonresident alien, check the Single box.*

City or town, state, and ZIP code
Jacksonville, FL 33490

4 If your last name differs from that on your social security card, check here. You must call 1-800-772-1213 for a new card. ▶ ☐

5 Total number of allowances you are claiming (from line **H** above **or** from the applicable worksheet on page 2) **5** 1

6 Additional amount, if any, you want withheld from each paycheck . . . . **6** $ 0

7 I claim exemption from withholding for 2001, and I certify that I meet **both** of the following conditions for exemption:
- Last year I had a right to a refund of **all** Federal income tax withheld because I had **no** tax liability **and**
- This year I expect a refund of **all** Federal income tax withheld because I expect to have **no** tax liability.

If you meet both conditions, write "Exempt" here . . . . ▶ **7**

Under penalties of perjury, I certify that I am entitled to the number of withholding allowances claimed on this certificate, or I am entitled to claim exempt status.

Employee's signature
(Form is not valid unless you sign it.) ▶ *John A. Smith*

Date ▶ *June 6* *2001*

8 Employer's name and address (Employer: Complete lines 8 and 10 only if sending to the IRS.)	**9** Office code (optional)	**10** Employer identification number

Cat. No. 10220Q

SAMPLE FORM 8109-B: FEDERAL TAX DEPOSIT COUPONS

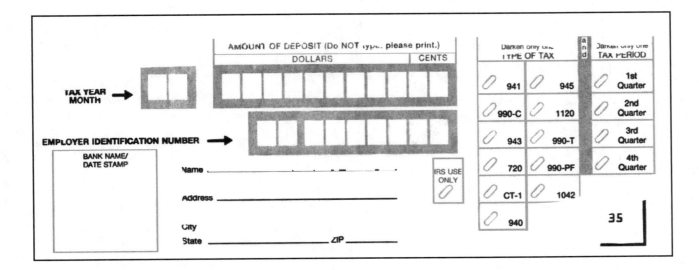

SAMPLE FORM 1040-ES: ESTIMATED TAX PAYMENT VOUCHER

Cat. No. 61900V

OMB No. 1545-0087

Form 1040-ES (OCR)

Department of the Treasury
Internal Revenue Service

2000 Estimated Tax

Payment Voucher **4**

Calendar year—
Due Jan. 15, 2001

Cross out any errors and print the correct information. Get **Form 8822** to report a new address (see instructions). For Paperwork Reduction Act Notice, see instructions.

0746497

07 234-56-7890 DC

9712

234-56-7890 DC WARD 30 0 9712 430 07

JOHN DOE
123 ANYWHERE STREET
LONG BEACH, CA 90807

LONG BEACH, CA 90807

Enter the amount of your payment. File this voucher only if you are making a payment of **estimated** tax.

$

► Make your check or money order payable to **"Internal Revenue Service."**
► Write your social security number and "1997 Form 1040-ES" on your payment.
► Send your payment and payment voucher to the address above.
► Do not send cash. Do not staple your payment to the voucher.

SAMPLE FORM W-2: WAGE AND TAX STATEMENT

a Control number	22222	Void ☐	For Official Use Only ▶ OMB No. 1545-0008	

b Employer's identification number 59-123456	**1** Wages, tips, other compensation 25,650.00	**2** Federal income tax withheld 5,050.00

c Employer's name, address, and ZIP code Doe Company 123 Main Street Long Beach, CA 90807	**3** Social security wages 25,650.00	**4** Social security tax withheld 1,590.30
	5 Medicare wages and tips 25,650.00	**6** Medicare tax withheld 371.93
	7 Social security tips 0	**8** Allocated tips 0

d Employee's social security number 123-45-6789	**9** Advance EIC payment 0	**10** Dependent care benefits 0

e Employee's name (first, middle initial, last) John A. Smith	**11** Nonqualified plans 0	**12** Benefits included in box 1 0
567 Wharf Boulevard Long Beach, CA 90807	**13** See Instrs. for box 13	**14** Other

	15 Statutory employee ☐	Deceased ☐	Pension plan ☐	Legal rep. ☐	Hshld. emp. ☐	Subtotal ☐	Deferred compensation ☐
f Employee's address and ZIP code							

16 State	Employer's state I.D. No.	**17** State wages, tips, etc.	**18** State income tax	**19** Locality name	**20** Local wages, tips, etc.	**21** Local income tax

Cat. No. 10134D

Department of the Treasury—Internal Revenue Service

Form **W-2** **Wage and Tax Statement** **2000**

Copy A For Social Security Administration

For Paperwork Reduction Act Notice, see separate instructions.

SAMPLE FORMS 1099 AND 1096: MISCELLANEOUS INCOME

9595 ☐ VOID ☐ CORRECTED

PAYER'S name, street address, city, state, and ZIP code		1 Rents	OMB No. 1545-0115	
Doe Company		$ 12,000.00		
123 Main Street		2 Royalties	**20**00	**Miscellaneous Income**
		$		
Long Beach, CA 90807		3 Other income		
		$	Form **1099-MISC**	

PAYER'S Federal identification number	RECIPIENT'S identification number	4 Federal income tax withheld	5 Fishing boat proceeds	Copy A
59-123456	9876532	$	$	For
RECIPIENT'S name		6 Medical and health care payments	7 Nonemployee compensation	**Internal Revenue Service Center**
John A. Smith		$	$ 21,000	File with Form 1096.
Street address (including apt. no.)		8 Substitute payments in lieu of dividends or interest	9 Payer made direct sales of $5,000 or more of consumer products to a buyer (recipient) for resale ▶ ☐	For Paperwork Reduction Act Notice and instructions for completing this form, see **Instructions for Forms 1099, 1098, 5498, and W-2G.**
567 Wharf Boulevard		$		
City, state, and ZIP code		10 Crop insurance proceeds	11 State income tax withheld	
Long Beach, CA 90807		$	$ 00.00	
Account number (optional)	2nd TIN Not. ☐	12 State/Payer's state number 8884444		

Form **1099-MISC**　　　　　　　Cat. No. 14425J　　　　Department of the Treasury - Internal Revenue Service

Do NOT Cut or Separate Forms on This Page

DO NOT STAPLE **6969**

Form **1096** Department of the Treasury Internal Revenue Service	**Annual Summary and Transmittal of U.S. Information Returns**	OMB No. 1545-0108 **20**00

A T T A C H　I R S　L A B E L　H E R E

FILER'S name

　Doe Company

Street address (including room or suite number)

　123 Main Street

City, state, and ZIP code
　Long Beach, CA 90807

If you are not using a preprinted label, enter in box 1 or 2 below the identification number you used as the filer on the information returns being transmitted. Do not fill in both boxes 1 and 2.	Name of person to contact if the IRS needs more information John Doe Telephone number (562) 5550000	**For Official Use Only** ☐☐☐☐☐☐☐ ☐☐

1 Employer identification number 59-123456	2 Social security number	3 Total number of forms 3	4 Federal income tax withheld $ 0	5 Total amount reported with this Form 1096 $ $63,000

Enter an "X" in only one box below to indicate the type of form being filed.　　If this is your FINAL return, enter an "X" here . ▶ ☒

W-2G 32	1098 81	1099-A 80	1099-B 79	1099-C 85	1099-DIV 91	1099-G 86	1099-INT 92	1099-MISC 95	1099-OID 96	1099-PATR 97	1099-R 98	1099-S 75	5498 28
☐	☐	☐	☐	☐	☐	☐	☐	☒	☐	☐	☐	☐	☐

PAYING CALIFORNIA TAXES 18

SALES AND USE TAX

If you are going to sell or lease personal property that would ordinarily be subject to a retail sales tax, you must obtain a seller's permit." There are two types. First is the regular permit that allows you to purchase inventory without paying sales tax called an Application for Seller's Permit and Registration as a Retailer. (see form 11, p.257.) The second is the same except that it is temporary. If you're going to sell only Easter baskets or Christmas trees, get a temporary permit. This also applies to the "yard sale." Obviously, there are many violations without much enforcement. However, if you are going to have a "business" like a Christmas tree lot, get a permit. To receive an application for a permit, contact the California State Board of Equalization at 800-400-7115 or one of the local offices listed on p.207. The process takes about one week after submitting the application. The board will send you a packet with instructions. A sample filled-in form is at the end of this chapter. A blank one is in the appendix. (see form 11, p.257.)

SELLING TO TAX
EXEMPT
PURCHASERS

The burden of sales tax is placed on the seller. The seller may choose not to collect the tax from the buyer. If you are selling to a buyer who will resell the goods and has a seller's permit, you should obtain a California Resale Certificate to avoid having to pay the tax. If you do not have a proper California Resale Certificate form at the time of the sale, something in writing and signed by the buyer giving the buyer's address, the buyer's seller permit number or note as to the exempt status of the buyer, a description of the goods and the words "for resale" will be sufficient until you can get the proper form.

If the buyer gives a resale certificate and then stores or uses the property other than for inventory or display in the regular course of business, the buyer must pay a use tax. The tax must be filed with the tax return for the period during which the property was first stored or used. Get the complete rules when you call for your seller's permit.

The California Revenue and Taxation Code is long and not easily understood without some educational background. If you have no accounting background, it is wise to consult an accountant for initial setup of your business. If you do not want to spend the money, at least see if a SCORE representative can walk you through it.

UNEMPLOYMENT COMPENSATION TAX

California's Unemployment Insurance Program is much like that of other states since they all adhere to certain federal standards.

The basic idea is that if an employee loses a job through no fault of his own, weekly unemployment insurance benefits will be paid temporarily. The payments are made for twenty-six weeks, which can be extended to fifty-two weeks.

Employer's tax is paid on up to $7,000 paid to each worker. The tax rate varies based on the prior number of claims against that employer.

To qualify for benefits a claimant must have earned a certain amount during a base period, which is one year. The amount is the lower of $1,300 during the highest quarter of the base period or at least $900 during the base period and 1.25 times that amount for the entire base period.

The Employment Development Department handles unemployment compensation regulations. You can get further information from them and also attend a seminar to help you get set up properly in your new business. Note that some of these are combination Franchise Tax Board and State Board of Equalization offices. The Unemployment Insurance Program Fact Sheet can be ordered. See the Publications Order in the appendix, to order publications with tax tips for many specific business. (see form 9, p.253.)

TANGIBLE AND INTANGIBLE PROPERTY TAXES

This is a tax on all personal property used in a business with the exception of inventory. It includes such things as dishes, machinery, furniture, tools, signs, carpeting, appliances, laboratory equipment, and just about everything else.

BUSINESS PERSONAL PROPERTY

Unlike real property, business personal property is reappraised annually. Each person owning taxable personal property (other than mobile homes) with an aggregate cost of $100,000 or more must file a Business Property Statement (BPS) with the County Assessor Department annually. Upon request of the Assessor Department, the owners of all other businesses must file a BPS. The BPS filing includes detailing the cost, by year of acquisition, of all equipment and fixtures, and the cost of supplies on hand at each business location.

Personal property is negatively defined as all property that is not real property. There are two types of personal property: tangible and intangible. Taxable tangible property would include such things as machines and equipment, furniture and tools. Exempt intangible property would include stocks and bonds, copyrights, notes, and licenses.

Contact your county assessor's office for forms and details if you believe that you should be filing.

INCOME TAX

California does have a state income tax, both for individuals and corporations. The corporate tax is 8.4% with an $800 minimum alternative tax. Form 100 is used for C corporations, 100S for S corporations.

The California Franchise Tax Board can be contacted at:

> Franchise Tax Board
> P.O. Box 942840
> Sacramento, CA 94240-0040

The Employment Development Department (EDD) of California requires that you also file a Registration Form. A sample filled-in Registration Form for Commercial Employers is at the end of this chapter. There is also a blank form in the appendix. (see form 14, p.269.) There is a separate Registration Form for other industries, so if you are not commercial, do not file this form. Contact the EDD at 916-654-7041 to get the appropriate form.

EXCISE TAX

California imposes an excise tax on such items as alcohol, tobacco, and fuel. From time to time there is a temporary tax imposed on top of the excise tax.

The Franchise Tax Board can help with information on special tax programs.

BOARD OF EQUALIZATION OFFICES

Sacramento Headquarters
P.O. Box 942879
Sacramento, CA 94279-0090
800-400-7115

1800 30th Street, Suite 380
P.O. Box 1728
Bakersfield, CA 93302-1728
661-395-2880

5901 Green Valley Circle
P.O. Box 3652
Culver City, CA 90231-3652
310-342-1000

1550 W. Main Street
El Centro, CA 92243-2832
760-352-3431

134 D Street, Suite 301
P.O. Box 4884
Eureka, CA 95502-4884
707-445-6500

5070 N. Sixth Street, Suite 110
P.O. Box 28580
Fresno, CA 93729-8580
559-248-4219

5473 Kearney Villa Road, Suite 300
San Diego, CA 92123
858-636-3191

23141 Moulton Parkway, Suite 100
P.O. Box 30890
Laguna Hills, CA 92654-0890
949-461-5711

12440 E. Imperial Highway, Suite 201
P.O. Box 409
Norwalk, CA 90651-0409
562-466-1694

1515 Clay Street, Suite 303
Oakland, CA 94612-1432
510-622-4100

42-700 Bob Hope Drive, Suite 301
Rancho Mirage, CA 92270-7167
760-346-8096

391 Hemstead Drive
P.O. Box 492529
Redding, CA 96049-2529
530-224-4729

3737 Main Street, Suite 1000
Riverside, CA 92501-3395
909-680-6400

3321 Power Inn Road, Suite 210
Sacramento, CA 95826-3889
916-227-6700

111 E. Navajo Drive, Suite 100
Salinas, CA 93906-2452
831-443-3003

1350 Front Street, Rm 5047
San Diego, CA 92101-3698
619-525-4526

455 Golden Gate Avenue, Suite 7500
San Francisco, CA 94102-3625
415-703-5400

250 South Second Street
San Jose, CA 95113-2706
408-277-1231

334 Via Vera Cruz, Suite 107
San Marcos, CA 92069-2694
760-510-5850

28 Civic Center Plaza, Rm 239
P.O. Box 12040
Santa Ana, CA 92712-2040
714-558-4059

50 D Street, Rm 230
P.O. Box 730
Santa Rosa, CA 95402-0730
707-576-2100

31 East Channel Street, Rm 264
P.O. Box 1890
Stockton, CA 95201-1890
209-948-7720

333 Sunset Avenue, Suite 330
Suisun City, CA 94585-2003
707-428-2041

680 W. Knox Street, Suite 200
P.O. Box T
Torrance, CA 90508-0270
310-516-4300

15350 Sherman Way, Suite 250
Van Nuys, CA 91406
818-904-2300

4820 McGrath Street, Suite 260
Ventura, CA 93003-7778
805-677-2700

1521 W. Cameron Avenue, Suite 300
West Covina, CA 91790-2738
626-480-7200

Out-of State Field Offices

3321 Power Inn Road, Suite 130
P.O. Box 188268
Sacramento, CA 95818-8268
916-227-6600

120 N. La Salle, Suite 1600
Chicago, IL 60602-2412
312-201-5300

205 East 42nd Street, Suite 1100
New Tork, NY 10017-5706
212-697-4680

1155 Dairy Ashford, Suite 550
Houston, TX 77079-3007
281-531-3450

TDD - 800-735-2929
voice operated-800-735-2922

TAXPAYER SERVICE CENTERS

1800 30th Street
Bakersfield, CA 93301-1935
661-395-2896
Fax: 661-395-2563

4300 Long Beach Blvd., Suite 700A
Long Beach, CA 90807
562-428-0021
Fax: 562-422-6698

3321 Power Inn Road, Suite 220
Sacramento, CA 95826
916-464-3502
Fax: 916-464-3504

464 West 4th Street, 4th Floor
San Bernardino, CA 92401
909-383-4176
Fax: 909-383-7900

31 East Channel Street, Room 219
Stockton, CA 95202-2314
209-956-1438
Fax: 209-948-3633

4820 McGrath Street, Suite 250
Ventura, CA 93003
805-654-4506
Fax: 805-677-2790

 **Employment Development Department**
State of California

This form will be the basic record of YOUR ACCOUNT. **DO NOT FILE THIS FORM UNTIL YOU HAVE PAID WAGES THAT EXCEED $100.00.** Please read the **INSTRUCTIONS** on page 2 before completing this form. **PLEASE PRINT OR TYPE.** Return this form to: ➔	EMPLOYMENT DEVELOPMENT DEPARTMENT ACCOUNT SERVICES GROUP MIC 28 PO BOX 826880 SACRAMENTO CA 94280-0001 **(916) 654-7041 FAX (916) 654-9211**

REGISTRATION FORM FOR COMMERCIAL EMPLOYERS

DEPT USE	ACCOUNT NUMBER	QUARTER	ETCSO	FED CODE	ON-LINE PROCESS DATE	TAS CODE

A. BUSINESS NAME Sam's Sporting Goods	**OWNERSHIP BEGAN OPERATING** MONTH: 10 DAY: 10 YEAR: 00	**FEDERAL I.D. NUMBER** 123-45-6789
B. OWNER, CORPORATION, LLC, LLP NAME Sam's Sport	**SSA/CORP/LLC/LLP I.D. NO.** 123-45-6789	**DRIVER'S LICENSE NUMBER** Cal 1234567

List all partners* or corporate officers or LLC members/managers/officers	TITLE (partner, officer title, LLC member/manager)	SOCIAL SECURITY NUMBER	DRIVER'S LICENSE NUMBER
none			

*If entity is a **Limited Partnership**, indicate General Partner with an (*). List additional partners, LLC members/officers/managers on a separate sheet.

C. BUSINESS LOCATION Street and Number (see instructions) 1234 Main St.	**CITY OR TOWN** Sportsville	**STATE** Ca	**ZIP CODE** 90000	**COUNTY** Los Angeles
MAILING ADDRESS (in care of P.O. Box or Street and Number) P.O. Box 11234	**CITY OR TOWN** Sportsville	**STATE** Ca	**ZIP CODE** 90000	**PHONE NUMBER** (555) 555-5555

D. HAVE YOU EVER BEEN REGISTERED WITH THE DEPARTMENT? ☒ No ☐ Yes	IF YES, ENTER EMPLOYER ACCOUNT NUMBER, BUSINESS NAME AND ADDRESS ACCT NUMBER BUSINESS NAME ADDRESS

E. INDICATE FIRST QUARTER AND YEAR IN WHICH WAGES EXCEED $100. ☐ Jan.-Mar. 20___ ☐ Apr.-June 20___ ☐ July-Sept. 20___ ☒ Oct.-Dec. 20___	**F. WILL YOU BE SUBJECT TO FEDERAL MONTHLY/SEMI-WEEKLY DEPOSITS?** ☒ No ☐ Yes

G. ORGANIZATION TYPE

☒ (IN) INDIVIDUAL OWNER	☐ (JV) JOINT VENTURE	☐ (LQ) LIQUIDATION	☐ (LC) LIMITED LIABILITY CO.
☐ (HW) HUS/WIFE CO-OWNERSHIP	☐ (RC) RECEIVERSHIP	☐ (LP) LIMITED PARTNERSHIP	☐ (PL) LIMITED LIABILITY PARTNERSHIP
☐ (GP) GENERAL PARTNERSHIP	☐ (BK) BANKRUPTCY	☐ (TR) TRUSTEESHIP	
☐ (CP) CORPORATION	☐ (AS) ASSOCIATION	☐ (EA) ESTATE ADMINISTRATION	☐ (OT) OTHER (Specify)

H. EMPLOYER TYPE (see instructions) ☒ (01) Commercial ☐ (10) Church ☐ (11) Indian Reservation ☐ (22) Pacific Maritime ☐ (25) Fishing Boat	**NUMBER OF EMPLOYEES**

I. BUSINESS TYPE ☐ (N) Mining ☐ (F) Finance ☐ (I) Insurance ☐ (C) Construction ☐ (B) Communications ☐ (E) Real Estate ☐ (M) Manufacturing ☐ (S) Services ☐ (O) Other ☐ (T) Transportation ☐ (L) Utilities ☒ (R) Retail Trade ☐ (W) Wholesale Trade	1) Describe kind of product or type of service: _____ 2) If MANUFACTURING, list principal products in order of importance.

J. CONTACT PERSON FOR BUSINESS   NAME   ADDRESS   PHONE Sam Sport, 1234 Main St. Sportsville, CA 90000   (555) 555-5555

K. SUPPORTIVE SERVICES
If you are part of a larger organization and you are primarily engaged in providing supportive services to other establishments of the larger organization, check one of these boxes.
(1) ☐ Control Administrative (headquarters, etc.) (3) ☐ Storage (warehouse) (5) ☒ Does not apply
(2) ☐ Research, development, or testing (4) ☐ Other (specify) _____

L. IS THIS A(N):
☒ New business ☐ On-going business just purchased ☐ All ☐ Part ☐ Other _____
☐ Change of partner(s) ☐ Change in form - (Sole proprietor to partnership; partnership to corporation; merger; corporation to LLC, etc.)
IF THE BUSINESS WAS PREVIOUSLY OWNED, PROVIDE THE FOLLOWING INFORMATION:

Previous Owner	Business Name	Purchase Price	Date of Transfer	EDD Account Number

M. DECLARATION
These Statements are hereby declared to be correct to the best knowledge and belief of the undersigned.

Signature _____ Date 1/6/01 _____ Residence Phone 555 555-5555

Title owner _____ Residence Address _____
(Owner, Partner, Officer, Member, Manager, etc.)   Street   City   State   ZIP Code

DE 1 Rev. 68 (1-00) **(INTERNET)**   CU

209

**APPLICATION FOR SELLER'S PERMIT AND REGISTRATION
AS A RETAILER (INDIVIDUALS/PARTNERSHIPS)**

STATE OF CALIFORNIA
BOARD OF EQUALIZATION

Use additional sheet(s) to include information for more than two partners

SECTION I: OWNERSHIP INFORMATION

1. PLEASE CHECK TYPE OF OWNERSHIP

☒ Sole Owner   ☐ Husband/Wife Co-ownership

☐ General Partnership   ☐ Limited Partnership
Provide documents filed with Secretary of State.

☐ Limited Liability Partnership *(registered to practice law, accounting or architecture) Provide documents filed with Secretary of State.*

Enter Federal Employer Identification Number (FEIN), if any

FOR BOARD USE ONLY			
TAX	IND	OFFICE	NUMBER
SR			
BUSINESS CODE			AREA CODE
APPLICATION PROCESSED BY			VERIFICATION: ☐ SSN ☐ DL ☐ Other

OWNER OR PARTNER

2. FULL NAME *(first, middle, last)*

Ralph Retailer

3. SOCIAL SECURITY NUMBER *(attach verification)*

123-45-6789

4. DRIVER'S LICENSE NUMBER *(attach verification)*

Cal 123456

5. RESIDENCE ADDRESS *(street, city, state, zip code)*

123 Main St. Anytown, CA 90000

6. RESIDENCE TELEPHONE NUMBER

(123)555-5555

7. NAME, ADDRESS & TELEPHONE NUMBER OF A PERSONAL REFERENCE

Fred Friend 321 Main St. Anytown, CA 90000

8. PARTNERSHIP NAME *(complete if business name [DBA] is different than name of partnership.)*

None

9. ☐ Check here if you have included a copy of your partnership agreement.

CO-OWNER OR PARTNER

10. FULL NAME *(first, middle, last)*

None

11. SOCIAL SECURITY NUMBER *(attach verification)*

12. DRIVER'S LICENSE NUMBER *(attach verification)*

13. RESIDENCE ADDRESS *(street, city, state, zip code)*

14. RESIDENCE TELEPHONE NUMBER

(   )

15. NAME, ADDRESS & TELEPHONE NUMBER OF A PERSONAL REFERENCE

SECTION II: BUSINESS INFORMATION

16. BUSINESS NAME [DBA] *(if any)*

Ralph's Rugs

17. BUSINESS ADDRESS *(street, city, state, zip code)* [do not list P.O. Box or mailing service]

123 Carpet St. Anytown, CA 90000

18. BUSINESS TELEPHONE NUMBER

(123)555-1234

19. MAILING ADDRESS *(street, city, state, zip code)* [if different from business address]

Same

20. DATE YOU WILL BEGIN SALES *(month, day & year)*

10/01/2001

21. TYPE OF ITEMS SOLD

22. NUMBER OF SELLING LOCATIONS *(if 2 or more, attach list of all locations)*

one

23. TYPE OF BUSINESS *(check one)*

☒ Retail ☐ Wholesale ☐ Mfg. ☐ Repair ☐ Service ☐ Construction Contractor

CHECK ONE

☒ Full Time ☐ Part Time

24. OWNERSHIP CHANGES

Are you buying an existing business? ☐ Yes ☒ No If yes, complete items 25 through 29 below.

Are you changing from one type of business organization to another (for example, from a sole owner to a general partnership or from a general partnership to a limited partnership, etc.)? ☐ Yes ☒ No If yes, complete items 27 and 28 below.

Other: _____

25. PURCHASE PRICE

$

26. VALUE OF FIXTURES & EQUIPMENT

$

27. FORMER OWNER'S NAME

28. SELLER'S PERMIT ACCOUNT NUMBER

29. IF AN ESCROW COMPANY IS REQUESTING A TAX CLEARANCE ON YOUR BEHALF, PLEASE LIST THEIR NAME, ADDRESS, TELEPHONE NUMBER AND THE ESCROW NUMBER

30. DO YOU MAKE INTERNET SALES?

☒ Yes ☐ No If yes, answer 31.

31. WEBSITE ADDRESS

www.ralphsrugs.com

32. IF ALCOHOLIC BEVERAGES ARE SOLD, PLEASE LIST YOUR ALCOHOLIC BEVERAGE CONTROL LICENSE NO. AND TYPE

None

33. NAME, ADDRESS & TELEPHONE NUMBER OF ACCOUNTANT/BOOKKEEPER

Arthur Asset 123 Number St. Anytown, CA 90000 (123) 555-0005

34. NAME, ADDRESS & TELEPHONE NUMBER OF BUSINESS LANDLORD

Oswald Owner 123 Wealthy Way Anytown, CA 9000 (123) 555-0000

35. NAME & LOCATION OF BANK OR OTHER FINANCIAL INSTITUTION (*Note whether business or personal*)

Bank of Anytown 1000 Main St. Anytown, CA 90000 (business)

CHECKING ACCOUNT NUMBER(S)

12345678

SAVINGS ACCOUNT NUMBER(S)

87654321

36. NAMES & ADDRESSES OF MAJOR SUPPLIERS

Rudy's Wholesale Rugs 123 Weaver Rd. Anytown, CA 90000

PRODUCTS PURCHASED

Rugs

SECTION III: SALES AND EMPLOYER INFORMATION

37. PROJECTED MONTHLY SALES (*if unknown, enter an estimated amount*)

Total gross sales $ 10,000   Taxable sales $ 2,000

38. INFORMATION CONCERNING EMPLOYMENT DEVELOPMENT DEPARTMENT (*EDD*)

Are you registered with EDD? .... ☒ Yes ☐ No

If no, will your payroll exceed $100 per quarter? .... ☒ Yes ☐ No

If yes, you must make application with EDD.

Number of employees one   (See pamphlet DE 44, *California Employer's Guide*)

I have already received pamphlet DE 44, *California Employer's Guide*. .... ☒ Yes ☐ No

CERTIFICATION

The statements contained herein are hereby certified to be correct to the best knowledge and belief of the undersigned who is duly authorized to sign this application. (All owners' and partners' signatures are required.)

NAME (*typed or printed*)

Ralph Retailer

TITLE

owner

SIGNATURE

Ralph Retailer

DATE

7/1/01

NAME (*typed or printed*)

TITLE

SIGNATURE

DATE

FOR BOARD USE ONLY
Furnished to Taxpayer

REPORTING BASIS

SECURITY REVIEW	FORMS		PUBLICATIONS	
	☐ BOE-8	☐ BOE-400-Y	☐ PUB 73	☐ PUB DE 44
☐ BOE-598-LZ $ _____	☐ BOE-467	☐ BOE-519		
☐ BOE-1009	☐ BOE-1241-D			

BY

APPROVED BY

REMOTE INPUT DATE

BY

	REGULATIONS		RETURNS
	☐ REG. 1668	☐ REG. 1698	
	☐ REG. 1700		

☐ Permit Issued   Date _____

211

OUT-OF-STATE TAXES 19

STATE SALES TAXES

In 1992, the United States Supreme Court ruled that state tax authorities cannot force small businesses to collect sales taxes on interstate mail orders. (*Quill Corporation v. North Dakota*).

Unfortunately, the court left open the possibility that Congress could allow interstate taxation of mail order sales, and since then several bills have been introduced that would do so. One, introduced by Arkansas senator Dale Bumpers was given the Orwellian "newspeak" title, *The Consumer and Main Street Protection Act.*

At present, companies are only required to collect sales taxes for states in which they *do business*. Exactly what business is enough to trigger taxation is a legal question and some states try to define it as broadly as possible.

If you have an office in a state, you are doing business there and any goods shipped to consumers in that state are subject to sales taxes. If you have a full time employee working in the state much of the year many states will consider you doing business there. In some states, attending a two-day trade show is enough business to trigger taxation for the entire year for every order shipped to the state. One loophole that often works is to be represented at shows by persons who are not your employees.

Because the laws are different in each state you will have to do some research on a state-by-state basis to find out how much business you can do in a state without being subject to their taxation. You can request a state's rules from its department of revenue, but keep in mind that what a department of revenue wants the law to be is not always what the courts will rule that it is.

Business Taxes

Even worse than being subject to a state's sales taxes is to be subject to their income or other business taxes. For example, California charges every company doing business in the state a minimum $800 a year fee and charges income tax on a portion of the company's worldwide income. Doing a small amount of business in the state is clearly not worth getting mired in California taxation.

For this reason some trade shows have been moved from the state and this has resulted in a review of the tax policies and some "safe-harbor" guidelines to advise companies on what they can do without becoming subject to taxation.

Write to the department of revenue of any state with which you have business contacts to see what might trigger your taxation.

Internet Taxes

State revenue departments want the possibility of taxing commerce on the Internet. Theories have already been proposed that websites available to state residents mean a company is doing business in a state.

Fortunately, Congress has passed a moratorium on taxation of the Internet. This will be extended, hopefully, and will give us a new tax-free world. A government has never let a new source of revenue go untapped. It would take a tremendous outcry to keep the Internet tax-free. Keep an eye out for any news stories on proposals to tax the Internet and petition your representatives against them.

CANADIAN TAXES

Apparently oblivious to the logic of the U.S. Supreme Court, the Canadian government expects American companies, which sell goods by mail order to Canadians, to collect taxes for them and file returns with Revenue Canada, their tax department.

Those that receive an occasional unsolicited order are not expected to register and Canadian customers, who order things from the U.S., pay the tax plus a $5 fee upon receipt of the goods. But companies that solicit Canadian orders are expected to be registered if their worldwide income is $30,000 or more per year. In some cases, a company may be required to post a bond and to pay for the cost of Canadian auditors visiting its premises and auditing its books. For these reasons you may notice that some companies decline to accept orders from Canada.

THE END...AND THE BEGINNING 20

If you have read through this whole book, you know more about the rules and laws for operating a California business than most people in business today. However, after learning about all the governmental regulations, you may become discouraged. You are probably wondering how you can keep track of all the laws and how you will have any time left to make money after complying with the laws. People are starting businesses every day and they are making money. American business owners are lucky, some countries have marginal tax rates as high as 105%.

The regulations that exist right now are enough to strangle some businesses. Consider the Armour meat-packing plant. The Federal Meat Inspection Service required that an opening be made in a conveyor to allow inspection or they would shut down the plant. OSHA told them that if they made that opening they would be shut down for safety reasons. Government regulations made it impossible for that plant to be in business.

But what you have to realize is that the same bureaucrats who are creating laws to slow down businesses are the ones who are responsible for enforcing the laws. And just as most government programs cost more than expected and fail to achieve their goals, most government regulations cannot be enforced against millions of people who do not wish to be controlled.

While serving on jury duty, the authors and other jurors were told by the judge that the jury must enforce the law whether it is considered to be a fair and sensible law or not. Actually, this instruction was erroneous. The jury has the full power to pardon a person in spite of what any law says. One of the benefits of the jury system is that it may refuse to enforce a law that it considers unfair.

In a pure democracy, fifty-one percent of the voters can decide that all left-handed people must wear green shirts and that everyone must go to church three days a week. It is the Bill of Rights in our constitution that protects us from this.

In America today, there are no laws regarding left-handed people or going to church but there are laws controlling minute aspects of our personal and business lives. Does a majority have the right to decide what hours you can work, what you can sell or where you can sell it? You must decide for yourself and act accordingly.

One way to avoid problems with the government is to keep a low profile and avoid open confrontation. For a lawyer, it can be fun going to appeals court over an unfair parking ticket or making a federal case out of a $25 fine. But for most people the expenses of a fight with the government are unbearable. If you start a mass protest against the IRS or OSHA they will have to make an example of you so that no one else gets any ideas.

The important thing is that you know the laws and the penalties for violations before making your decision. Knowing the laws will also allow you to use the loopholes in the laws to avoid violations.

Congratulations on deciding to start a business in California! We hope you get rich in record time. If you have any unusual experiences along the way, drop us a line at the following address. The information may be useful for a future book.

Sphinx Publishing
P.O. Box 4410
Naperville, IL 60567-4410

GLOSSARY

A

acceptance. An agreement that the terms of an offer are acceptable and that the contract can be considered formed. Offer, acceptance and consideration form a contract.

affirmative action. A movement that attempts to eliminate or remedy past, present, and future acts of discrimination or the effects of discrimination.

articles of incorporation. The document filed with the secretary of state that sets up the by-laws and terms of a corporation.

B

bait advertising. An illegal ploy to entice a customer to buy a higher-priced item by advertising for a lower-priced item, especially where the lower-priced item was never really available.

bulk sales. Selling larger than usual quantities.

C

C corporation.   A business where the entity, rather than the shareholders, is taxed.

collections.   That part of a business that ensures that payment comes into the business in a timely, accurate manner.

consideration.   That thing of value offered between parties that is essential to a contract in order to make it legally enforceable.

copyright.   The right to reproduce, sell, display or perform original work that is expressed in writing, photographs, sound, etc.

corporation.   An entity comprised of shareholders, recognized by law as a separate person with rights and duties that a person under the law would have.

D

deceptive pricing.   Misleading a consumer into believing that something costs one price, while other hidden costs are added to that price.

discrimination.   Denying a person or group, or granting a person or group, privileges based on sex, religion, race, creed, or disability.

domain name.   On the Internet, it is the name that identifies a website.

E

endorsements.   A way of bolstering the credibility of your product or service, usually by having someone notable make a statement about it, or appear on its behalf.

excise tax.   Money paid to the government for the manufacture, use or sale of goods, or on licenses and occupation fees.

express warranty.   A guarantee overtly made by a seller. It can be a promise ("If it break's, I'll fix it free"), a description of the goods or a sample or model.

F

fictitious name.   The name a business is known by, or does business as.

G

general partner.   A partner who shares profit, loss and liability. A general partner, unlike a limited partner, may be active in running the business.

goods.   Tangible items like a chair or a car. Contracts for goods are controlled by Article 2 of the Uniform Commercial Code and differ from those for real property, services and paper rights (stocks, bonds, insurance, etc.).

guarantee.   The promise that a future commitment will be fulfilled, or to promise that a future contract will be carried out.

guaranty.   The assurance that a duty or obligation will be carried out if the original party fails to carry it out.

I

implied warranty.   A guarantee inferred from the actions and words of a seller.

independent contractor.   A person hired to do work, but does so under his or her own business, using his or her own methods and equipment, and not as an employee of the one hiring.

intangible property.   An asset that is not physical in nature, such as a good will, copyrights, and patents.

intellectual property. An abstract asset such as copyrights, trademarks, patents, trade-secrets, and publicity.

L

liability. Legal obligation or responsibility.

limited liability company. A business that restricts the amount of money an investor risks to the amount that they contribute.

limited liability partnership. A partnership that restricts the amount of money a partner is liable for to the amount that they have in the business, and excludes personal assets of the partners.

limited partner. A partner who shares in the profits but whose losses are limited to his investment in the business. To keep this limited liability, a limited partner may not participate in managing the business.

limited partnership. A partnership with an active manager (general partner) and limited partners (investors). The general partner has personal liability. The limited partners can lose only their investment in the business.

limited warranty. A promise covering only limited labor, materials and repairs. The terms "full" and "limited" warranty were created by the Magnuson-Moss Warranty Act of 1975.

M

merchant. One who deals regularly in the subject goods or is an expert in these goods. The Uniform Commercial Code sets higher standards for merchants than for those who only occasionally deal in the subject goods.

merchant's firm offer. A written and signed offer by a merchant, stating that it will remain open. The offer cannot be withdrawn (revoked) even though no consideration was given to keep it open. The offer remains open for the time stated or a reasonable time if none is stated. Regardless of the stated time, the seller does not have to keep the offer open more that three months.

N

nonprofit corporation. A business not designed for making a profit and is afforded special tax treatment.

O

occupational license. A license required for certain occupations. There are two types. First is the license obtained by education, experience and testing (Doctor, Lawyer, Contractor, Etc.). A contract with such a person who is unlicensed is an illegal contract and unenforceable. The second type is a "revenue raising" license. All that is really required is the payment of a fee to get the license. A contract made with an unlicensed person in this category is not illegal and is enforceable.

offer. The act of setting up the possibility for acceptance of a contract or agreement. There must be serious intent, communication, and definite terms.

P

partnership. Two or more people doing business as an entity for profit.

personal property. Any possession not classified as real property.

professional corporation. A business that requires its members to have a professional license, such as a doctor, lawyer, or certified public accountant.

R

real property. Land and all of its attachments, growths, and structures.

S

S corporation. A business that is taxed through the shareholders rather than through the entity itself.

sale on approval. Completion of a sale depends upon the buyer's approval and subsequent use. Title and risk of loss stay with the seller until approval.

sale or return. If goods are bought primarily for resale, then under sale or return terms, the unsold goods can be returned to the seller. Title and risk of loss pass to the buyer until returned.

security/securities. The goods given as a collateral guarantee that the contracted price will be paid.

sexual harassment. Employment discrimination of a verbal or physical nature centered on the sex of an individual, or on the topic of sex.

shares. A representation of a part ownership in a corporation.

sole proprietorship. A business owned by one person who does not share profits and is liable for all debts.

Statute of Frauds. That part of the law that requires certain transactions to be in writing to be valid.

stock. The certificate that represents ownership in a corporation.

sublease. A rental agreement where the first tenant remains liable to the landlord, and the second tenant is liable to the first tenant for rent and care of the premises.

T

tangible property.   Moveable, non-abstract assets, such as equipment and automobiles.

trade secrets.   Confidential information about the products, procedure, formula, method, etc that a business uses to accomplish some goal.

trademark.   The rights to the use of a symbol or words connected to a specific product or service to set one business apart from another.

U

unemployment compensation.   State-funded pay to a person who has been laid off from a job.

Uniform Commercial Code.   A set of laws used to unify business contracts from state to state. The code covers such things as goods (Article 2) and negotiable instruments, such as checks and notes (Article 3). The California version is simply called the Commercial Code.

usury.   Charging illegally high interest rates on a loan.

W

warranty.   The promise that something conforms to the legal specifications of a certain contract.

warranty of fitness for a particular purpose.   A warranty that the goods are fit for the buyer's intended use rather than only for their ordinary use. The seller must know of the buyer's intended use and the buyer must rely on the seller's choice of the goods.

warranty of merchantability.   The promise that the goods are fit for their ordinary use, are adequately packaged and labeled, must be of average quality and pass without objection in the trade.

warranty of title.   The promise that the seller has good title and transfers that title to the buyer in a rightful manner free of liens unless disclosed to the buyer.

worker's compensation.   Payments for those employees injured due to work-related activity.

FOR FURTHER REFERENCE

The following books will provide valuable information to those who are starting new businesses. Some are out of print, but they are classics that are worth tracking down.

For inspiration to give you the drive to succeed:

Hill, Napoleon, *Think and Grow Rich*. New York: Fawcett Books, 1990, 233 pages.

Karbo, Joe, *The Lazy Man's Way to Riches*. Sunset Beach: F P Publishing, 1974, 156 pages.

Schwartz, David J., *The Magic of Thinking Big*. Fireside, 1987, 234 pages.

For hints on what it takes to be successful:

Carnegie, Dale, *How to Win Friends and Influence People*. New York: Pocket Books, 1994, 276 pages.

Ringer, Robert J., *Looking Out for #1*. New York: Fawcett Books, 1993.

Ringer, Robert J., *Million Dollar Habits*. New York: Fawcett Books, 1991.

Ringer, Robert J., *Winning Through Intimidation*. New York: Fawcett Books, 1993.

For advice on bookkeeping and organization:

Kamoroff, Bernard, *Small Time Operator (25th Edition)*. Bell Springs Publishing, 2000, 200 pages.

For a very practical guide to investing:

Tobias, Andrew, *The Only Investment Guide You'll Ever Need*. Harvest Books, 1999, 239 pages.

For advice on how to avoid problems with government agencies:

Browne, Harry, *How I Found Freedom in an Unfree World*. Great Falls: Liam Works, 1998, 387 pages.

The following are other books published by **Sphinx Publishing** that may be helpful to your business:

Eckert, W. Kelsea, Sartorius, Arthur, III, & Warda, Mark, *How to Form Your Own Corporation*. 2001.

Haman, Edward A., *How to Form Your Own Partnership*. 1999.

Ray, James C., *The Most Valuable Business Legal Forms You'll Ever Need*. 2001.

Ray, James C., *The Complete Book of Corporate Forms*. 2001.

Warda, Mark, *How to Form a Delaware Corporation from Any State*. 1999.

Warda, Mark, *Incorporate in Nevada from Any State*. 2001.

Warda, Mark, *How to Form a Limited Liability Company*. 1999.

Warda, Mark, *How to Register Your Own Copyright*. 2000.

Warda, Mark, *How to Register Your Own Trademark.*. 1999.

The following are books published by **Sourcebooks, Inc.** that may be helpful to your business:

Fleury, Robert E., *The Small Business Survival Guide.*. 1995.

Gutman, Jean E., *Accounting Made Easy*. 1998.

Milling, Bryan E., *How to Get a Small Business Loan (2nd Edition)*. 1998.

The following websites provide information that may be useful to you in starting your business:

Internal Revenue Service: http://www.irs.gov

Small Business Administration: http://www.sba.gov

Social Security Administration: http://www.ssa.gov

U. S. Business Advisor: http://www.business.gov

Appendix: Tax Timetable Business Startup Checklist & Ready-to-use Forms

The following forms may be photocopied or removed from this book and used immediately. We recommend that you photocopy them and save the originals in case you make a mistake, or for future use. Some of the tax forms explained in this book are not included here because you should use original returns provided by the IRS (940, 941) or the California Department of Revenue (quarterly unemployment compensation form).

These forms are included on the following pages:

TAX TIMETABLE

	California					Federal			
	Sales	Unemployment	Tangible	Intangible	Corp. Income	Est. Payment	Annual Return	Form 941*	Misc.
JAN.	20th	31st				15th		31st	940 31st W-2 508 1099
FEB.	20th			28th 4% disc.					28th W-3
MAR.	20th		31st	31st 3% disc.			15th Corp. & Partnership		
APR.	20th	30th	1st	30th 2% disc.	1st	15th	15th Personal	30th	30th 508
MAY	20th			31st 1% disc.					
JUN.	20th			30th tax due		15th			
JUL.	20th	31st						31st	31st 508
AUG.	20th								
SEP.	20th					15th			
OCT.	20th	31st						31st	31st 508
NOV.	20th								
DEC.	20th								

* In addition to form 941, deposits must be made regularly if withholding exceeds $500 in any month

FICTITIOUS BUSINESS NAME STATEMENT

The following person (persons) is (are) doing business as

* _____

at ** _____:

*** _____

_____

_____

_____

This business is conducted by **** _____

The registrant commenced to transact business under the fictitious business name or names listed above on ***** _____

Signed _____

Statement filed with the County Clerk of _____ County

on _____

NOTICE

THIS FICTITIOUS BUSINESS NAME STATEMENT EXPIRES FIVE YEARS FROM THE DATE IT WAS FILED IN THE OFFICE OF THE COUNTY CLERK. A NEW FICTITIOUS BUSINESS NAME STATEMENT MUST BE FILED BEFORE THAT TIME. THE FILING OF THIS STATEMENT DOES NOT OF ITSELF AUTHORIZE THE USE IN THIS STATE OF A FICTITIOUS BUSINESS NAME IN VIOLATION OF THE RIGHTS OF ANOTHER UNDER FEDERAL, STATE, OR COMMON LAW (SEE SECTION 14400 ET SEQ., BUSINESS AND PROFESSIONAL CODE).

INSTRUCTIONS

1.   Where the asterisk (*) appears in the form, insert the fictitious business name or names. Only those businesses operated at the same address may be listed on one statement.

2.   Where the two asterisks (**) appear on the form: If the registrant has a place of business in this state, insert the street address of his or her principal place of business in this state. If the registrant has no place of business in this state, insert the street address of his or her principal place of business outside this state.

3.   Where the three asterisks (***) appear in the form: If the registrant is an individual, insert his or her full name and residence address. If the registrant is a partnership or other association of persons, insert the full name and residence address of each general partner. If the registrant is a limited liability company, insert the name of the limited liability company as set out in its articles of organization and the state of organization. If the registrant is a business trust, insert the full name and address of each trustee. If the registrant is a corporation, insert the name of the corporation as set out in its articles of incorporation and the state of incorporation.

4.   Where four asterisks (****) appear in the form, insert whichever of the following best describes the nature of the business: (i) "an individual," (ii) "a general partnership," (iii) "a limited partnership," (iv) "a limited liability company," (v) "an unincorporated association other than a partnership," (vi) "a corporation," (vii) "a business trust," (viii) "copartners," (ix) "husband and wife," (x) "joint venture," or (xi) "other--please specify."

5.   Where the five asterisks (*****) appear in the form, insert the date on which the registrant first commenced to transact business under the fictitious business name or names listed, if already transacting business under that name or names. If the registrant has not yet commenced to transact business under the fictitious business name or names listed, insert the statement, "Not applicable."

If the registrant is an individual, the statement shall be signed by the individual; if a partnership or other association of persons, by a general partner; if a limited liability company, by a manager or officer; if a business trust, by a trustee; if a corporation, by an officer.

Publication of notice pursuant to this section shall be once a week for four successive weeks. Four publications in a newspaper regularly published once a week or more often, with at least five days intervening between the respective publication dates not counting such publication dates, are sufficient. The period of notice commences with the first day of publication and terminates at the end of the twenty-eighth day, including therein the first day.

The newspaper selected for the publication of the statement should be one that circulates in the area where the business is to be conducted. Where a new statement is required because the prior statement has expired, the new statement need not be published unless there has been a change in the information required in the expired statement.

PTO Form 1478 (Rev 9/98)
OMB No. 0651-0009 (Exp. 08/31/01)

Trademark/Service Mark Application, Principal Register, with Declaration

PrinTEAS - Version 1.22: 08/22/2000

Each field name links to the relevant section of the "HELP" instructions that will appear at the bottom of the screen. Fields containing the symbol "*" must be completed; all other relevant fields should be completed if the information is known.

Note: ☐ check here if you do not want the scrolling help to be automatically shown at the bottom of the screen.

Important:

For general trademark information, please telephone the Trademark Assistance Center, at 703-308-9000. For automated status information on an application that has an assigned serial number, please telephone 703-305-8747, or use http://tarr.uspto.gov.

If you need help in resolving technical glitches, you can e-mail us at PrinTEAS@uspto.gov. Please include your telephone number in your Email, so we can talk to you directly, if necessary.

Applicant Information

* Name	

Entity Type: Click on the one appropriate circle to indicate the applicant's entity type and enter the corresponding information.

○ Individual	Country of Citizenship	
○ Corporation	State or Country of Incorporation	
○ Partnership	State or Country Where Organized	
	Name and Citizenship of all General Partners	▲ ▼
○ Other	Specify Entity Type	▲ ▼
	State or Country Where Organized	
* Address	* Street Address	▲ ▼
	* City	
	State	Select State ▼ If not listed above, please select 'OTHER' and specify here:
	* Country	Select Country ▼ If not listed above, please select 'OTHER' and specify here:
	Zip/Postal Code	
Phone Number		
Fax Number		
Internet E-Mail Address	☐ Check here to authorize the USPTO to communicate with the applicant or its representative via e-mail. NOTE: While the application may list an e-mail address for the applicant, applicant's attorney, and/or applicant's domestic representative, only one e-mail address may be used for correspondence, in accordance with Office policy. The applicant must keep this address current in the Office's records.	

Mark Information

Before the USPTO can register your mark, we must know exactly what it is. You can display a mark in one of two formats:
(1) typed; or (2) stylized or design. When you click on one of the two circles below, and follow the relevant instructions, the program will create a separate page that displays your mark once you validate the application (using the Validate Form button at the end of this form). You must print out and submit this separate page with the application form (even if you have listed the "mark" in the body of the application). If you have a stylized mark or design, but either you do NOT have a GIF or JPG image file or your browser does not permit this function, check the box to indicate you do NOT have the image in a GIF or JPG image file (and then see the special help instructions).

WARNING: AFTER SEARCHING THE USPTO DATABASE, EVEN IF YOU THINK THE RESULTS ARE "O.K.," DO NOT ASSUME THAT YOUR MARK CAN BE REGISTERED AT THE USPTO. AFTER YOU FILE AN APPLICATION, THE USPTO MUST DO ITS OWN SEARCH AND OTHER REVIEW, AND MIGHT REFUSE TO REGISTER YOUR MARK.

* Mark	○ Typed Format	Click on this circle if you wish to register a word(s), letter(s), and/or number(s) in a format that can be reproduced using a typewriter. Also, only the following common punctuation marks and symbols are acceptable in a typed drawing (any other symbol, including a <u>foreign diacritical mark</u>, requires a stylized format): . ? " - ; ( ) % $ @ + , ! ' : / & # * = [ ] Enter the mark here: NOTE: The mark must be entered in ALL upper case letters, regardless of how you actually use the mark. E.g., MONEYWISE, not MoneyWise.
	○ Stylized or Design Format	Click on this circle if you wish to register a stylized word(s), letter(s), number(s), and/or a design. Click on the 'Browse' button to select GIF or JPG image file from your local drive. ☐ Check this box if you do NOT have the image in a GIF or JPG image file, and click here for further instructions. For a stylized word(s) or letter(s), or a design that also includes a word(s), enter the LITERAL element only of the mark here:

BASIS FOR FILING AND GOODS AND/OR SERVICES INFORMATION

✓	Section 1(b), Intent to Use: Applicant has a bona fide intention to use or use through a related company the mark in commerce on or in connection with the goods and/or services identified below (15 U.S.C. §1051(b)).
	International Class
	If known, enter class number 001 - 042, A, B, or 200
	* Listing of Goods and/or Services

235

Fee Information

Number of Classes Paid   1 ▼

Note: The total fee is computed based on the Number of Classes in which the goods and/or services associated with the mark are classified. $ 325   = **Number of Classes Paid x $325 (per class)**

* Amount $

Declaration

The undersigned, being hereby warned that willful false statements and the like so made are punishable by fine or imprisonment, or both, under 18 U.S.C. §1001, and that such willful false statements may jeopardize the validity of the application or any resulting registration, declares that he/she is properly authorized to execute this application on behalf of the applicant; he/she believes the applicant to be the owner of the trademark/service mark sought to be registered, or, if the application is being filed under 15 U.S.C. §1051(b), he/she believes applicant to be entitled to use such mark in commerce; to the best of his/her knowledge and belief no other person, firm, corporation, or association has the right to use the mark in commerce, either in the identical form thereof or in such near resemblance thereto as to be likely, when used on or in connection with the goods/services of such other person, to cause confusion, or to cause mistake, or to deceive; and that all statements made of his/her own knowledge are true; and that all statements made on information and belief are believed to be true.

Signature _____   Date Signed _____

Signatory's Name _____

Signatory's Position _____

Click on the desired action:

The "Validate Form" function allows you to run an automated check to ensure that all mandatory fields have been completed. You will receive an "error" message if you have not filled in one of the five (5) fields that are considered "minimum filing requirements" under the Trademark Law Treaty Implementation Act of 1998. For other fields that the USPTO believes are important, but not mandatory, you will receive a "warning" message if the field is left blank. This warning is a courtesy, if non-completion was merely an oversight. If you so choose, you may by-pass that "warning" message and validate the form (however, you cannot by-pass an "error" message).

| Validate Form | | Reset Form |

Note: To print the completed application AND the separate sheet showing the representation of the mark, click on the Validate Form button, and follow the steps on the Validation Screen.

* Instructions

To file a **complete** application, you must submit the following items:
- the signed and dated form (the "Scannable Form");
- a representation of the mark, preferably on a single sheet of paper (See information under the "Mark Information" section, above);
- a check or money order for $325.00 per each class of goods and services, made out to the Commissioner of Patents and Trademarks (unless using a USPTO deposit account);
- if the application is based on use in commerce, one specimen for each class of goods and services;
- if the application is based on Section 44(e), a certified copy (and English translation, if applicable) of the certificate of foreign registration.

NOTE: If your application does not include the following five (5) items, we will return your application and refund the filing fee. You would then need to correct the deficiency and re-file, resulting in a new filing date: (1) the name of the applicant; (2) a name and address for correspondence; (3) a clear representation of the mark; (4) a list of the goods or services; and (5) the filing fee for at least one class of goods or services.

You may also wish to include a self-addressed stamped postcard on which you list every item that you are submitting. This will confirm receipt of your submission.

The mailing address for standard mail is:
> Commissioner for Trademarks
> Box-New App-Fee
> 2900 Crystal Drive
> Arlington, Virginia 22202-3513

The mailing address for courier delivery is:
> Commissioner for Trademarks
> USPTO- New App-Fee
> 2900 Crystal Drive, Suite 3B-30
> Arlington, Virginia 22202-3513

*

Privacy Policy Statement

The information collected on this form allows the PTO to determine whether a mark may be registered on the Principal or Supplemental register, and provides notice of an applicant's claim of ownership of the mark. Responses to the request for information are required to obtain the benefit of a registration on the Principal or Supplemental register. 15 U.S.C. §1051 et seq. and 37 C.F.R. Part 2. All information collected will be made public. Gathering and providing the information will require an estimated 12 or 18 minutes (depending if the application is based on an intent to use the mark in commerce, use of the mark in commerce, or a foreign application or registration). Please direct comments on the time needed to complete this form, and/or suggestions for reducing this burden to the Chief Information Officer, U.S. Patent and Trademark Office, U.S. Department of Commerce, Washington D.C. 20231. Please note that the PTO may not conduct or sponsor a collection of information using a form that does not display a valid OMB control number.

APPLICATION FOR EMPLOYMENT

We consider applicants for all positions without regard to race, color, religion, sex, national origin, age, marital or veteran status, the presence of a non-job-related medical condition or handicap, or any other legally protected status. Proof of citizenship or immigration status will be required upon employment.

(PLEASE TYPE OR PRINT)

Position Applied For   Date of Application

Last Name	First Name	Middle Name or Initial

Is there any other information regarding your name that will be needed to check work or school records? ❏ Yes ❏ No

Address   *Number Street*   *City*   *State*   *Zip Code*

Telephone Number(s) [indicate home or work]	Social Security Number

Date Available:_____   Are you available: ❏ Full Time   ❏ Part Time   ❏ Weekends

Are you 18 years of age or older?   ❏ Yes   ❏ No

Have you been convicted of a felony within the past 7 years?   ❏ Yes   ❏ No

    Conviction will not necessarily disqualify an applicant from employment.

If Yes, attach explanation.

Can you produce documents proving you are authorized to work in the United States? ❏ Yes   ❏ No

Education

	High School	Undergraduate	Graduate
School Name & Location			
Years Completed	1 2 3 4	1 2 3 4	1 2 3 4
Diploma / Degree			
Course of Study			

State any additional information you feel may be helpful to us in considering your application (such as any specialized training; skills; apprenticeships; honors received; professional, trade, business or civic organizations or activities; job-related military training or experience; foreign language abilities; etc.)

_____

_____

_____

_____

Employment Experience

Start with your present or last job. Include any job-related military service assignments and voluntary activities. You may exclude organizations which indicate race, color, religion, gender, national origin, handicap, or other protected status.

1.

Employer Name & Address	Dates Employed	Job Title/Duties
	Hourly Rate/Salary	
May we contact this employer? ❑ Yes ❑ No	Hours Per Week	
Employer Phone		
Supervisor		
Reason for Leaving		

2.

Employer Name & Address	Dates Employed	Job Title/Duties
	Hourly Rate/Salary	
Employer Phone	Hours Per Week	
Supervisor		
Reason for Leaving		

3.

Employer Name & Address	Dates Employed	Job Title/Duties
	Hourly Rate/Salary	
Employer Phone	Hours Per Week	
Supervisor		
Reason for Leaving		

References: Name   Occupation   Address   Phone #   Relationship   Years known

1. _____
2. _____
3. _____

If you need additional space, continue on a separate sheet of paper.

Applicant's Statement

I certify that the information given on this application is true and complete to the best of my knowledge. I authorize investigation of all statements contained in this application, and understand that false or misleading information given in my application or interview(s) may result in discharge.

I understand and acknowledge that, unless otherwise defined by applicable law, any employment relationship with this organization is "at will," which means that I may resign at any time and the employer may discharge me at any time with or without cause. I further understand that this "at will" employment relationship may not be changed orally, by any written document, or by conduct, unless such change is specifically acknowledged in writing by an authorized executive of this organization.

_____
Signature of Applicant

_____
Date

U.S. Department of Justice
Immigration and Naturalization Service

OMB No. 1115-0136

Employment Eligibility Verification

Please read instructions carefully before completing this form. The instructions must be available during completion of this form. ANTI-DISCRIMINATION NOTICE: It is illegal to discriminate against work eligible individuals. Employers CANNOT specify which document(s) they will accept from an employee. The refusal to hire an individual because of a future expiration date may also constitute illegal discrimination.

Section 1. Employee Information and Verification. To be completed and signed by employee at the time employment begins.

Print Name: Last	First	Middle Initial	Maiden Name

Address *(Street Name and Number)*	Apt. #	Date of Birth *(month/day/year)*

City	State	Zip Code	Social Security #

I am aware that federal law provides for imprisonment and/or fines for false statements or use of false documents in connection with the completion of this form.

I attest, under penalty of perjury, that I am (check one of the following):

☐ A citizen or national of the United States
☐ A Lawful Permanent Resident (Alien # A_____)
☐ An alien authorized to work until ___/___/___
(Alien # or Admission #) _____

Employee's Signature	Date *(month/day/year)*

Preparer and/or Translator Certification. *(To be completed and signed if Section 1 is prepared by a person other than the employee.) I attest, under penalty of perjury, that I have assisted in the completion of this form and that to the best of my knowledge the information is true and correct.*

Preparer's/Translator's Signature	Print Name

Address *(Street Name and Number, City, State, Zip Code)*	Date *(month/day/year)*

Section 2. Employer Review and Verification. To be completed and signed by employer. Examine one document from List A OR examine one document from List B and one from List C, as listed on the reverse of this form, and record the title, number and expiration date, if any, of the document(s)

List A	OR	List B	AND	List C
Document title: _____		_____		_____
Issuing authority: _____		_____		_____
Document #: _____		_____		_____
Expiration Date *(if any):* ___/___/___		___/___/___		___/___/___
Document #: _____				
Expiration Date *(if any):* ___/___/___				

CERTIFICATION - I attest, under penalty of perjury, that I have examined the document(s) presented by the above-named employee, that the above-listed document(s) appear to be genuine and to relate to the employee named, that the employee began employment on *(month/day/year)* ___/___/___ **and that to the best of my knowledge the employee is eligible to work in the United States. (State employment agencies may omit the date the employee began employment.)**

Signature of Employer or Authorized Representative	Print Name	Title

Business or Organization Name	Address *(Street Name and Number, City, State, Zip Code)*	Date *(month/day/year)*

Section 3. Updating and Reverification. To be completed and signed by employer.

A. New Name *(if applicable)*	B. Date of rehire *(month/day/year) (if applicable)*

C. If employee's previous grant of work authorization has expired, provide the information below for the document that establishes current employment eligibility.

Document Title:_____   Document #: _____   Expiration Date (if any): ___/___/___

I attest, under penalty of perjury, that to the best of my knowledge, this employee is eligible to work in the United States, and if the employee presented document(s), the document(s) I have examined appear to be genuine and to relate to the individual.

Signature of Employer or Authorized Representative	Date *(month/day/year)*

Form I-9 (Rev. 11-21-91)N

INSTRUCTIONS
PLEASE READ ALL INSTRUCTIONS CAREFULLY BEFORE COMPLETING THIS FORM.

Anti-Discrimination Notice. It is illegal to discriminate against any individual (other than an alien not authorized to work in the U.S.) in hiring, discharging, or recruiting or referring for a fee because of that individual's national origin or citizenship status. It is illegal to discriminate against work eligible individuals. Employers **CANNOT** specify which document(s) they will accept from an employee. The refusal to hire an individual because of a future expiration date may also constitute illegal discrimination.

Section 1 - Employee.
All employees, citizens and noncitizens, hired after November 6, 1986, must complete Section 1 of this form at the time of hire, which is the actual beginning of employment. **The employer is responsible for ensuring that Section 1 is timely and properly completed.**

Preparer/Translator Certification. The Preparer/Translator Certification must be completed if Section 1 is prepared by a person other than the employee. A preparer/translator may be used only when the employee is unable to complete Section 1 on his/her own. However, the employee must still sign Section 1.

Section 2 - Employer.
For the purpose of completing this form, the term "employer" includes those recruiters and referrers for a fee who are agricultural associations, agricultural employers or farm labor contractors.

Employers must complete Section 2 by examining evidence of identity and employment eligibility within three (3) business days of the date employment begins. If employees are authorized to work, but are unable to present the required document(s) within three business days, they must present a receipt for the application of the document(s) within three business days and the actual document(s) within ninety (90) days. However, if employers hire individuals for a duration of less than three business days, Section 2 must be completed at the time employment begins. **Employers must record: 1)** document title; **2)** issuing authority; **3)** document number, **4)** expiration date, if any; and **5)** the date employment begins. Employers must sign and date the certification. Employees must present original documents. Employers may, but are not required to, photocopy the document(s) presented. These photocopies may only be used for the verification process and must be retained with the I-9. **However, employers are still responsible for completing the I-9.**

Section 3 - Updating and Reverification.
Employers must complete Section 3 when updating and/or reverifying the I-9. Employers must reverify employment eligibility of their employees on or before the expiration date recorded in Section 1. Employers **CANNOT** specify which document(s) they will accept from an employee.

- If an employee's name has changed at the time this form is being updated/ reverified, complete Block A.

- If an employee is rehired within three (3) years of the date this form was originally completed and the employee is still eligible to be employed on the same basis as previously indicated on this form (updating), complete Block B and the signature block.

- If an employee is rehired within three (3) years of the date this form was originally completed and the employee's work authorization has expired **or** if a current employee's work authorization is about to expire (reverification), complete Block B and:
  - examine any document that reflects that the employee is authorized to work in the U.S. (see List A or C),
  - record the document title, document number and expiration date (if any) in Block C, and
  - complete the signature block.

Photocopying and Retaining Form I-9. A blank I-9 may be reproduced, provided both sides are copied. The Instructions must be available to all employees completing this form. Employers must retain completed I-9s for three (3) years after the date of hire or one (1) year after the date employment ends, whichever is later.

For more detailed information, you may refer to the INS Handbook for Employers, (Form M-274). You may obtain the handbook at your local INS office.

Privacy Act Notice. The authority for collecting this information is the Immigration Reform and Control Act of 1986, Pub. L. 99-603 (8 USC 1324a).

This information is for employers to verify the eligibility of individuals for employment to preclude the unlawful hiring, or recruiting or referring for a fee, of aliens who are not authorized to work in the United States.

This information will be used by employers as a record of their basis for determining eligibility of an employee to work in the United States. The form will be kept by the employer and made available for inspection by officials of the U.S. Immigration and Naturalization Service, the Department of Labor and the Office of Special Counsel for Immigration Related Unfair Employment Practices.

Submission of the information required in this form is voluntary. However, an individual may not begin employment unless this form is completed, since employers are subject to civil or criminal penalties if they do not comply with the Immigration Reform and Control Act of 1986.

Reporting Burden. We try to create forms and instructions that are accurate, can be easily understood and which impose the least possible burden on you to provide us with information. Often this is difficult because some immigration laws are very complex. Accordingly, the reporting burden for this collection of information is computed as follows: **1)** learning about this form, 5 minutes; **2)** completing the form, 5 minutes; and **3)** assembling and filing (recordkeeping) the form, 5 minutes, for an average of 15 minutes per response. If you have comments regarding the accuracy of this burden estimate, or suggestions for making this form simpler, you can write to the Immigration and Naturalization Service, HQPDI, 425 I Street, N.W., Room 4307r, Washington, DC 20536. OMB No. 1115-0136.

EMPLOYERS MUST RETAIN COMPLETED FORM I-9
PLEASE DO NOT MAIL COMPLETED FORM I-9 TO INS

Form I-9 (Rev. 11-21-91)N

LISTS OF ACCEPTABLE DOCUMENTS

LIST A	LIST B	LIST C
Documents that Establish Both Identity and Employment Eligibility	**Documents that Establish Identity**	**Documents that Establish Employment Eligibility**

OR ... **AND**

LIST A
Documents that Establish Both Identity and Employment Eligibility

1. U.S. Passport (unexpired or expired)

2. Certificate of U.S. Citizenship (INS Form N-560 or N-561)

3. Certificate of Naturalization (INS Form N-550 or N-570)

4. Unexpired foreign passport, with I-551 stamp or attached INS Form I-94 indicating unexpired employment authorization

5. Alien Registration Receipt Card with photograph (INS Form I-151 or I-551)

6. Unexpired Temporary Card (INS Form I-688)

7. Unexpired Employment Authorization Card (INS Form I-688A)

8. Unexpired Reentry Permit (INS Form I-327)

9. Unexpired Refugee Travel Document (INS Form I-571)

10. Unexpired Employment Authorization Document issued by the INS which contains a photograph (INS Form I-688B)

LIST B
Documents that Establish Identity

1. Driver's license or ID card issued by a state or outlying possession of the United States provided it contains a photograph or information such as name, date of birth, sex, height, eye color and address

2. ID card issued by federal, state or local government agencies or entities, provided it contains a photograph or information such as name, date of birth, sex, height, eye color and address

3. School ID card with a photograph

4. Voter's registration card

5. U.S. Military card or draft record

6. Military dependent's ID card

7. U.S. Coast Guard Merchant Mariner Card

8. Native American tribal document

9. Driver's license issued by a Canadian government authority

For persons under age 18 who are unable to present a document listed above:

10. School record or report card

11. Clinic, doctor or hospital record

12. Day-care or nursery school record

LIST C
Documents that Establish Employment Eligibility

1. U.S. social security card issued by the Social Security Administration (other than a card stating it is not valid for employment)

2. Certification of Birth Abroad issued by the Department of State (Form FS-545 or Form DS-1350)

3. Original or certified copy of a birth certificate issued by a state, county, municipal authority or outlying possession of the United States bearing an official seal

4. Native American tribal document

5. U.S. Citizen ID Card (INS Form I-197)

6. ID Card for use of Resident Citizen in the United States (INS Form I-179)

7. Unexpired employment authorization document issued by the INS (other then those listed under List A)

Illustrations of many of these documents appear in Part 8 of the Handbook for Employers (M-274)

form 6

Form SS-4
Application for Employer Identification Number

(Rev. April 2000)
Department of the Treasury
Internal Revenue Service

(For use by employers, corporations, partnerships, trusts, estates, churches, government agencies, certain individuals, and others. See instructions.)

► Keep a copy for your records.

EIN

OMB No. 1545-0003

Please type or print clearly.

1 Name of applicant (legal name) (see instructions)

2 Trade name of business (if different from name on line 1)

3 Executor, trustee, "care of" name

4a Mailing address (street address) (room, apt., or suite no.)

5a Business address (if different from address on lines 4a and 4b)

4b City, state, and ZIP code

5b City, state, and ZIP code

6 County and state where principal business is located

7 Name of principal officer, general partner, grantor, owner, or trustor—SSN or ITIN may be required (see instructions) ►

8a Type of entity (Check only one box.) (see instructions)

Caution: *If applicant is a limited liability company, see the instructions for line 8a.*

☐ Sole proprietor (SSN) _____
☐ Partnership
☐ REMIC
☐ State/local government
☐ Church or church-controlled organization
☐ Other nonprofit organization (specify) ►
☐ Other (specify) ►

☐ Personal service corp.
☐ National Guard
☐ Farmers' cooperative

☐ Estate (SSN of decedent) _____
☐ Plan administrator (SSN) _____
☐ Other corporation (specify) ►
☐ Trust
☐ Federal government/military
(enter GEN if applicable) _____

8b If a corporation, name the state or foreign country (if applicable) where incorporated

State

Foreign country

9 Reason for applying (Check only one box.) (see instructions)
☐ Started new business (specify type) ►_____
☐ Hired employees (Check the box and see line 12.)
☐ Created a pension plan (specify type) ►

☐ Banking purpose (specify purpose) ►_____
☐ Changed type of organization (specify new type) ►_____
☐ Purchased going business
☐ Created a trust (specify type) ►_____
☐ Other (specify) ►

10 Date business started or acquired (month, day, year) (see instructions)

11 Closing month of accounting year (see instructions)

12 First date wages or annuities were paid or will be paid (month, day, year). **Note:** *If applicant is a withholding agent, enter date income will first be paid to nonresident alien. (month, day, year)* . . . . ►

13 Highest number of employees expected in the next 12 months. **Note:** *If the applicant does not expect to have any employees during the period, enter -0-. (see instructions)* . . . . ►

Nonagricultural	Agricultural	Household

14 Principal activity (see instructions) ►

15 Is the principal business activity manufacturing? . . . . ☐ Yes ☐ No
If "Yes," principal product and raw material used ►

16 To whom are most of the products or services sold? Please check one box.
☐ Public (retail)   ☐ Other (specify) ►   ☐ Business (wholesale)   ☐ N/A

17a Has the applicant ever applied for an employer identification number for this or any other business? . . . . ☐ Yes ☐ No
Note: *If "Yes," please complete lines 17b and 17c.*

17b If you checked "Yes" on line 17a, give applicant's legal name and trade name shown on prior application, if different from line 1 or 2 above.
Legal name ►   Trade name ►

17c Approximate date when and city and state where the application was filed. Enter previous employer identification number if known.
Approximate date when filed (mo., day, year) | City and state where filed | Previous EIN

Under penalties of perjury, I declare that I have examined this application, and to the best of my knowledge and belief, it is true, correct, and complete.

Business telephone number (include area code) ( )
Fax telephone number (include area code) ( )

Name and title (Please type or print clearly.) ►

Signature ►   Date ►

Note: *Do not write below this line. For official use only.*

Please leave blank ►	Geo.	Ind.	Class	Size	Reason for applying

For Privacy Act and Paperwork Reduction Act Notice, see page 4.   Cat. No. 16055N   Form **SS-4** (Rev. 4-2000)

243

General Instructions

Section references are to the Internal Revenue Code unless otherwise noted.

Purpose of Form

Use Form SS-4 to apply for an employer identification number (EIN). An EIN is a nine-digit number (for example, 12-3456789) assigned to sole proprietors, corporations, partnerships, estates, trusts, and other entities for tax filing and reporting purposes. The information you provide on this form will establish your business tax account.

Caution: *An EIN is for use in connection with your business activities only. Do **not** use your EIN in place of your social security number (SSN).*

Who Must File

You must file this form if you have not been assigned an EIN before and:

● You pay wages to one or more employees including household employees.

● You are required to have an EIN to use on any return, statement, or other document, even if you are not an employer.

● You are a withholding agent required to withhold taxes on income, other than wages, paid to a nonresident alien (individual, corporation, partnership, etc.). A withholding agent may be an agent, broker, fiduciary, manager, tenant, or spouse, and is required to file **Form 1042,** Annual Withholding Tax Return for U.S. Source Income of Foreign Persons.

● You file **Schedule C,** Profit or Loss From Business, **Schedule C-EZ,** Net Profit From Business, or **Schedule F,** Profit or Loss From Farming, of **Form 1040,** U.S. Individual Income Tax Return, **and** have a Keogh plan or are required to file excise, employment, or alcohol, tobacco, or firearms returns.

The following must use EINs even if they do not have any employees:

● State and local agencies who serve as tax reporting agents for public assistance recipients, under Rev. Proc. 80-4, 1980-1 C.B. 581, should obtain a separate EIN for this reporting. See **Household employer** on page 3.

● Trusts, except the following:

1. Certain grantor-owned trusts. (See the **Instructions for Form 1041,** U.S. Income Tax Return for Estates and Trusts.)

2. Individual retirement arrangement (IRA) trusts, unless the trust has to file **Form 990-T,** Exempt Organization Business Income Tax Return. (See the **Instructions for Form 990-T.)**

● Estates

● Partnerships

● REMICs (real estate mortgage investment conduits) (See the **Instructions for Form 1066,** U.S. Real Estate Mortgage Investment Conduit (REMIC) Income Tax Return.)

● Corporations

● Nonprofit organizations (churches, clubs, etc.)

● Farmers' cooperatives

● Plan administrators (A plan administrator is the person or group of persons specified as the administrator by the instrument under which the plan is operated.)

When To Apply for a New EIN

New Business. If you become the new owner of an existing business, **do not** use the EIN of the former owner. **If you already have an EIN, use that number.** If you do not have an EIN, apply for one on this form. If you become the "owner" of a corporation by acquiring its stock, use the corporation's EIN.

Changes in Organization or Ownership. If you already have an EIN, you may need to get a new one if either the organization or ownership of your business changes. If you incorporate a sole proprietorship or form a partnership, you must get a new EIN. However, **do not** apply for a new EIN if:

● You change only the name of your business,

● You elected on **Form 8832,** Entity Classification Election, to change the way the entity is taxed, or

● A partnership terminates because at least 50% of the total interests in partnership capital and profits were sold or exchanged within a 12-month period. (See Regulations section 301.6109-1(d)(2)(iii).) The EIN for the terminated partnership should continue to be used.

Note: *If you are electing to be an "S corporation," be sure you file **Form 2553,** Election by a Small Business Corporation.*

File Only One Form SS-4. File only one Form SS-4, regardless of the number of businesses operated or trade names under which a business operates. However, each corporation in an affiliated group must file a separate application.

EIN Applied for, But Not Received. If you do not have an EIN by the time a return is due, write "Applied for" and the date you applied in the space shown for the number. **Do not** show your social security number (SSN) as an EIN on returns.

If you do not have an EIN by the time a tax deposit is due, send your payment to the Internal Revenue Service Center for your filing area. (See **Where To Apply** below.) Make your check or money order payable to "United States Treasury" and show your name (as shown on Form SS-4), address, type of tax, period covered, and date you applied for an EIN. Send an explanation with the deposit.

For more information about EINs, see **Pub. 583,** Starting a Business and Keeping Records, and **Pub. 1635,** Understanding Your EIN.

How To Apply

You can apply for an EIN either by mail or by telephone. You can get an EIN immediately by calling the Tele-TIN number for the service center for your state, or you can send the completed Form SS-4 directly to the service center to receive your EIN by mail.

Application by Tele-TIN. Under the Tele-TIN program, you can receive your EIN by telephone and use it immediately to file a return or make a payment. To receive an EIN by telephone, complete Form SS-4, then call the Tele-TIN number listed for your state under **Where To Apply.** The person making the call must be authorized to sign the form. (See **Signature** on page 4.)

An IRS representative will use the information from the Form SS-4 to establish your account and assign you an EIN. Write the number you are given on the upper right corner of the form and sign and date it.

*Mail or fax (facsimile) the signed Form SS-4 **within 24 hours** to the Tele-TIN Unit at the service center address for your state.* The IRS representative will give you the fax number. The fax numbers are also listed in Pub. 1635.

Taxpayer representatives can receive their client's EIN by telephone if they first send a fax of a completed **Form 2848,** Power of Attorney and Declaration of Representative, or **Form 8821,** Tax Information Authorization, to the Tele-TIN unit. The Form 2848 or Form 8821 will be used solely to release the EIN to the representative authorized on the form.

Application by Mail. Complete Form SS-4 at least 4 to 5 weeks before you will need an EIN. Sign and date the application and mail it to the service center address for your state. You will receive your EIN in the mail in approximately 4 weeks.

Where To Apply

The Tele-TIN numbers listed below will involve a long-distance charge to callers outside of the local calling area and can be used only to apply for an EIN. **The numbers may change without notice.** Call 1-800-829-1040 to verify a number or to ask about the status of an application by mail.

If your principal business, office or agency, or legal residence in the case of an individual is located in: ▼	Call the Tele-TIN number shown or file with the Internal Revenue Service Center at: ▼
Florida, Georgia, South Carolina	Attn: Entity Control Atlanta, GA 39901 770-455-2360
New Jersey, New York (New York City and counties of Nassau, Rockland, Suffolk, and Westchester)	Attn: Entity Control Holtsville, NY 00501 516-447-4955
New York (all other counties), Connecticut, Maine, Massachusetts, New Hampshire, Rhode Island, Vermont	Attn: Entity Control Andover, MA 05501 978-474-9717
Illinois, Iowa, Minnesota, Missouri, Wisconsin	Attn: Entity Control Stop 6800 2306 E. Bannister Rd. Kansas City, MO 64999 816-926-5999
Delaware, District of Columbia, Maryland, Pennsylvania, Virginia	Attn: Entity Control Philadelphia, PA 19255 215-516-6999
Indiana, Kentucky, Michigan, Ohio, West Virginia	Attn: Entity Control Cincinnati, OH 45999 859-292-5467

Kansas, New Mexico, Oklahoma, Texas	Attn: Entity Control Austin, TX 73301 512-460-7843
Alaska, Arizona, California (counties of Alpine, Amador, Butte, Calaveras, Colusa, Contra Costa, Del Norte, El Dorado, Glenn, Humboldt, Lake, Lassen, Marin, Mendocino, Modoc, Napa, Nevada, Placer, Plumas, Sacramento, San Joaquin, Shasta, Sierra, Siskiyou, Solano, Sonoma, Sutter, Tehama, Trinity, Yolo, and Yuba), Colorado, Idaho, Montana, Nebraska, Nevada, North Dakota, Oregon, South Dakota, Utah, Washington, Wyoming	Attn: Entity Control Mail Stop 6271 P.O. Box 9941 Ogden, UT 84201 801-620-7645
California (all other counties), Hawaii	Attn: Entity Control Fresno, CA 93888 559-452-4010
Alabama, Arkansas, Louisiana, Mississippi, North Carolina, Tennessee	Attn: Entity Control Memphis, TN 37501 901-546-3920
If you have no legal residence, principal place of business, or principal office or agency in any state	Attn: Entity Control Philadelphia, PA 19255 215-516-6999

Specific Instructions

The instructions that follow are for those items that are not self-explanatory. Enter N/A (nonapplicable) on the lines that do not apply.

Line 1. Enter the legal name of the entity applying for the EIN exactly as it appears on the social security card, charter, or other applicable legal document.

Individuals. Enter your first name, middle initial, and last name. If you are a sole proprietor, enter your individual name, not your business name. Enter your business name on line 2. Do not use abbreviations or nicknames on line 1.

Trusts. Enter the name of the trust.

Estate of a decedent. Enter the name of the estate.

Partnerships. Enter the legal name of the partnership as it appears in the partnership agreement. **Do not** list the names of the partners on line 1. See the specific instructions for line 7.

Corporations. Enter the corporate name as it appears in the corporation charter or other legal document creating it.

Plan administrators. Enter the name of the plan administrator. A plan administrator who already has an EIN should use that number.

Line 2. Enter the trade name of the business if different from the legal name. The trade name is the "doing business as" name.

Note: *Use the full legal name on line 1 on all tax returns filed for the entity. However, if you enter a trade name on line 2 and choose to use the trade name instead of the legal name, enter the trade name on all returns you file. To prevent processing delays and errors, **always** use either the legal name only or the trade name only on all tax returns.*

Line 3. Trusts enter the name of the trustee. Estates enter the name of the executor, administrator, or other fiduciary. If the entity applying has a designated person to receive tax information, enter that person's name as the "care of" person. Print or type the first name, middle initial, and last name.

Line 7. Enter the first name, middle initial, last name, and SSN of a principal officer if the business is a corporation; of a general partner if a partnership; of the owner of a single member entity that is disregarded as an entity separate from its owner; or of a grantor, owner, or trustor if a trust. If the person in question is an alien individual with a previously assigned individual taxpayer identification number (ITIN), enter the ITIN in the space provided, instead of an SSN. You are not required to enter an SSN or ITIN if the reason you are applying for an EIN is to make an entity classification election (see Regulations section 301.7701-1 through 301.7701-3), and you are a nonresident alien with no effectively connected income from sources within the United States.

Line 8a. Check the box that best describes the type of entity applying for the EIN. If you are an alien individual with an ITIN previously assigned to you, enter the ITIN in place of a requested SSN.

Caution: *This is not an election for a tax classification of an entity. See "Limited liability company (LLC)" below.*

If not specifically mentioned, check the "Other" box, enter the type of entity and the type of return that will be filed (for example, common trust fund, Form 1065). Do not enter N/A. If you are an alien individual applying for an EIN, see the **Line 7** instructions above.

Sole proprietor. Check this box if you file Schedule C, C-EZ, or F (Form 1040) and have a qualified plan, or are required to file excise, employment, or alcohol, tobacco, or firearms returns, or are a payer of gambling winnings. Enter your SSN (or ITIN) in the space provided. If you are a nonresident alien with are a nonresident alien with no effectively

connected income from sources within the United States, you do not need to enter an SSN or ITIN.

REMIC. Check this box if the entity has elected to be treated as a real estate mortgage investment conduit (REMIC). See the Instructions for Form 1066 for more information.

Other nonprofit organization. Check this box if the nonprofit organization is other than a church or church-controlled organization and specify the type of nonprofit organization (for example, an educational organization).

If the organization also seeks tax-exempt status, you must file either **Package 1023,** Application for Recognition of Exemption, or **Package 1024,** Application for Recognition of Exemption Under Section 501(a). Get **Pub. 557,** Tax Exempt Status for Your Organization, for more information.

Group exemption number (GEN). If the organization is covered by a group exemption letter, enter the four-digit GEN. (Do not confuse the GEN with the nine-digit EIN.) If you do not know the GEN, contact the parent organization. Get Pub. 557 for more information about group exemption numbers.

Withholding agent. If you are a withholding agent required to file Form 1042, check the "Other" box and enter "Withholding agent."

Personal service corporation. Check this box if the entity is a personal service corporation. An entity is a personal service corporation for a tax year only if:

● The principal activity of the entity during the testing period (prior tax year) for the tax year is the performance of personal services substantially by employee-owners, and

● The employee-owners own at least 10% of the fair market value of the outstanding stock in the entity on the last day of the testing period.

Personal services include performance of services in such fields as health, law, accounting, or consulting. For more information about personal service corporations, see the **Instructions for Forms 1120 and 1120-A,** and **Pub. 542,** Corporations.

Limited liability company (LLC). See the definition of limited liability company in the **Instructions for Form 1065,** U.S. Partnership Return of Income. An LLC with two or more members can be a partnership or an association taxable as a corporation. An LLC with a single owner can be an association taxable as a corporation or an entity disregarded as an entity separate from its owner. See Form 8832 for more details.

Note: *A domestic LLC with at least two members that does not file Form 8832 is classified as a partnership for Federal income tax purposes.*

● If the entity is classified as a partnership for Federal income tax purposes, check the "partnership" box.

● If the entity is classified as a corporation for Federal income tax purposes, check the "Other corporation" box and write "limited liability co." in the space provided.

● If the entity is disregarded as an entity separate from its owner, check the "Other" box and write in "disregarded entity" in the space provided.

Plan administrator. If the plan administrator is an individual, enter the plan administrator's SSN in the space provided.

Other corporation. This box is for any corporation other than a personal service corporation. If you check this box, enter the type of corporation (such as insurance company) in the space provided.

Household employer. If you are an individual, check the "Other" box and enter "Household employer" and your SSN. If you are a state or local agency serving as a tax reporting agent for public assistance recipients who become household employers, check the "Other" box and enter "Household employer agent." If you are a trust that qualifies as a household employer, you do not need a separate EIN for reporting tax information relating to household employees; use the EIN of the trust.

QSub. For a qualified subchapter S subsidiary (QSub) check the "Other" box and specify "QSub."

Line 9. Check only **one** box. Do not enter N/A.

Started new business. Check this box if you are starting a new business that requires an EIN. If you check this box, enter the type of business being started. **Do not** apply if you already have an EIN and are only adding another place of business.

Hired employees. Check this box if the existing business is requesting an EIN because it has hired or is hiring employees and is therefore required to file employment tax returns. **Do not** apply if you already have an EIN and are only hiring employees. For information on the applicable employment taxes for family members, see **Circular E,** Employer's Tax Guide (Publication 15).

Created a pension plan. Check this box if you have created a pension plan and need an EIN for reporting purposes. Also, enter the type of plan.

Note: *Check this box if you are applying for a trust EIN when a new pension plan is established.*

Banking purpose. Check this box if you are requesting an EIN for banking purposes only, and enter the banking purpose (for example, a bowling league for depositing dues or an investment club for dividend and interest reporting).

Changed type of organization. Check this box if the business is changing its type of organization, for example, if the business was a sole proprietorship and has been incorporated or has become a partnership. If you check this box, specify in the space provided the type of change made, for example, "from sole proprietorship to partnership."

Purchased going business. Check this box if you purchased an existing business. **Do not** use the former owner's EIN. **Do not** apply for a new EIN if you already have one. Use your own EIN.

Created a trust. Check this box if you created a trust, and enter the type of trust created. For example, indicate if the trust is a nonexempt charitable trust or a split-interest trust.

Note: *Do not check this box if you are applying for a trust EIN when a new pension plan is established. Check "Created a pension plan."*

Exception. Do **not** file this form for certain grantor-type trusts. The trustee does not need an EIN for the trust if the trustee furnishes the name and TIN of the grantor/owner and the address of the trust to all payors. See the Instructions for Form 1041 for more information.

Other (specify). Check this box if you are requesting an EIN for any other reason, and enter the reason.

Line 10. If you are starting a new business, enter the starting date of the business. If the business you acquired is already operating, enter the date you acquired the business. Trusts should enter the date the trust was legally created. Estates should enter the date of death of the decedent whose name appears on line 1 or the date when the estate was legally funded.

Line 11. Enter the last month of your accounting year or tax year. An accounting or tax year is usually 12 consecutive months, either a calendar year or a fiscal year (including a period of 52 or 53 weeks). A calendar year is 12 consecutive months ending on December 31. A fiscal year is either 12 consecutive months ending on the last day of any month other than December or a 52-53 week year. For more information on accounting periods, see **Pub. 538,** Accounting Periods and Methods.

Individuals. Your tax year generally will be a calendar year.

Partnerships. Partnerships generally must adopt one of the following tax years:
- The tax year of the majority of its partners,
- The tax year common to all of its principal partners,
- The tax year that results in the least aggregate deferral of income, or
- In certain cases, some other tax year.

See the Instructions for Form 1065 for more information.

REMIC. REMICs must have a calendar year as their tax year.

Personal service corporations. A personal service corporation generally must adopt a calendar year unless:
- It can establish a business purpose for having a different tax year, or
- It elects under section 444 to have a tax year other than a calendar year.

Trusts. Generally, a trust must adopt a calendar year except for the following:
- Tax-exempt trusts,
- Charitable trusts, and
- Grantor-owned trusts.

Line 12. If the business has or will have employees, enter the date on which the business began or will begin to pay wages. If the business does not plan to have employees, enter N/A.

Withholding agent. Enter the date you began or will begin to pay income to a nonresident alien. This also applies to individuals who are required to file Form 1042 to report alimony paid to a nonresident alien.

Line 13. For a definition of agricultural labor (farmwork), see **Circular A,** Agricultural Employer's Tax Guide (Publication 51).

Line 14. Generally, enter the exact type of business being operated (for example, advertising agency, farm, food or beverage establishment, labor union, real estate agency, steam laundry, rental of coin-operated vending machine, or investment club). Also state if the business will involve the sale or distribution of alcoholic beverages.

Governmental. Enter the type of organization (state, county, school district, municipality, etc.).

Nonprofit organization (other than governmental). Enter whether organized for religious, educational, or humane purposes, and the principal activity (for example, religious organization—hospital, charitable).

Mining and quarrying. Specify the process and the principal product (for example, mining bituminous coal, contract drilling for oil, or quarrying dimension stone).

Contract construction. Specify whether general contracting or special trade contracting. Also, show the type of work normally performed (for example, general contractor for residential buildings or electrical subcontractor).

Food or beverage establishments. Specify the type of establishment and state whether you employ workers who receive tips (for example, lounge—yes).

Trade. Specify the type of sales and the principal line of goods sold (for example, wholesale dairy products, manufacturer's representative for mining machinery, or retail hardware).

Manufacturing. Specify the type of establishment operated (for example, sawmill or vegetable cannery).

Signature. The application must be signed by (a) the individual, if the applicant is an individual, (b) the president, vice president, or other principal officer, if the applicant is a corporation, (c) a responsible and duly authorized member or officer having knowledge of its affairs, if the applicant is a partnership or other unincorporated organization, or (d) the fiduciary, if the applicant is a trust or an estate.

How To Get Forms and Publications

Phone. You can order forms, instructions, and publications by phone 24 hours a day, 7 days a week. Just call 1-800-TAX-FORM (1-800-829-3676). You should receive your order or notification of its status within 10 workdays.

Personal computer. With your personal computer and modem, you can get the forms and information you need using IRS's Internet Web Site at **www.irs.gov** or File Transfer Protocol at **ftp.irs.gov.**

CD-ROM. For small businesses, return preparers, or others who may frequently need tax forms or publications, a CD-ROM containing over 2,000 tax products (including many prior year forms) can be purchased from the National Technical Information Service (NTIS).

To order **Pub. 1796,** Federal Tax Products on CD-ROM, call **1-877-CDFORMS** (1-877-233-6767) toll free or connect to **www.irs.gov/cdorders**

Privacy Act and Paperwork Reduction Act Notice. We ask for the information on this form to carry out the Internal Revenue laws of the United States. We need it to comply with section 6109 and the regulations thereunder which generally require the inclusion of an employer identification number (EIN) on certain returns, statements, or other documents filed with the Internal Revenue Service. Information on this form may be used to determine which Federal tax returns you are required to file and to provide you with related forms and publications. We disclose this form to the Social Security Administration for their use in determining compliance with applicable laws. We will be unable to issue an EIN to you unless you provide all of the requested information which applies to your entity.

You are not required to provide the information requested on a form that is subject to the Paperwork Reduction Act unless the form displays a valid OMB control number. Books or records relating to a form or its instructions must be retained as long as their contents may become material in the administration of any Internal Revenue law. Generally, tax returns/return information are confidential, as required by section 6103.

The time needed to complete and file this form will vary depending on individual circumstances. The estimated average time is:

Recordkeeping	7 min.
Learning about the law or the form	22 min.
Preparing the form	46 min.
Copying, assembling, and sending the form to the IRS . .	20 min.

If you have comments concerning the accuracy of these time estimates or suggestions for making this form simpler, we would be happy to hear from you. You can write to the Tax Forms Committee, Western Area Distribution Center, Rancho Cordova, CA 95743-0001. **Do not** send the form to this address. Instead, see **Where To Apply** on page 2.

| Form **SS-8** (Rev. June 1997) Department of the Treasury Internal Revenue Service | **Determination of Employee Work Status for Purposes of Federal Employment Taxes and Income Tax Withholding** | OMB No. 1545-0004 |

Paperwork Reduction Act Notice

We ask for the information on this form to carry out the Internal Revenue laws of the United States. You are required to give us the information. We need it to ensure that you are complying with these laws and to allow us to figure and collect the right amount of tax.

You are not required to provide the information requested on a form that is subject to the Paperwork Reduction Act unless the form displays a valid OMB control number. Books or records relating to a form or its instructions must be retained as long as their contents may become material in the administration of any Internal Revenue law. Generally, tax returns and return information are confidential, as required by Code section 6103.

The time needed to complete and file this form will vary depending on individual circumstances. The estimated average time is: **Recordkeeping, 34 hr., 55 min.; Learning about the law or the form, 12 min.;** and **Preparing and sending the form to the IRS, 46 min.** If you have comments concerning the accuracy of these time estimates or suggestions for making this form simpler, we would be happy to hear from you. You can write to the Tax Forms Committee, Western Area Distribution Center, Rancho Cordova, CA 95743-0001. **DO NOT send the tax form to this address. Instead, see General Information for where to file.**

Purpose

Employers and workers file Form SS-8 to get a determination as to whether a worker is an employee for purposes of Federal employment taxes and income tax withholding.

General Information

Complete this form carefully. If the firm is completing the form, complete it for **ONE** individual who is representative of the class of workers whose status is in question. If you want a written determination for more than one class of workers, complete a separate Form SS-8 for one worker

from each class whose status is typical of that class. A written determination for any worker will apply to other workers of the same class if the facts are not materially different from those of the worker whose status was ruled upon.

Caution: Form SS-8 is not a claim for refund of social security and Medicare taxes or Federal income tax withholding. Also, a determination that an individual is an employee does not necessarily reduce any current or prior tax liability. A worker must file his or her income tax return even if a determination has not been made by the due date of the return.

Where to file.—In the list below, find the state where your legal residence, principal place of business, office, or agency is located. Send Form SS-8 to the address listed for your location.

Location:	Send to:
Alaska, Arizona, Arkansas, California, Colorado, Hawaii, Idaho, Illinois, Iowa, Kansas, Minnesota, Missouri, Montana, Nebraska, Nevada, New Mexico, North Dakota, Oklahoma, Oregon, South Dakota, Texas, Utah, Washington, Wisconsin, Wyoming	Internal Revenue Service SS-8 Determinations P.O. Box 1231, Stop 4106 AUSC Austin, TX 78767
Alabama, Connecticut, Delaware, District of Columbia, Florida, Georgia, Indiana, Kentucky, Louisiana, Maine, Maryland, Massachusetts, Michigan, Mississippi, New Hampshire, New Jersey, New York, North Carolina, Ohio, Pennsylvania, Rhode Island, South Carolina, Tennessee, Vermont, Virginia, West Virginia, All other locations not listed	Internal Revenue Service SS-8 Determinations Two Lakemont Road Newport, VT 05855-1555
American Samoa, Guam, Puerto Rico, U.S. Virgin Islands	Internal Revenue Service Mercantile Plaza 2 Avenue Ponce de Leon San Juan, Puerto Rico 00918

Name of firm (or person) for whom the worker performed services	Name of worker
Address of firm (include street address, apt. or suite no., city, state, and ZIP code)	Address of worker (include street address, apt. or suite no., city, state, and ZIP code)

Trade name	Telephone number (include area code) ( )	Worker's social security number
Telephone number (include area code) ( )	Firm's employer identification number	

Check type of firm for which the work relationship is in question:

☐ Individual   ☐ Partnership   ☐ Corporation   ☐ Other (specify) ▶ ....

Important Information Needed To Process Your Request

This form is being completed by: ☐ Firm   ☐ Worker

If this form is being completed by the worker, the IRS **must** have your permission to disclose your name to the firm.

Do you object to disclosing your name and the information on this form to the firm? . . . .   ☐ Yes   ☐ No

If you answer "Yes," the IRS cannot act on your request. **Do not complete the rest of this form unless the IRS asks for it.**

Under section 6110 of the Internal Revenue Code, the information on this form and related file documents will be open to the public if any ruling or determination is made. However, names, addresses, and taxpayer identification numbers will be removed before the information is made public.

Is there any other information you want removed? . . . .   ☐ Yes   ☐ No

If you check "Yes," we cannot process your request unless you submit a copy of this form and copies of all supporting documents showing, in brackets, the information you want removed. Attach a separate statement showing which specific exemption of section 6110(c) applies to each bracketed part.

Cat. No. 16106T   Form **SS-8** (Rev. 6-97)

This form is designed to cover many work activities, so some of the questions may not apply to you. You must answer ALL items or mark them "Unknown" or "Does not apply." If you need more space, attach another sheet.

Total number of workers in this class. (Attach names and addresses. If more than 10 workers, list only 10.) ▶ _____

This information is about services performed by the worker from _____ to _____
(month, day, year)   (month, day, year)

Is the worker still performing services for the firm? . . . . ☐ Yes ☐ No

● If "No," what was the date of termination? ▶ _____
(month, day, year)

1a Describe the firm's business ....

 b Describe the work done by the worker ....

2a If the work is done under a written agreement between the firm and the worker, attach a copy.

 b If the agreement is not in writing, describe the terms and conditions of the work arrangement ....
....

 c If the actual working arrangement differs in any way from the agreement, explain the differences and why they occur ....
....

3a Is the worker given training by the firm? . . . . ☐ Yes ☐ No
 ● If "Yes," what kind? ....
 ● How often? ....

 b Is the worker given instructions in the way the work is to be done (exclusive of actual training in 3a)? . ☐ Yes ☐ No
 ● If "Yes," give specific examples ....

 c Attach samples of any written instructions or procedures.

 d Does the firm have the right to change the methods used by the worker or direct that person on how to
do the work? . . . . ☐ Yes ☐ No
 ● Explain your answer ....
....

 e Does the operation of the firm's business require that the worker be supervised or controlled in the
performance of the service? . . . . ☐ Yes ☐ No
 ● Explain your answer ....
....

4a The firm engages the worker:
 ☐ To perform and complete a particular job only
 ☐ To work at a job for an indefinite period of time
 ☐ Other (explain) ....

 b Is the worker required to follow a routine or a schedule established by the firm? . . . . ☐ Yes ☐ No
 ● If "Yes," what is the routine or schedule? ....
....

 c Does the worker report to the firm or its representative?. . . . . ☐ Yes ☐ No
 ● If "Yes," how often? ....
 ● For what purpose? ....
 ● In what manner (in person, in writing, by telephone, etc.)? ....
 ● Attach copies of any report forms used in reporting to the firm.

 d Does the worker furnish a time record to the firm? . . . . ☐ Yes ☐ No
 ● If "Yes," attach copies of time records.

5a State the kind and value of tools, equipment, supplies, and materials furnished by:
 ● The firm ....
....
 ● The worker ....
....

 b What expenses are incurred by the worker in the performance of services for the firm? ....

 c Does the firm reimburse the worker for any expenses? . . . . ☐ Yes ☐ No
 ● If "Yes," specify the reimbursed expenses ....

6a Will the worker perform the services personally? . . . . ☐ Yes ☐ No

b Does the worker have helpers? . . . . ☐ Yes ☐ No

   • If "Yes," who hires the helpers? ☐ Firm ☐ Worker

   • If the helpers are hired by the worker, is the firm's approval necessary? . . . . ☐ Yes ☐ No

   • Who pays the helpers? ☐ Firm ☐ Worker

   • If the worker pays the helpers, does the firm repay the worker? . . . . ☐ Yes ☐ No

   • Are social security and Medicare taxes and Federal income tax withheld from the helpers' pay? . . ☐ Yes ☐ No

   • If "Yes," who reports and pays these taxes? ☐ Firm ☐ Worker

   • Who reports the helpers' earnings to the Internal Revenue Service? ☐ Firm ☐ Worker

   • What services do the helpers perform? ....

7 At what location are the services performed? ☐ Firm's ☐ Worker's ☐ Other (specify) ....

8a Type of pay worker receives:

   ☐ Salary   ☐ Commission ☐ Hourly wage   ☐ Piecework ☐ Lump sum   ☐ Other (specify) ....

b Does the firm guarantee a minimum amount of pay to the worker? . . . . ☐ Yes ☐ No

c Does the firm allow the worker a drawing account or advances against pay? . . . . ☐ Yes ☐ No

   • If "Yes," is the worker paid such advances on a regular basis? . . . . ☐ Yes ☐ No

d How does the worker repay such advances? ....

9a Is the worker eligible for a pension, bonus, paid vacations, sick pay, etc.? . . . . ☐ Yes ☐ No

   • If "Yes," specify ....

b Does the firm carry worker's compensation insurance on the worker? . . . . ☐ Yes ☐ No

c Does the firm withhold social security and Medicare taxes from amounts paid the worker? . . . . ☐ Yes ☐ No

d Does the firm withhold Federal income tax from amounts paid the worker? . . . . ☐ Yes ☐ No

e How does the firm report the worker's earnings to the Internal Revenue Service?

   ☐ Form W-2 ☐ Form 1099-MISC ☐ Does not report ☐ Other (specify) ....

   • Attach a copy.

f Does the firm bond the worker? . . . . ☐ Yes ☐ No

10a Approximately how many hours a day does the worker perform services for the firm? ....

b Does the firm set hours of work for the worker? . . . . ☐ Yes ☐ No

   • If "Yes," what are the worker's set hours? _____ a.m./p.m. to _____ a.m./p.m. (Circle whether a.m. or p.m.)

c Does the worker perform similar services for others? . . . . ☐ Yes ☐ No ☐ Unknown

   • If "Yes," are these services performed on a daily basis for other firms? . . . . . ☐ Yes ☐ No ☐ Unknown

   • Percentage of time spent in performing these services for:

   This firm .... % Other firms .... % ☐ Unknown

   • Does the firm have priority on the worker's time? . . . . ☐ Yes ☐ No

   • If "No," explain ....

d Is the worker prohibited from competing with the firm either while performing services or during any later
period? . . . . ☐ Yes ☐ No

11a Can the firm discharge the worker at any time without incurring a liability? . . . . ☐ Yes ☐ No

   • If "No," explain ....

b Can the worker terminate the services at any time without incurring a liability? . . . . ☐ Yes ☐ No

   • If "No," explain ....

12a Does the worker perform services for the firm under:

   ☐ The firm's business name ☐ The worker's own business name ☐ Other (specify) ....

b Does the worker advertise or maintain a business listing in the telephone directory, a trade
journal, etc.? . . . . ☐ Yes ☐ No ☐ Unknown

   • If "Yes," specify ....

c Does the worker represent himself or herself to the public as being in business to perform
the same or similar services? . . . . ☐ Yes ☐ No ☐ Unknown

   • If "Yes," how? ....

d Does the worker have his or her own shop or office? . . . . ☐ Yes ☐ No ☐ Unknown

   • If "Yes," where? ....

e Does the firm represent the worker as an employee of the firm to its customers? . . . . ☐ Yes ☐ No

   • If "No," how is the worker represented? ....

f How did the firm learn of the worker's services? ....

13 Is a license necessary for the work? . . . . ☐ Yes ☐ No ☐ Unknown

   • If "Yes," what kind of license is required? ....

   • Who issues the license?

   • Who pays the license fee?

14 Does the worker have a financial investment in a business related to the services
    performed? . . . . ☐ Yes   ☐ No   ☐ Unknown
    • If "Yes," specify and give amount of the investment ....

15 Can the worker incur a loss in the performance of the service for the firm? . . . . ☐ Yes   ☐ No
    • If "Yes," how? ....

16a Has any other government agency ruled on the status of the firm's workers? . . . . ☐ Yes   ☐ No
    • If "Yes," attach a copy of the ruling.

  b Is the same issue being considered by any IRS office in connection with the audit of the worker's tax
    return or the firm's tax return, or has it been considered recently? . . . . ☐ Yes   ☐ No
    • If "Yes," for which year(s)? ....

17 Does the worker assemble or process a product at home or away from the firm's place of business? ☐ Yes ☐ No
    • If "Yes," who furnishes materials or goods used by the worker? ☐ Firm   ☐ Worker   ☐ Other
    • Is the worker furnished a pattern or given instructions to follow in making the product? . . . . . ☐ Yes ☐ No
    • Is the worker required to return the finished product to the firm or to someone designated by the firm? ☐ Yes ☐ No

18 Attach a detailed explanation of any other reason why you believe the worker is an employee or an independent contractor.

    Answer items 19a through o only if the worker is a salesperson or provides a service directly to customers.

19a Are leads to prospective customers furnished by the firm? . . . . ☐ Yes   ☐ No   ☐ Does not apply
  b Is the worker required to pursue or report on leads? . . . . ☐ Yes   ☐ No   ☐ Does not apply
  c Is the worker required to adhere to prices, terms, and conditions of sale established by the firm? . . ☐ Yes ☐ No
  d Are orders submitted to and subject to approval by the firm? . . . . ☐ Yes   ☐ No
  e Is the worker expected to attend sales meetings? . . . . ☐ Yes   ☐ No
    • If "Yes," is the worker subject to any kind of penalty for failing to attend? . . . . ☐ Yes   ☐ No
  f Does the firm assign a specific territory to the worker? . . . . ☐ Yes   ☐ No
  g Whom does the customer pay?   ☐ Firm   ☐ Worker
    • If worker, does the worker remit the total amount to the firm? . . . . ☐ Yes   ☐ No
  h Does the worker sell a consumer product in a home or establishment other than a permanent retail
    establishment? . . . . ☐ Yes   ☐ No
  i List the products and/or services distributed by the worker, such as meat, vegetables, fruit, bakery products, beverages (other
    than milk), or laundry or dry cleaning services. If more than one type of product and/or service is distributed, specify the
    principal one ....
  j Did the firm or another person assign the route or territory and a list of customers to the worker? . . ☐ Yes   ☐ No
    • If "Yes," enter the name and job title of the person who made the assignment ....
  k Did the worker pay the firm or person for the privilege of serving customers on the route or in the territory? ☐ Yes ☐ No
    • If "Yes," how much did the worker pay (not including any amount paid for a truck or racks, etc.)? $ ....
    • What factors were considered in determining the value of the route or territory? ....
  l How are new customers obtained by the worker? Explain fully, showing whether the new customers called the firm for service,
    were solicited by the worker, or both ....
  m Does the worker sell life insurance? . . . . ☐ Yes   ☐ No
    • If "Yes," is the selling of life insurance or annuity contracts for the firm the worker's entire business
    activity? . . . . ☐ Yes   ☐ No
    • If "No," list the other business activities and the amount of time spent on them ....
  n Does the worker sell other types of insurance for the firm? . . . . ☐ Yes   ☐ No
    • If "Yes," state the percentage of the worker's total working time spent in selling other types of insurance .... %
    • At the time the contract was entered into between the firm and the worker, was it their intention that the worker sell life
    insurance for the firm: ☐ on a full-time basis   ☐ on a part-time basis
    • State the manner in which the intention was expressed ....
  o Is the worker a traveling or city salesperson? . . . . ☐ Yes   ☐ No
    • If "Yes," from whom does the worker principally solicit orders for the firm? ....
    • If the worker solicits orders from wholesalers, retailers, contractors, or operators of hotels, restaurants, or other similar
    establishments, specify the percentage of the worker's time spent in the solicitation .... %
    • Is the merchandise purchased by the customers for resale or for use in their business operations? If used by the customers
    in their business operations, describe the merchandise and state whether it is equipment installed on their premises or a
    consumable supply

Under penalties of perjury, I declare that I have examined this request, including accompanying documents, and to the best of my knowledge and belief, the facts
presented are true, correct, and complete.

Signature ▶   Title ▶   Date ▶

If the firm is completing this form, an officer or member of the firm must sign it. If the worker is completing this form, the worker must sign it. If the worker wants a
written determination about services performed for two or more firms, a separate form must be completed and signed for each firm. Additional copies of this form may
be obtained by calling 1-800-TAX-FORM (1-800-829-3676).

Form W-4 (2001)

Purpose. Complete Form W-4 so your employer can withhold the correct Federal income tax from your pay. Because your tax situation may change, you may want to refigure your withholding each year.

Exemption from withholding. If you are exempt, complete only lines 1, 2, 3, 4, and 7, and sign the form to validate it. Your exemption for 2001 expires February 18, 2002.

Note: *You cannot claim exemption from withholding if (1) your income exceeds $750 and includes more than $250 of unearned income (e.g., interest and dividends) and (2) another person can claim you as a dependent on their tax return.*

Basic instructions. If you are not exempt, complete the **Personal Allowances Worksheet** below. The worksheets on page 2 adjust your withholding allowances based on itemized deductions, certain credits, adjustments to income, or two-earner/two-job situations. Complete all worksheets that apply. They will help you figure the number of withholding allowances you are entitled to claim. **However, you may claim fewer (or zero) allowances.**

Head of household. Generally, you may claim head of household filing status on your tax return only if you are unmarried and pay more than 50% of the costs of keeping up a home for yourself and your dependent(s) or other qualifying individuals. See line E below.

Tax credits. You can take projected tax credits into account in figuring your allowable number of withholding allowances. Credits for child or dependent care expenses and the child tax credit may be claimed using the **Personal Allowances Worksheet** below. See **Pub. 919**, How Do I Adjust My Tax Withholding? for information on converting your other credits into withholding allowances.

Nonwage income. If you have a large amount of nonwage income, such as interest or dividends, consider making estimated tax payments using **Form 1040-ES**, Estimated Tax for Individuals. Otherwise, you may owe additional tax.

Two earners/two jobs. If you have a working spouse or more than one job, figure the total number of allowances you are entitled to claim on all jobs using worksheets from only one Form W-4. Your withholding usually will be most accurate when all allowances are claimed on the Form W-4 for the highest paying job and zero allowances are claimed on the others.

Check your withholding. After your Form W-4 takes effect, use Pub. 919 to see how the dollar amount you are having withheld compares to your projected total tax for 2001. Get Pub. 919 especially if you used the **Two-Earner/Two-Job Worksheet** on page 2 and your earnings exceed $150,000 (Single) or $200,000 (Married).

Recent name change? If your name on line 1 differs from that shown on your social security card, call 1-800-772-1213 for a new social security card.

Personal Allowances Worksheet (Keep for your records.)

A Enter "1" for **yourself** if no one else can claim you as a dependent . . . . **A** _____

B Enter "1" if:
- You are single and have only one job; or
- You are married, have only one job, and your spouse does not work; or
- Your wages from a second job or your spouse's wages (or the total of both) are $1,000 or less.

B _____

C Enter "1" for your **spouse**. But, you may choose to enter -0- if you are married and have either a working spouse or more than one job. (Entering -0- may help you avoid having too little tax withheld.) . . . . **C** _____

D Enter number of **dependents** (other than your spouse or yourself) you will claim on your tax return . . . . . . **D** _____

E Enter "1" if you will file as **head of household** on your tax return (see conditions under **Head of household** above) . **E** _____

F Enter "1" if you have at least $1,500 of **child or dependent care expenses** for which you plan to claim a credit . . **F** _____
(Note: Do **not** include child support payments. See **Pub. 503**, *Child and Dependent Care Expenses*, for details.)

G **Child Tax Credit** (including additional child tax credit):
- If your total income will be between $18,000 and $50,000 ($23,000 and $63,000 if married), enter "1" for each eligible child.
- If your total income will be between $50,000 and $80,000 ($63,000 and $115,000 if married), enter "1" if you have two eligible children, enter "2" if you have three or four eligible children, or enter "3" if you have five or more eligible children. **G** _____

H Add lines A through G and enter total here. (**Note:** *This may be different from the number of exemptions you claim on your tax return.*) ▶ **H** _____

For accuracy, complete all worksheets that apply.
- If you plan to **itemize or claim adjustments to income** and want to reduce your withholding, see the **Deductions and Adjustments Worksheet** on page 2.
- If you are **single**, have **more than one job** and your combined earnings from all jobs exceed $35,000, **or** if you are **married** and have a **working spouse or more than one job** and the combined earnings from all jobs exceed $60,000, see the **Two-Earner/Two-Job Worksheet** on page 2 to avoid having too little tax withheld.
- If **neither** of the above situations applies, **stop here** and enter the number from line H on line 5 of Form W-4 below.

- - - - - - - - - - - - - - - - **Cut here and give Form W-4 to your employer. Keep the top part for your records.** - - - - - - - - - - - - - - - -

Form **W-4** Department of the Treasury Internal Revenue Service	**Employee's Withholding Allowance Certificate** ▶ **For Privacy Act and Paperwork Reduction Act Notice, see page 2.**	OMB No. 1545-0010 **2001**

1 Type or print your first name and middle initial / Last name

2 Your social security number

Home address (number and street or rural route)

3 ☐ Single ☐ Married ☐ Married, but withhold at higher Single rate.
Note: *If married, but legally separated, or spouse is a nonresident alien, check the Single box.*

City or town, state, and ZIP code

4 If your last name differs from that on your social security card, check here. You must call 1-800-772-1213 for a new card. ▶ ☐

5 Total number of allowances you are claiming (from line **H** above **or** from the applicable worksheet on page 2) — **5** _____

6 Additional amount, if any, you want withheld from each paycheck . . . . **6** $ _____

7 I claim exemption from withholding for 2001, and I certify that I meet **both** of the following conditions for exemption:
- Last year I had a right to a refund of **all** Federal income tax withheld because I had **no** tax liability **and**
- This year I expect a refund of **all** Federal income tax withheld because I expect to have **no** tax liability.

If you meet both conditions, write "Exempt" here . . . . ▶ **7** _____

Under penalties of perjury, I certify that I am entitled to the number of withholding allowances claimed on this certificate, or I am entitled to claim exempt status.

Employee's signature
(Form is not valid unless you sign it.) ▶

Date ▶

8 Employer's name and address (Employer: Complete lines 8 and 10 only if sending to the IRS.)

9 Office code (optional)

10 Employer identification number

Cat. No. 10220Q

Deductions and Adjustments Worksheet

Note: *Use this worksheet only if you plan to itemize deductions, claim certain credits, or claim adjustments to income on your 2001 tax return.*

1   Enter an estimate of your 2001 itemized deductions. These include qualifying home mortgage interest, charitable contributions, state and local taxes, medical expenses in excess of 7.5% of your income, and miscellaneous deductions. (For 2001, you may have to reduce your itemized deductions if your income is over $132,950 ($66,475 if married filing separately). See **Worksheet 3** in Pub. 919 for details.) . . .   **1** $ _____

2   Enter: { $7,600 if married filing jointly or qualifying widow(er)
             $6,650 if head of household
             $4,550 if single
             $3,800 if married filing separately }   . . .   **2** $ _____

3   **Subtract** line 2 from line 1. If line 2 is greater than line 1, enter -0- . . .   **3** $ _____

4   Enter an estimate of your 2001 adjustments to income, including alimony, deductible IRA contributions, and student loan interest   **4** $ _____

5   **Add** lines 3 and 4 and enter the total (Include any amount for credits from **Worksheet 7** in Pub. 919.)   **5** $ _____

6   Enter an estimate of your 2001 nonwage income (such as dividends or interest) . . .   **6** $ _____

7   **Subtract** line 6 from line 5. Enter the result, but not less than -0- . . .   **7** $ _____

8   **Divide** the amount on line 7 by $3,000 and enter the result here. Drop any fraction . . .   **8**   _____

9   Enter the number from the **Personal Allowances Worksheet,** line H, page 1 . . .   **9**   _____

10   **Add** lines 8 and 9 and enter the total here. If you plan to use the **Two-Earner/Two-Job Worksheet,** also enter this total on line 1 below. Otherwise, **stop here** and enter this total on Form W-4, line 5, page 1 .   **10**   _____

Two-Earner/Two-Job Worksheet

Note: *Use this worksheet only if the instructions under line H on page 1 direct you here.*

1   Enter the number from line H, page 1 (or from line 10 above if you used the **Deductions and Adjustments Worksheet**)   **1**   _____

2   Find the number in **Table 1** below that applies to the **lowest** paying job and enter it here . . .   **2**   _____

3   If line 1 is **more than or equal to** line 2, subtract line 2 from line 1. Enter the result here (if zero, enter -0-) and on Form W-4, line 5, page 1. **Do not** use the rest of this worksheet . . .   **3**   _____

Note: *If line 1 is **less than** line 2, enter -0- on Form W-4, line 5, page 1. Complete lines 4–9 below to calculate the additional withholding amount necessary to avoid a year end tax bill.*

4   Enter the number from line 2 of this worksheet . . .   **4**   _____

5   Enter the number from line 1 of this worksheet . . .   **5**   _____

6   **Subtract** line 5 from line 4 . . .   **6**   _____

7   Find the amount in **Table 2** below that applies to the **highest** paying job and enter it here . . .   **7** $ _____

8   **Multiply** line 7 by line 6 and enter the result here. This is the additional annual withholding needed . .   **8** $ _____

9   Divide line 8 by the number of pay periods remaining in 2001. For example, divide by 26 if you are paid every two weeks and you complete this form in December 2000. Enter the result here and on Form W-4, line 6, page 1. This is the additional amount to be withheld from each paycheck . . .   **9** $ _____

Table 1: Two-Earner/Two-Job Worksheet

Married Filing Jointly				**All Others**			
If wages from **LOWEST** paying job are—	Enter on line 2 above	If wages from **LOWEST** paying job are—	Enter on line 2 above	If wages from **LOWEST** paying job are—	Enter on line 2 above	If wages from **LOWEST** paying job are—	Enter on line 2 above
$0 - $4,000	0	42,001 - 47,000	8	$0 - $6,000	0	65,001 - 80,000	8
4,001 - 8,000	1	47,001 - 55,000	9	6,001 - 12,000	1	80,001 - 105,000	9
8,001 - 14,000	2	55,001 - 65,000	10	12,001 - 17,000	2	105,001 and over	10
14,001 - 19,000	3	65,001 - 70,000	11	17,001 - 22,000	3		
19,001 - 25,000	4	70,001 - 90,000	12	22,001 - 28,000	4		
25,001 - 32,000	5	90,001 - 105,000	13	28,001 - 40,000	5		
32,001 - 38,000	6	105,001 - 115,000	14	40,001 - 50,000	6		
38,001 - 42,000	7	115,001 and over	15	50,001 - 65,000	7		

Table 2: Two-Earner/Two-Job Worksheet

Married Filing Jointly		**All Others**	
If wages from **HIGHEST** paying job are—	Enter on line 7 above	If wages from **HIGHEST** paying job are—	Enter on line 7 above
$0 - $50,000	$440	$0 - $30,000	$440
50,001 - 100,000	800	30,001 - 60,000	800
100,001 - 130,000	900	60,001 - 120,000	900
130,001 - 250,000	1,000	120,001 - 270,000	1,000
250,001 and over	1,100	270,001 and over	1,100

BOE-663 (FRONT) REV. 5 (10-00)
PUBLICATIONS ORDER

STATE OF CALIFORNIA
BOARD OF EQUALIZATION

Please enter the quantity of each publication you wish to order and send your completed order form to the State Board of Equalization, Supply Unit, 3920 West Capitol Avenue, West Sacramento, CA 95691 or FAX your order to (916) 372-6078.

NAME OF BUSINESS	FOR OFFICE USE ONLY	REQUEST ☐ New ☐ One Time ☐ Replacement
ATTENTION	RECEIVED BY	IS FOR ☐ Distribution Change
MAILING ADDRESS	DATE REQUEST RECEIVED	
CITY STATE ZIP	SHIPPED BY	
TELEPHONE NUMBER ( )	DATE MATERIAL SHIPPED	

PAMPHLETS *(No Charge)*

QTY.	NO.	TITLE
_____	1	Sales and Use Tax Law
_____	2	Uniform Local Sales & Use Tax Law and Transactions & Use Tax Law
_____	3	Use Fuel Tax Law
_____	4	Cigarette Tax Law
_____	5	Alcoholic Beverage Tax Law
_____	6	Motor Vehicle Fuel License Tax Law
_____	7	Tax on Insurers Law
_____	8	Private Railroad Car Tax Law
_____	9	Tax Tips for Construction and Building Contractors
_____	10	Energy Resources Surcharge Law
_____	11	Energy Resources Surcharge Regulations
_____	12	Use Fuel Tax for Vendors and Users
_____	14	Motor Vehicle Fuel License Tax Regulations
_____	15	Cigarette Tax Regulations
_____	16	Alcoholic Beverage Tax Regulations and Instructions
_____	17	Appeals Procedures: Sales & Use Taxes and Special Taxes
_____	18	Tax Tips for Nonprofit Organizations
_____	19	Diesel Fuel Tax Law
_____	20	California Emergency Telephone Users Surcharge Law
_____	21	State Board of Equalization
_____	22	Tax Tips for the Dining and Beverage Industry
_____	22K	Tax Tips for the Dining and Beverage Industry (Korean)
_____	22S	Tax Tips for the Dining and Beverage Industry (Spanish)
_____	24	Tax Tips for Liquor Stores
_____	24K	Tax Tips for Liquor Stores (Korean)
_____	25	Tax Tips for Auto Repair Garages and Service Stations
_____	25S	Tax Tips for Auto Repair Garages and Service Stations (Spanish)
_____	26	Tax Information Bulletin Index
_____	27	Tax Tips for Drug Stores
_____	28	Tax Information for City and County Officials Sales and Use Tax
_____	29	California Property Tax: An Overview
_____	30	Residential Property Assessment Appeals
_____	31	Tax Tips for Grocery Stores

QTY.	NO.	TITLE
_____	31C	Tax Tips for Grocery Stores (Chinese)
_____	31K	Tax Tips for Grocery Stores (Korean)
_____	31S	Tax Tips for Grocery Stores (Spanish)
_____	31V	Tax Tips for Grocery Stores (Vietnamese)
_____	32	Tax Tips for Purchasers from Mexico
_____	32S	Tax Tips for Purchasers from Mexico (Spanish)
_____	34	Tax Tips for Motor Vehicle Dealers (New & Used)
_____	35	Tax Tips for Interior Designers and Decorators
_____	36	Tax Tips for Veterinarians
_____	37	Tax Tips for the Graphic Arts Industry
_____	38	Tax Tips for Advertising Agencies
_____	39	Emergency Telephone Users Surcharge Regulations
_____	40	Tax Tips for the Watercraft Industry
_____	41	Taxes and Fees Administered by Board of Equalization
_____	42	Resale Certificate Tips
_____	43	Timber Yield Tax Law
_____	44	Tax Tips for District Taxes
_____	45	Tax Tips for Hospitals
_____	46	Tax Tips for Leasing of Tangible Personal Property in California
_____	47	Tax Tips for Mobilehomes and Factory-Built Housing
_____	48	Property Tax Exemptions for Religious Organizations
_____	49	California Underground Storage Tank Maintenance Fee Law
_____	50	Guide to the International Fuel Tax Agreement
_____	50S	Guide to the International Fuel Tax Agreement (Spanish)
_____	50-A	Introduction to the International Fuel Tax Agreement
_____	50-A-S	Introduction to the International Fuel Tax Agreement (Spanish)
_____	51	Guide to Board of Equalization Services
_____	51C	Guide to Board of Equalization Services (Chinese)
_____	51K	Guide to Board of Equalization Services (Korean)
_____	51S	Guide to Board of Equalization Services (Spanish)
_____	51V	Guide to Board of Equalization Services (Vietnamese)
_____	52	Vehicles and Vessels: How to Request an Exemption from California Use Tax

QTY.	NO.	TITLE		QTY.	NO.	TITLE
_____	53	Guide to the Managed Audit Program		_____	86	Timber Yield Tax (brochure)
_____	54	Collections		_____	87	Guide to the Timber Yield Tax
_____	58-A	How to Inspect & Correct Your Records		_____	88	Underground Storage Tank Fee
_____	59	Local Motor Vehicle Fuel Taxation Law		_____	90	Environmental Fee
_____	60	Hazardous Substances Tax Law		_____	91	Tire Recycling Fee
_____	61	Sales and Use Taxes: Exemptions and Exclusions		_____	92	Alcoholic Beverage Tax
_____	62	Tax Tips for Locksmiths		_____	93	Cigarette & Tobacco Products Tax
_____	64	Tax Tips for Jewelry Stores		_____	94	Occupational Lead Poisoning Prevention Fee
_____	66	Tax Tips for Retail Feed and Farm Supply Stores		_____	100	Shipping and Delivery Charges
_____	68	Tax Tips for Photographers, Photo Finishers and Film Processing Laboratories		_____	101	Sales Delivered Outside California
_____	69	California Integrated Waste Management Fee Law		_____	102	Sales to the U.S. Government
_____	70	The California Taxpayers' Bill of Rights		_____	103	Sales for Resale
_____	70C	The California Taxpayers' Bill of Rights (Chinese)		_____	104	Sales to Residents of Other Countries
_____	70K	The California Taxpayers' Bill of Rights (Korean)		_____	105	District Taxes and Delivered Sales
_____	70S	The California Taxpayers' Bill of Rights (Spanish)		_____	106	Gift Wrapping Charges
_____	70V	The California Taxpayers' Bill of Rights (Vietnamese)		_____	107	Do You Need a California Seller's Permit?
_____	71	California City and County Sales and Use Tax Rates		_____	108	When Is Labor Taxable?
_____	72	Summary of Statutory & Constitutional Authorities		_____	109	Are Your Internet Sales Taxable?
_____	73	Your California Seller's Permit		_____	110	California Use Tax Basics
_____	73C	Your California Seller's Permit (Chinese)		_____	111	Swap Meets and Flea Markets
_____	73K	Your California Seller's Permit (Korean)		_____	112	Purchases From Out-of-State Vendors
_____	73S	Your California Seller's Permit (Spanish)		_____	113	Coupons and Sales Tax
_____	73V	Your California Seller's Permit (Vietnamese)		_____	115	Applying Sales Tax to Tips
_____	74	Closing Out Your Seller's Permit		_____	Other	_____
_____	74S	Closing Out Your Seller's Permit (Spanish)				_____
_____	75	Interest and Penalty Payments				_____
_____	76	Audits				_____
_____	76K	Audits (Korean)				_____
_____	76S	Audits (Spanish)				_____
_____	78	Certification Program for Property Tax Appraisers				_____
_____	79	Documented Vessels & California Tax				_____
_____	79A	Aircraft and California Tax				_____
_____	79B	California Individual Use Tax				_____
_____	80	Electronic Funds Transfer Program				
_____	80A	EFT Program ACH Credit Information				
_____	80B	ACH Debit Information				
_____	81	Franchise and Personal Income Tax Appeals				
_____	82	Prepaid Sales Tax on Sales of Fuel				
_____	83	Tire Recycling Fee Law				
_____	84	Use Fuel Permit Requirements				

MISCELLANEOUS (No Charge)

_____ Annual Calendar of Board Meetings

_____ Annual Report of the State Board of Equalization

_____ State of California Sales Tax Reimbursement Schedules

_____ Tax Information Bulletin (published quarterly)
Issue (mo./year) _____

_____ Other _____

BOE-663-D (FRONT) REV. 5 (4-00)
REGULATIONS ORDER

Please enter the quantity of each publication you wish to order and send your completed order form to the State Board of Equalization, Supply Unit, 3920 West Capitol Avenue, West Sacramento, CA 95691 or FAX your order to (916) 372-6078.

NAME OF BUSINESS	FOR OFFICE USE ONLY	REQUEST ☐ New ☐ One Time
		☐ Replacement
ATTENTION	RECEIVED BY	IS FOR ☐ Distribution Change
MAILING ADDRESS	DATE REQUEST RECEIVED	
CITY STATE ZIP	SHIPPED BY	
TELEPHONE NUMBER ( )	DATE MATERIAL SHIPPED	

SALES AND USE TAX REGULATIONS *(No Charge)*

QTY.	NO.	TITLE
	1500.	Foreword

SERVICE ENTERPRISES

QTY.	NO.	TITLE
	1501.	Service Enterprises Generally
	1501.1.	Research and Development Contracts
	1502.	Computers, Programs, and Data Processing
	1502.1.	Word Processing
	1503.	Hospitals, Institutions and Homes for the Care of Persons
	1504.	Mailing Lists and Services
	1505.	Morticians
	1506.	Miscellaneous Service Enterprises

CONTRACTORS AND SUBCONTRACTORS

QTY.	NO.	TITLE
	1521.	Construction Contractors
	1521.4.	Factory-Built Housing

MANUFACTURERS, PRODUCERS, PROCESSORS

QTY.	NO.	TITLE
	1524.	Manufacturers of Personal Property
	1525.	Property Used in Manufacturing
	1525.1.	Manufacturing Aids
	1525.2.	Manufacturing Equipment
	1525.3.	Manufacturing Equipment — Leases of Tangible Personal Property
	1525.5.	Manufacturing By-Products and Joint-Products
	1526.	Producing, Fabricating and Processing Property Furnished By Consumers – General Rules
	1527.	Sound Recording
	1528.	Photographers, Photostat Producers, Photo Finishers and X-Ray Laboratories
	1529.	Motion Pictures
	1530.	Foundries
	1531.	Fur Dressers and Dyers
	1532.	Teleproduction or Other Postproduction Service Equipment

GRAPHIC ARTS AND RELATED ENTERPRISES

QTY.	NO.	TITLE
	1540.	Advertising Agencies, Commercial Artists and Designers
	1541.	Printing and Related Arts
	1541.5.	Printed Sales Messages
	1543.	Publishers

INSTALLERS, REPAIRERS, RECONDITIONERS

QTY.	NO.	TITLE
	1546.	Installing, Repairing, Reconditioning in General
	1548.	Retreading and Recapping Tires
	1549.	Fur Repairers, Alterers and Remodelers
	1550.	Reupholsterers
	1551.	Repainting and Refinishing
	1553.	Miscellaneous Repair Operations

SPECIFIC BUSINESSES ENGAGED IN RETAILING

QTY.	NO.	TITLE
	1565.	Auctioneers
	1566.	Automobile Dealers and Salesmen
	1567.	Banks and Insurance Companies
	1568.	Beer, Wine, and Liquor Dealers
	1569.	Consignees and Lienors of Tangible Personal Property for Sale
	1570.	Charitable Organizations
	1571.	Florists
	1572.	Memorial Dealers
	1573.	Court Ordered Sales, Foreclosures and Repossessions
	1574.	Vending Machine Operators

SPECIFIC KINDS OF PROPERTY AND EXEMPTIONS GENERALLY

QTY.	NO.	TITLE
	1583.	Modular Systems Furniture
	1584.	Membership Fees
	1585.	Cellular Telephones, Pagers, and other Wireless Telecommunication Devices
	1586.	Works of Art and Museum Pieces for Public Display
	1587.	Animal Life, Feed, Drugs and Medicines
	1588.	Seeds, Plants and Fertilizer
	1589.	Containers and Labels
	1590.	Newspapers and Periodicals
	1591.	Medicines and Medical Supplies, Devices and Appliances
	1591.1	Medical Devices, Appliances and Supplies
	1591.2	Wheelchairs, Crutches, Canes, and Walkers
	1591.3	Vehicles for Physically Handicapped Persons
	1591.4	Medical Oxygen Delivery Systems
	1592.	Eyeglasses and Other Ophthalmic Materials
	1593.	Aircraft
	1594.	Watercraft

QTY.	NO.	TITLE
	1595.	Occasional Sales – Sale of a Business – Business Reorganization
	1596.	Buildings and Other Property Affixed to Realty
	1597.	Property Transferred or Sold by Certain Nonprofit Organizations
	1598.	Motor Vehicle and Aircraft Fuels
	1599.	Coins and Bullion

ARTICLE 8. FOOD PRODUCTS

	1602.	Food Products
	1602.5.	Reporting Methods for Grocers
	1603.	Taxable Sales of Food Products

SPECIAL PROVISIONS AFFECTING VEHICLES, VESSELS AND AIRCRAFT

	1610.	Vehicles, Vessels, and Aircraft
	1610.2.	Mobilehomes and Commercial Coaches

MATTERS INVOLVING THE FEDERAL GOVERNMENT

	1614.	Sales to the United States and Its Instrumentalities
	1616.	Federal Areas
	1617.	Federal Taxes
	1618.	United States Government Supply Contracts
	1619.	Foreign Consuls

INTERSTATE AND FOREIGN COMMERCE

	1620.	Interstate and Foreign Commerce
	1620.2	Beverages Sold or Served by Carriers
	1621.	Sales to Common Carriers

MATTERS INVOLVING TRANSPORTATION OF PROPERTY

	1628.	Transportation Charges
	1629.	Goods Damaged in Transit
	1630.	Packers, Loaders, and Shippers
	1632.	C.O.D. Fees

CREDIT TRANSACTIONS

	1641.	Credit Sales and Repossessions
	1642.	Bad Debts
	1643.	Debit Card Fees

EXCHANGES, RETURNS, DEFECTS

	1654.	Barter, Exchange, "Trade-ins" and Foreign Currency Transaction
	1655.	Returns, Defects and Replacements

LEASES OF TANGIBLE PERSONAL PROPERTY

	1660.	Leases of Tangible Personal Property – In General
	1661.	Leases of Mobile Transportation Equipment

RESALE CERTIFICATES; DEMONSTRATION; GIFTS AND PROMOTIONS

	1667.	Exemption Certificates
	1668.	Resale Certificates
	1669.	Demonstration, Display and Use of Property Held for Resale – General
	1669.5.	Demonstration, Display and Use of Property Held for Resale – Vehicles

QTY.	NO.	TITLE
	1670.	Gifts, Marketing Aids, Premiums and Prizes
	1671.	Trading Stamps and Related Promotional Plans

PAYMENT AND COLLECTION OF USE TAX

	1684.	Collection of Use Tax by Retailers
	1685.	Payment of Tax by Purchasers
	1686.	Receipts for Tax Paid to Retailers
	1687.	Information Returns

ADMINISTRATION – MISCELLANEOUS

	1698.	Records
	1699.	Permits
	1699.5.	Direct Payment Permits
	1699.6.	Use Tax Direct Payment Permits
	1700.	Reimbursement for Sales Tax
	1701.	"Tax-Paid Purchases Resold"
	1702.	Successor's Liability
	1702.5.	Responsible Person Liability
	1703.	Interest and Penalties
	1704.	Whole Dollar Reporting - Computations on Returns or Other Documents
	1705.	Relief from Liability
	1705.1.	Innocent Spouse Relief

BRADLEY-BURNS UNIFORM LOCAL SALES AND USE TAX

	1802.	Place of Sale for Purposes of Bradley-Burns Uniform Local Sales and Use Taxes
	1803.	Application of Tax
	1805.	Aircraft Common Carriers
	1806.	Construction Contractors

TRANSACTIONS (SALES) AND USE TAXES

	1821.	Foreword
	1822.	Place of Sale for Purposes of Transactions (Sales) and Use Taxes
	1823.	Application of Transactions (Sales) Tax and Use Tax
	1823.5.	Place of Delivery of Certain Vehicles, Aircraft and Undocumented Vessels
	1825.	Aircraft Common Carriers
	1826.	Construction Contractors
	1827.	Collection of Use Tax by Retailers

HEARING PROCEDURES

	5010-5095 -	Rules of Practice
		(offered as a set only)
	7001-7011 -	Contribution Disclosure
		(offered as a set only)
	Other	_____
		_____
		_____
		_____
		_____
		_____
		_____
		_____

BOE-400-MIP (FRONT) REV. 15 (9-00)

**APPLICATION FOR SELLER'S PERMIT AND REGISTRATION
AS A RETAILER (INDIVIDUALS/PARTNERSHIPS)**

STATE OF CALIFORNIA
BOARD OF EQUALIZATION

Use additional sheet(s) to include information for more than two partners

SECTION I: OWNERSHIP INFORMATION

FOR BOARD USE ONLY			
TAX	IND	OFFICE	NUMBER

1. PLEASE CHECK TYPE OF OWNERSHIP

☐ Sole Owner   ☐ Husband/Wife Co-ownership

☐ General Partnership   ☐ Limited Partnership
Provide documents filed with Secretary of State.

☐ Limited Liability Partnership *(registered to practice law, accounting or architecture) Provide documents filed with Secretary of State.*

Enter Federal Employer Identification Number (FEIN), if any

SR

BUSINESS CODE

AREA CODE

APPLICATION PROCESSED BY

VERIFICATION:
☐ SSN ☐ DL ☐ Other

OWNER OR PARTNER

2. FULL NAME *(first, middle, last)*

3. SOCIAL SECURITY NUMBER *(attach verification)*

4. DRIVER'S LICENSE NUMBER *(attach verification)*

5. RESIDENCE ADDRESS *(street, city, state, zip code)*

6. RESIDENCE TELEPHONE NUMBER
(   )

7. NAME, ADDRESS & TELEPHONE NUMBER OF A PERSONAL REFERENCE

8. **PARTNERSHIP NAME** *(complete if business name [DBA] is different than name of partnership.)*

9. ☐ Check here if you have included a copy of your partnership agreement.

CO-OWNER OR PARTNER

10. FULL NAME *(first, middle, last)*

11. SOCIAL SECURITY NUMBER *(attach verification)*

12. DRIVER'S LICENSE NUMBER *(attach verification)*

13. RESIDENCE ADDRESS *(street, city, state, zip code)*

14. RESIDENCE TELEPHONE NUMBER
(   )

15. NAME, ADDRESS & TELEPHONE NUMBER OF A PERSONAL REFERENCE

SECTION II: BUSINESS INFORMATION

16. BUSINESS NAME [DBA] *(if any)*

17. BUSINESS ADDRESS *(street, city, state, zip code) [do not list P.O. Box or mailing service]*

18. BUSINESS TELEPHONE NUMBER
(   )

19. MAILING ADDRESS *(street, city, state, zip code) [if different from business address]*

20. DATE YOU WILL BEGIN SALES *(month, day & year)*

21. TYPE OF ITEMS SOLD

22. NUMBER OF SELLING LOCATIONS *(if 2 or more, attach list of all locations)*

23. TYPE OF BUSINESS *(check one)*

☐ Retail ☐ Wholesale ☐ Mfg. ☐ Repair ☐ Service ☐ Construction Contractor

CHECK ONE
☐ Full Time ☐ Part Time

24. OWNERSHIP CHANGES

Are you buying an existing business?   ☐ Yes ☐ No If yes, complete items 25 through 29 below.

Are you changing from one type of business organization to another (for example, from a sole owner to a general partnership or from a general partnership to a limited partnership, etc.)? ☐ Yes ☐ No If yes, complete items 27 and 28 below.

Other: _____

25. PURCHASE PRICE
$

26. VALUE OF FIXTURES & EQUIPMENT
$

27. FORMER OWNER'S NAME

28. SELLER'S PERMIT ACCOUNT NUMBER

29. IF AN ESCROW COMPANY IS REQUESTING A TAX CLEARANCE ON YOUR BEHALF, PLEASE LIST THEIR NAME, ADDRESS, TELEPHONE NUMBER AND THE ESCROW NUMBER

30. DO YOU MAKE INTERNET SALES?
☐ Yes ☐ No If yes, answer 31.

31. WEBSITE ADDRESS

32. IF ALCOHOLIC BEVERAGES ARE SOLD, PLEASE LIST YOUR ALCOHOLIC BEVERAGE CONTROL LICENSE NO. AND TYPE

33. NAME, ADDRESS & TELEPHONE NUMBER OF ACCOUNTANT/BOOKKEEPER

34. NAME, ADDRESS & TELEPHONE NUMBER OF BUSINESS LANDLORD

35. NAME & LOCATION OF BANK OR OTHER FINANCIAL INSTITUTION (Note whether business or personal)	CHECKING ACCOUNT NUMBER(S)
	SAVINGS ACCOUNT NUMBER(S)
36. NAMES & ADDRESSES OF MAJOR SUPPLIERS	PRODUCTS PURCHASED

SECTION III: SALES AND EMPLOYER INFORMATION

37. PROJECTED MONTHLY SALES (if unknown, enter an estimated amount)

Total gross sales $ Taxable sales $

38. INFORMATION CONCERNING EMPLOYMENT DEVELOPMENT DEPARTMENT (EDD)

Are you registered with EDD? .... ☐ Yes ☐ No

If no, will your payroll exceed $100 per quarter? .... ☐ Yes ☐ No

If yes, you must make application with EDD.

Number of employees   (See pamphlet DE 44, California Employer's Guide)

I have already received pamphlet DE 44, California Employer's Guide. .... ☐ Yes ☐ No

CERTIFICATION

The statements contained herein are hereby certified to be correct to the best knowledge and belief of the undersigned who is duly authorized to sign this application. (All owners' and partners' signatures are required.)

NAME (typed or printed)	TITLE	
SIGNATURE		DATE
NAME (typed or printed)	TITLE	
SIGNATURE		DATE

FOR BOARD USE ONLY
Furnished to Taxpayer

REPORTING BASIS	FORMS	PUBLICATIONS
SECURITY REVIEW	☐ BOE-8 ☐ BOE-400-Y	☐ PUB 73 ☐ PUB DE 44
☐ BOE-598-LZ $	☐ BOE-467 ☐ BOE-519	
☐ BOE-1009	☐ BOE-1241-D	
BY		
APPROVED BY	REGULATIONS	RETURNS
REMOTE INPUT DATE	☐ REG. 1668 ☐ REG. 1698	
	☐ REG. 1700	
BY		
☐ Permit Issued Date		

258

Section I: Ownership Information

Items 1-15: Type of Ownership and Owner Information

All applicants. You must provide the information requested for each owner or partner (attach additional sheets if necessary).

All partnerships. Partnerships should provide a copy of their written partnership agreement, if one exists. If you file your agreement with us *at the time you apply for a permit* and your agreement specifies that all business assets are held *in the name of the partnership*, the law requires the Board to attempt to collect any delinquent tax liability from the partnership assets before it attempts to collect from the partners' personal assets.

You should notify us immediately if you add or drop partners (see pg. 2).

Items 3,4,11,12: Driver's License/Social Security Number

You must provide copies of your Social Security card and driver's license or California Identification Card. If your Social Security card is not readily available, you can attach copies of other documents that show your Social Security number, such as employer paycheck stubs, preprinted income tax labels, or withholding statements (W-2 forms). This information is kept in strictist confidence.

Section II: Business Information

Item 21: Types of Items Sold

Be specific. For example, for a beauty supply business, you would write "beauty supplies," rather than "general merchandise." If you use a broad description, such as "market-driven products," you should list examples of the types of products sold — for example, sports equipment, household appliances, or garden supplies.

Item 24: Ownership Changes

If you are purchasing an existing business, we need to know the previous owner's name and seller's permit number. To make sure you won't have to pay any unpaid taxes owed by the previous owner, you should write to us and request a tax clearance before you buy.

If you are changing from one type of business organization to another (for example, from a sole owner to a general partnership or from a general partnership to a limited partnership), provide the previous owner's name and seller's permit number.

Section III: Sales and Employer Information

✐ Certification

This section *must* be signed by the owner or, in the case of a partnership or co-ownership, by each partner or co-owner.

Where Can I Get Help?

No doubt you will have questions about how the Sales and Use Tax Law applies to your business operations. For assistance, you may take advantage of the resources listed below.

INFORMATION CENTER

1-800-400-7115

FOR TDD ASSISTANCE
From TDD phones: 1-800-735-2929
From voice phones: 1-800-735-2922

Customer service representatives are available from 8 a.m. through 5 p.m., Monday-Friday, excluding State holidays.

Fax-Back Service. To order fax copies of selected forms and notices, call 1-800-400-7115 and choose the fax-back option. You can call at any time for this service.

Translator Services. We can provide bilingual services for persons who need assistance in a language other than English.

WRITTEN TAX ADVICE

It is best to get tax advice from the Board in writing. You may be relieved of tax, penalty, or interest charges if we determine you did not correctly report tax because you reasonably relied on our written advice regarding a transaction.

For this relief to apply, your request for advice must be in writing, identify the taxpayer to whom the advice applies, and fully describe the facts and circumstances of the transaction.

Send your request for written advice to: State Board of Equalization; Public Information and Administration Section, MIC:44; P.O. Box 942879, Sacramento, CA 94279-0044.

CLASSES

You may enroll in a basic sales and use tax class offered by some local Board offices. You should call ahead to find out when your local office conducts classes for beginning sellers.

INTERNET
www.boe.ca.gov

Our website includes lots of useful information. For example, you can find out what the tax rate is in a particular county, or you can download numerous publications — such as laws, regulations, pamphlets, and policy manuals — that will help you understand how the law applies to your business. You can also verify sellers' permit numbers on-line, read about upcoming Taxpayers' Bill of Rights hearings, and obtain information on Board field office addresses and telephone numbers.

Another good resource — especially for starting businesses — is the California Tax Information Center at www.taxes.ca.gov.

TAXPAYERS' RIGHTS ADVOCATE OFFICE

If you would like to know more about your rights as a taxpayer or if you are unable to resolve a disagreement with the Board, please contact the Taxpayers' Rights Advocate office for help. Call 916-324-2798 (or toll-free, 1-888-324-2798). Their fax number is 916-323-3319.

If you prefer, you can write to them at the following address: Taxpayers' Rights Advocate, MIC:70; State Board of Equalization; PO Box 942879; Sacramento, CA 94279-0070.

To request a copy of publication 70, *The California Taxpayers' Bill of Rights*, call the Information Center or visit our Internet site.

FIELD OFFICES

See page 4.

Application for Seller's Permit ■ Individuals/Partnerships (9-00)

Form 8300
(Rev. August 1997)

Department of the Treasury
Internal Revenue Service

Report of Cash Payments Over $10,000 Received in a Trade or Business

▶ See instructions for definition of cash.
▶ Use this form for transactions occurring after July 31, 1997.
Please type or print.

OMB No. 1545-0892

1 Check appropriate box(es) if: **a** ☐ Amends prior report; **b** ☐ Suspicious transaction.

Part I   Identity of Individual From Whom the Cash Was Received

2 If more than one individual is involved, check here and see instructions . . . . ▶ ☐

3 Last name	**4** First name	**5** M.I.	**6** Taxpayer identification number

7 Address (number, street, and apt. or suite no.)   **8** Date of birth ▶ M M D D Y Y Y Y (see instructions)

9 City	**10** State	**11** ZIP code	**12** Country (if not U.S.)	**13** Occupation, profession, or business

14 Document used to verify identity: **a** Describe identification ▶ ....
b Issued by   **c** Number

Part II   Person on Whose Behalf This Transaction Was Conducted

15 If this transaction was conducted on behalf of more than one person, check here and see instructions . . . . . ▶ ☐

16 Individual's last name or Organization's name	**17** First name	**18** M.I.	**19** Taxpayer identification number

20 Doing business as (DBA) name (see instructions)   Employer identification number

21 Address (number, street, and apt. or suite no.)   **22** Occupation, profession, or business

23 City	**24** State	**25** ZIP code	**26** Country (if not U.S.)

27 Alien identification: **a** Describe identification ▶ ....
b Issued by   **c** Number

Part III   Description of Transaction and Method of Payment

28 Date cash received M M D D Y Y Y Y	**29** Total cash received $ .00	**30** If cash was received in more than one payment, check here . . . ▶ ☐	**31** Total price if different from item 29 $ .00

32 Amount of cash received (in U.S. dollar equivalent) (must equal item 29) (see instructions):

a U.S. currency $ _____ .00 (Amount in $100 bills or higher $ _____ .00)
b Foreign currency $ _____ .00 (Country ▶ _____)
c Cashier's check(s) $ _____ .00   Issuer's name(s) and serial number(s) of the monetary instrument(s) ▶ ....
d Money order(s) $ _____ .00   ....
e Bank draft(s) $ _____ .00   ....
f Traveler's check(s) $ _____ .00

33 Type of transaction
a ☐ Personal property purchased
b ☐ Real property purchased
c ☐ Personal services provided
d ☐ Business services provided
e ☐ Intangible property purchased
f ☐ Debt obligations paid
g ☐ Exchange of cash
h ☐ Escrow or trust funds
i ☐ Bail bond
j ☐ Other (specify) ▶

34 Specific description of property or service shown in 33. (Give serial or registration number, address, docket number, etc.) ▶ ....
....
....

Part IV   Business That Received Cash

35 Name of business that received cash	**36** Employer identification number

37 Address (number, street, and apt. or suite no.)   Social security number

38 City	**39** State	**40** ZIP code	**41** Nature of your business

42 Under penalties of perjury, I declare that to the best of my knowledge the information I have furnished above is true, correct, and complete.

Signature of authorized official   Title of authorized official

43 Date of signature M M D D Y Y Y Y	**44** Type or print name of contact person	**45** Contact telephone number ( )

For Paperwork Reduction Act Notice, see page 4.   Cat. No. 62133S   Form **8300** (Rev. 8-97)

Multiple Parties

(Complete applicable parts below if box 2 or 15 on page 1 is checked)

Part I **Continued—Complete if box 2 on page 1 is checked**

3 Last name	**4** First name	**5** M.I.	**6** Taxpayer identification number

7 Address (number, street, and apt. or suite no.)

8 Date of birth . . ▶ M M D D Y Y Y Y
(see instructions)

9 City	**10** State	**11** ZIP code	**12** Country (if not U.S.)	**13** Occupation, profession, or business

14 Document used to verify identity: **a** Describe identification ▶ _____
b Issued by _____ **c** Number

3 Last name	**4** First name	**5** M.I.	**6** Taxpayer identification number

7 Address (number, street, and apt. or suite no.)

8 Date of birth . . ▶ M M D D Y Y Y Y
(see instructions)

9 City	**10** State	**11** ZIP code	**12** Country (if not U.S.)	**13** Occupation, profession, or business

14 Document used to verify identity: **a** Describe identification ▶ _____
b Issued by _____ **c** Number

Part II **Continued—Complete if box 15 on page 1 is checked**

16 Individual's last name or Organization's name	**17** First name	**18** M.I.	**19** Taxpayer identification number

20 Doing business as (DBA) name (see instructions)

Employer identification number

21 Address (number, street, and apt. or suite no.)	**22** Occupation, profession, or business

23 City	**24** State	**25** ZIP code	**26** Country (if not U.S.)

27 Alien identification: **a** Describe identification ▶ _____
b Issued by _____ **c** Number

16 Individual's last name or Organization's name	**17** First name	**18** M.I.	**19** Taxpayer identification number

20 Doing business as (DBA) name (see instructions)

Employer identification number

21 Address (number, street, and apt. or suite no.)	**22** Occupation, profession, or business

23 City	**24** State	**25** ZIP code	**26** Country (if not U.S.)

27 Alien identification: **a** Describe identification ▶ _____
b Issued by _____ **c** Number

Item You Should Note

Clerks of Federal or State courts must now file Form 8300 if more than $10,000 in cash is received as bail for an individual(s) charged with certain criminal offenses. For these purposes, a clerk includes the clerk's office or any other office, department, division, branch, or unit of the court that is authorized to receive bail. If a person receives bail on behalf of a clerk, the clerk is treated as receiving the bail.

If multiple payments are made in cash to satisfy bail and the initial payment does not exceed $10,000, the initial payment and subsequent payments must be aggregated and the information return must be filed by the 15th day after receipt of the payment that causes the aggregate amount to exceed $10,000 in cash. In such cases, the reporting requirement can be satisfied either by sending a single written statement with an aggregate amount listed or by furnishing a copy of each Form 8300 relating to that payer. Payments made to satisfy separate bail requirements are not required to be aggregated. See Treasury Regulations section 1.6050I-2.

Casinos must file Form 8300 for nongaming activities (restaurants, shops, etc.).

General Instructions

Who must file.—Each person engaged in a trade or business who, in the course of that trade or business, receives more than $10,000 in cash in one transaction or in two or more related transactions, must file Form 8300. Any transactions conducted between a payer (or its agent) and the recipient in a 24-hour period are related transactions. Transactions are considered related even if they occur over a period of more than 24 hours if the recipient knows, or has reason to know, that each transaction is one of a series of connected transactions.

Keep a copy of each Form 8300 for 5 years from the date you file it.

Voluntary use of Form 8300.—Form 8300 may be filed voluntarily for any suspicious transaction (see **Definitions**), even if the total amount does not exceed $10,000.

Exceptions.—Cash is not required to be reported if it is received:

● By a financial institution required to file **Form 4789,** Currency Transaction Report.

● By a casino required to file (or exempt from filing) **Form 8362,** Currency Transaction Report by Casinos, if the cash is received as part of its gaming business.

● By an agent who receives the cash from a principal, if the agent uses all of the cash within 15 days in a second transaction that is reportable on Form 8300 or on Form 4789, and discloses all the information necessary to complete Part II of Form 8300 or Form 4789 to the recipient of the cash in the second transaction.

● In a transaction occurring entirely outside the United States. See **Pub. 1544,** Reporting Cash Payments Over $10,000 (Received in a Trade or Business),

regarding transactions occurring in Puerto Rico, the Virgin Islands, and territories and possessions of the United States.

● In a transaction that is not in the course of a person's trade or business.

When to file.—File Form 8300 by the 15th day after the date the cash was received. If that date falls on a Saturday, Sunday, or legal holiday, file the form on the next business day.

Where to file.—File the form with the Internal Revenue Service, Detroit Computing Center, P.O. Box 32621, Detroit, MI 48232, or hand carry it to your local IRS office.

Statement to be provided.—You must give a written statement to each person named on a required Form 8300 on or before January 31 of the year following the calendar year in which the cash is received. The statement must show the name, telephone number, and address of the information contact for the business, the aggregate amount of reportable cash received, and that the information was furnished to the IRS. Keep a copy of the statement for your records.

Multiple payments.—If you receive more than one cash payment for a single transaction or for related transactions, you must report the multiple payments any time you receive a total amount that exceeds $10,000 within any 12-month period. Submit the report within 15 days of the date you receive the payment that causes the total amount to exceed $10,000. If more than one report is required within 15 days, you may file a combined report. File the combined report no later than the date the earliest report, if filed separately, would have to be filed.

Taxpayer identification number (TIN).—You must furnish the correct TIN of the person or persons from whom you receive the cash and, if applicable, the person or persons on whose behalf the transaction is being conducted. **You may be subject to penalties for an incorrect or missing TIN.**

The TIN for an individual (including a sole proprietorship) is the individual's social security number (SSN). For certain resident aliens who are not eligible to get an SSN and nonresident aliens who are required to file tax returns, it is an IRS Individual Taxpayer Identification Number (ITIN). For other persons, including corporations, partnerships, and estates, it is the employer identification number.

If you have requested but are not able to get a TIN for one or more of the parties to a transaction within 15 days following the transaction, file the report and attach a statement explaining why the TIN is not included.

Exception: *You are not required to provide the TIN of a person who is a nonresident alien individual or a foreign organization* **if** *that person does not have income effectively connected with the conduct of a U.S. trade or business* **and** *does not have an office or place of business, or fiscal or paying agent, in the United States. See Pub. 1544 for more information.*

Penalties.—You may be subject to penalties if you fail to file a correct and complete Form 8300 on time and you cannot show that the failure was due to reasonable cause. You may also be subject to penalties if you fail to furnish timely a correct and complete statement to each person named in a required report. A minimum penalty of $25,000 may be imposed if the failure is due to an intentional disregard of the cash reporting requirements.

Penalties may also be imposed for causing, or attempting to cause, a trade or business to fail to file a required report; for causing, or attempting to cause, a trade or business to file a required report containing a material omission or misstatement of fact; or for structuring, or attempting to structure, transactions to avoid the reporting requirements. These violations may also be subject to criminal prosecution which, upon conviction, may result in imprisonment of up to 5 years or fines of up to $250,000 for individuals and $500,000 for corporations or both.

Definitions

Cash.—The term "cash" means the following:

● U.S. and foreign coin and currency received in any transaction.

● A cashier's check, money order, bank draft, or traveler's check having a face amount of $10,000 or less that is received in a **designated reporting transaction** (defined below), or that is received in any transaction in which the recipient knows that the instrument is being used in an attempt to avoid the reporting of the transaction under section 6050I.

Note: *Cash does not include a check drawn on the payer's own account, such as a personal check, regardless of the amount.*

Designated reporting transaction.—A retail sale (or the receipt of funds by a broker or other intermediary in connection with a retail sale) of a consumer durable, a collectible, or a travel or entertainment activity.

*Retail sale.—*Any sale (whether or not the sale is for resale or for any other purpose) made in the course of a trade or business if that trade or business principally consists of making sales to ultimate consumers.

*Consumer durable.—*An item of tangible personal property of a type that, under ordinary usage, can reasonably be expected to remain useful for at least 1 year, and that has a sales price of more than $10,000.

*Collectible.—*Any work of art, rug, antique, metal, gem, stamp, coin, etc.

*Travel or entertainment activity.—*An item of travel or entertainment that pertains to a single trip or event if the combined sales price of the item and all other items relating to the same trip or event that are sold in the same transaction (or related transactions) exceeds $10,000.

*Exceptions.—*A cashier's check, money order, bank draft, or traveler's check is not considered received in a designated reporting transaction if it constitutes the proceeds of a bank loan or if it is received as a payment on certain promissory notes, installment sales contracts, or down payment plans. See Pub. 1544 for more information.

Person.—An individual, corporation, partnership, trust, estate, association, or company.

Recipient.—The person receiving the cash. Each branch or other unit of a person's trade or business is considered a separate recipient unless the branch receiving the cash (or a central office linking the branches), knows or has reason to know the identity of payers making cash payments to other branches.

Transaction.—Includes the purchase of property or services, the payment of debt, the exchange of a negotiable instrument for cash, and the receipt of cash to be held in escrow or trust. A single transaction may not be broken into multiple transactions to avoid reporting.

Suspicious transaction.—A transaction in which it appears that a person is attempting to cause Form 8300 not to be filed, or to file a false or incomplete form. The term also includes any transaction in which there is an indication of possible illegal activity.

Specific Instructions

You must complete all parts. However, you may skip Part II if the individual named in Part I is conducting the transaction on his or her behalf only.

Item 1.—If you are amending a prior report, check box 1a. Complete the appropriate items with the correct or amended information only. Complete all of Part IV. Staple a copy of the original report to the amended report.

To voluntarily report a suspicious transaction (see **Definitions**), check box 1b. You may also telephone your local IRS Criminal Investigation Division or call 1-800-800-2877.

Part I

Item 2.—If two or more individuals conducted the transaction you are reporting, check the box and complete Part I for any one of the individuals. Provide the same information for the other individual(s) on the back of the form. If more than three individuals are involved, provide the same information on additional sheets of paper and attach them to this form.

Item 6.—Enter the taxpayer identification number (TIN) of the individual named. See **Taxpayer identification number (TIN)** under **General Instructions** for more information.

Item 8.—Enter eight numerals for the date of birth of the individual named. For example, if the individual's birth date is July 6, 1960, enter 07 06 1960.

Item 13.—Fully describe the nature of the occupation, profession, or business (for example, "plumber," "attorney," or "automobile dealer"). Do not use general or nondescriptive terms such as "businessman" or "self-employed."

Item 14.—You must verify the name and address of the named individual(s). Verification must be made by examination of a document normally accepted as a means of identification when cashing checks (for example, a driver's license, passport, alien registration card, or other official document). In item 14a, enter the type of document examined. In item 14b, identify the issuer of the document. In item 14c, enter the document's number. For example, if the individual has a Utah driver's license, enter "driver's license" in item 14a, "Utah" in item 14b, and the number appearing on the license in item 14c.

Part II

Item 15.—If the transaction is being conducted on behalf of more than one person (including husband and wife or parent and child), check the box and complete Part II for any one of the persons. Provide the same information for the other person(s) on the back of the form. If more than three persons are involved, provide the same information on additional sheets of paper and attach them to this form.

Items 16 through 19.—If the person on whose behalf the transaction is being conducted is an individual, complete items 16, 17, and 18. Enter his or her TIN in item 19. If the individual is a sole proprietor and has an employer identification number (EIN), you must enter both the SSN and EIN in item 19. If the person is an organization, put its name as shown on required tax filings in item 16 and its EIN in item 19.

Item 20.—If a sole proprietor or organization named in items 16 through 18 is doing business under a name other than that entered in item 16 (e.g., a "trade" or "doing business as (DBA)" name), enter it here.

Item 27.—If the person is **NOT** required to furnish a TIN (see **Taxpayer identification number (TIN)** under **General Instructions),** complete this item. Enter a description of the type of official document issued to that person in item 27a (for example, "passport"), the country that issued the document in item 27b, and the document's number in item 27c.

Part III

Item 28.—Enter the date you received the cash. If you received the cash in more than one payment, enter the date you received the payment that caused the combined amount to exceed $10,000. See **Multiple payments** under **General Instructions** for more information.

Item 30.—Check this box if the amount shown in item 29 was received in more than one payment (for example, as installment payments or payments on related transactions).

Item 31.—Enter the total price of the property, services, amount of cash exchanged, etc. (for example, the total cost of a vehicle purchased, cost of catering service, exchange of currency) if different from the amount shown in item 29.

Item 32.—Enter the dollar amount of each form of cash received. Show foreign currency amounts in U.S. dollar equivalent at a fair market rate of exchange available to the public. **The sum of the amounts must equal item 29.** For cashier's check, money order, bank draft, or traveler's check, provide the name of the issuer and the serial number of each instrument. Names of all issuers and all serial numbers involved must be provided. If necessary, provide this information on additional sheets of paper and attach them to this form.

Item 33.—Check the appropriate box(es) that describe the transaction. If the transaction is not specified in boxes a–i, check box j and briefly describe the transaction (for example, car lease, boat lease, house lease, aircraft rental).

Part IV

Item 36.—If you are a sole proprietorship, you must enter your SSN. If your business also has an EIN, you must provide the EIN as well. All other business entities must enter an EIN.

Item 41.—Fully describe the nature of your business, for example, "attorney," "jewelry dealer." Do not use general or nondescriptive terms such as "business" or "store."

Item 42.—This form must be signed by an individual who has been authorized to do so for the business that received the cash.

Paperwork Reduction Act Notice

The requested information is useful in criminal, tax, and regulatory investigations, for instance, by directing the Federal Government's attention to unusual or questionable transactions. Trades or businesses are required to provide the information under 26 U.S.C. 6050I.

You are not required to provide the information requested on a form that is subject to the Paperwork Reduction Act unless the form displays a valid OMB control number. Books or records relating to a form or its instructions must be retained as long as their contents may become material in the administration of any Internal Revenue law. Generally, tax returns and return information are confidential, as required by Code section 6103.

The time needed to complete this form will vary depending on individual circumstances. The estimated average time is 21 minutes. If you have comments concerning the accuracy of this time estimate or suggestions for making this form simpler, you can write to the Tax Forms Committee, Western Area Distribution Center, Rancho Cordova, CA 95743-0001. DO NOT send this form to this office. Instead, see **Where To File** on page 3.

Form **8850**
(Rev. November 1998)
Department of the Treasury
Internal Revenue Service

Pre-Screening Notice and Certification Request for the Work Opportunity and Welfare-to-Work Credits

▶ See separate instructions.

OMB No. 1545-1500

Job applicant: Fill in the lines below and check any boxes that apply. Complete only this side.

Your name _____ Social security number ▶ _____

Street address where you live _____

City or town, state, and ZIP code _____

Telephone no. ( ) - _____

If you are under age 25, enter your date of birth (month, day, year) ___/___/___

Work Opportunity Credit

1 ☐ Check here if you received a conditional certification from the state employment security agency (SESA) or a participating local agency for the work opportunity credit.

2 ☐ Check here if **any** of the following statements apply to you.

- I am a member of a family that has received assistance from Aid to Families with Dependent Children (AFDC) or its successor program, Temporary Assistance for Needy Families (TANF), for any 9 months during the last 18 months.

- I am a veteran and a member of a family that received food stamps for at least a 3-month period within the last 15 months.
- I was referred here by a rehabilitation agency approved by the state or the Department of Veterans Affairs.

- I am at least age 18 but **not** over age 24 and I am a member of a family that:
  a Received food stamps for the last 6 months, OR
  b Received food stamps for at least 3 of the last 5 months, BUT is no longer eligible to receive them.

- Within the past year, I was convicted of a felony or released from prison for a felony AND during the last 6 months I was a member of a low-income family.

- I received supplemental security income (SSI) benefits for any month ending within the last 60 days.

Welfare-to-Work Credit

3 ☐ Check here if you received a conditional certification from the SESA or a participating local agency for the welfare-to-work credit.

4 ☐ Check here if you are a member of a family that:
- Received AFDC or TANF payments for at least the last 18 months, OR
- Received AFDC or TANF payments for any 18 months beginning after August 5, 1997, OR
- Stopped being eligible for AFDC or TANF payments after August 5, 1997, because Federal or state law limited the maximum time those payments could be made.

All Applicants

Under penalties of perjury, I declare that I gave the above information to the employer on or before the day I was offered a job, and it is, to the best of my knowledge, true, correct, and complete.

Job applicant's signature ▶   Date ___/___/___

For Privacy Act and Paperwork Reduction Act Notice, see page 2.   Cat. No. 22851L   Form **8850** (Rev. 11-98)

For Employer's Use Only

Employer's name _____ Telephone no. ( ) - ___ EIN ▶ _____

Street address _____

City or town, state, and ZIP code _____

Person to contact, if different from above _____ Telephone no. ( ) -

Street address _____

City or town, state, and ZIP code _____

If, based on the individual's age and home address, he or she is a member of group 4 or 6 (as described under **Members of Targeted Groups** in the separate instructions), enter that group number (4 or 6) . . . . ▶ ____

DATE APPLICANT: Gave   Was   Was   Started
                 information   /   /   offered job   /   /   hired   /   /   job   /   /

Under penalties of perjury, I declare that I completed this form on or before the day a job was offered to the applicant and that the information I have furnished is, to the best of my knowledge, true, correct, and complete. Based on the information the job applicant furnished on page 1, I believe the individual is a member of a targeted group or a long-term family assistance recipient. I hereby request a certification that the individual is a member of a targeted group or a long-term family assistance recipient.

Employer's signature ▶ _____ Title _____ Date   /   /

Privacy Act and Paperwork Reduction Act Notice

Section references are to the Internal Revenue Code.

Section 51(d)(12) permits a prospective employer to request the applicant to complete this form and give it to the prospective employer. The information will be used by the employer to complete the employer's Federal tax return. Completion of this form is voluntary and may assist members of targeted groups and long-term family assistance recipients in securing employment. Routine uses of this form include giving it to the state employment security agency (SESA), which will contact appropriate sources to confirm that the applicant is a member of a targeted group or a long-term family

assistance recipient. This form may also be given to the Internal Revenue Service for administration of the Internal Revenue laws, to the Department of Justice for civil and criminal litigation, to the Department of Labor for oversight of the certifications performed by the SESA, and to cities, states, and the District of Columbia for use in administering their tax laws.

You are not required to provide the information requested on a form that is subject to the Paperwork Reduction Act unless the form displays a valid OMB control number. Books or records relating to a form or its instructions must be retained as long as their contents may become material in the administration of any Internal Revenue law. Generally, tax returns and return information are confidential, as required by section 6103.

The time needed to complete and file this form will vary depending on individual circumstances. The estimated average time is:

Recordkeeping . . . . 2 hr., 47 min.
Learning about the law or the form . . . . 28 min.
Preparing and sending this form to the SESA . . . . 36 min.

If you have comments concerning the accuracy of these time estimates or suggestions for making this form simpler, we would be happy to hear from you. You can write to the Tax Forms Committee, Western Area Distribution Center, Rancho Cordova, CA 95743-0001.

DO NOT send this form to this address. Instead, see **When and Where To File** in the separate instructions.

Instructions for Form 8850

Department of the Treasury
Internal Revenue Service

(Revised November 1998)

Pre-Screening Notice and Certification Request for the Work Opportunity and Welfare-to-Work Credits

Section references are to the Internal Revenue Code unless otherwise noted.

General Instructions

A Change To Note

The Tax and Trade Relief Extension Act of 1998 extended the work opportunity credit and the welfare-to-work credit to cover individuals who begin work for the employer before July 1, 1999.

Purpose of Form

Employers use Form 8850 to pre-screen and to make a written request to a state employment security agency (SESA) to certify an individual as:

● A member of a targeted group for purposes of qualifying for the work opportunity credit, or

● A long-term family assistance recipient for purposes of qualifying for the welfare-to-work credit.

Submitting Form 8850 to the SESA is but one step in the employer qualifying for the work opportunity credit or the welfare-to-work credit. The SESA must certify the job applicant is a member of a targeted group or is a long-term family assistance recipient. After starting work, the employee must meet the minimum number-of-hours-worked requirement for the work opportunity credit or the minimum number-of-hours, number-of-days requirement for the welfare-to-work credit. The employer may elect to take the applicable credit by filing **Form 5884,** Work Opportunity Credit, or **Form 8861,** Welfare-to-Work Credit.

Who Should Complete and Sign the Form

The job applicant gives information to the employer on or before the day a job offer is made. This information is entered on Form 8850. Based on the applicant's information, the employer determines whether or not he or she believes the applicant is a member of a targeted group (as defined under **Members of Targeted Groups** below) or a long-term family assistance recipient (as defined under **Welfare-to-Work Job Applicants** on page 2). If the employer believes the applicant is a member of a targeted group or a long-term family assistance recipient, the employer completes the rest of the form no later than the day the job offer is made. Both the job applicant and the employer must sign Form 8850 no later than the date for submitting the form to the SESA.

Instructions for Employer

When and Where To File

Do not file Form 8850 with the Internal Revenue Service. Instead, send it to the work opportunity tax credit (WOTC) coordinator for your SESA no later than the 21st day after the job applicant begins work for you.

To get the name, address, and phone and fax numbers of the WOTC coordinator for your SESA, visit the Department of Labor, Employment and Training Administration (ETA) web site at **www.ttrc.doleta.gov/common/directories**, or call **202-219-9092** (not a toll-free number).

Additional Requirements for Certification

In addition to filing Form 8850, you must complete and send to your state's WOTC coordinator **either:**

● **ETA Form 9062,** Conditional Certification Form, if the job applicant received this form from a participating agency (e.g., the Jobs Corps), **or**

● **ETA Form 9061,** Individual Characteristics Form, if the job applicant did not receive a conditional certification.

Using the Department of Labor's fax on demand service, you can get a directory of WOTC coordinators and ETA Form 9061 by calling **703-365-0768** (not a toll-free number) from the telephone connected to your fax machine and following the prompts. You can also get ETA Form 9061 from your local public employment service office, or you can download it from the ETA web site at **www.doleta.gov**.

Recordkeeping

Keep copies of Forms 8850, along with any transmittal letters that you submit to your SESA, as long as they may be needed for the administration of the Internal Revenue Code provisions relating to the work opportunity credit and the welfare-to-work credit. Records that support these credits usually must be kept for 3 years from the date any income tax return claiming the credits is due or filed, whichever is later.

Members of Targeted Groups

A job applicant may be certified as a member of a targeted group if he or she is:

1. A member of a family receiving assistance under a state plan approved under part A of title IV of the Social Security Act relating to Aid to Families with Dependent Children (AFDC) or its successor program, Temporary Assistance for Needy Families (TANF). The assistance must be received for any 9 months during the 18-month period that ends on the hiring date.

2. A veteran who is a member of a family receiving assistance under the Food Stamp program for generally at least a 3-month period during the 15-month period ending on the hiring date. See section 51(d)(3).

To be considered a **veteran,** the applicant must:

● Have served on active duty (not including training) in the Armed Forces of the United States for more than 180 days OR have been discharged for a service-connected disability, AND

● Not have a period of active duty (not including training) of more than 90 days that ended during the 60-day period ending on the hiring date.

3. An ex-felon who:

● Has been convicted of a felony under any Federal or state law,

● Is hired not more than 1 year after the conviction or release from prison for that felony, AND

● Is a member of a family that had income on an annual basis of 70% or less of the Bureau of Labor Statistics lower living standard during the 6 months preceding the earlier of the month the income determination occurs or the month in which the hiring date occurs.

Cat. No. 24833J

4. An individual who is at least age 18 but not yet age 25 on the hiring date and lives in an empowerment zone or enterprise community.

The Secretary of Housing and Urban Development (HUD) designated parts of the following cities as urban empowerment zones:

- Atlanta, GA (9.29 square miles)
- Baltimore, MD (6.8 square miles)
- Philadelphia, PA/Camden, NJ (4.4 square miles)
- Chicago, IL (14.33 square miles)
- Detroit, MI (18.3 square miles)
- New York City, NY (the Bronx and Manhattan) (7.6 square miles)

The Secretary of Agriculture (USDA) designated the following rural empowerment zones:

- The Kentucky Highlands (part of Wayne and all of Clinton and Jackson counties)
- Mid-Delta, Mississippi (parts of Bolivar, Holmes, Humphreys, Leflore, Sunflower, and Washington counties)
- Rio Grande Valley, Texas (parts of Cameron, Hidalgo, Starr, and Willacy counties)

Under section 1400, parts of Washington, DC, are treated as an empowerment zone. For more details, see Notice 98-57, 1998-47 I.R.B. 9.

There are 64 urban and 30 rural enterprise communities located in 35 states. There are no empowerment zones or enterprise communities in Puerto Rico, Guam, or any U.S. possession.

You may call HUD at **1-800-998-9999** for information on the six urban empowerment zones and Washington, DC. You may call the USDA at **1-800-645-4712** about the rural empowerment zones. On the Internet, you can visit the EZ/EC Home Page at **www.ezec.gov**. Your SESA has information on where the enterprise communities are located. Also, many enterprise communities have their own web sites.

5. An individual who has a physical or mental disability resulting in a substantial handicap to employment and who was referred to the employer upon completion of (or while receiving) rehabilitation services under a state plan of employment or a program approved by the Department of Veterans Affairs.

6. An individual who:

- Performs services for the employer between May 1 and September 15,
- Is age 16 but not yet age 18 on the hiring date (or if later, on May 1),
- Has never worked for the employer before, AND
- Lives in an empowerment zone or enterprise community.

7. An individual who:

- Is at least age 18 but not yet age 25 AND
- Is a member of a family that—

   a. Has received food stamps for the 6-month period ending on the hiring date OR

   b. Is no longer eligible for such assistance under section 6(o) of the Food Stamp Act of 1977 and the family received food stamps for at least 3 months of the 5-month period ending on the hiring date.

8. An individual who is receiving supplemental security income benefits under title XVI of the Social Security Act (including benefits of the type described in section 1616 of the Social Security Act or section 212 of Public Law 93-66) for any month ending within the 60-day period ending on the hiring date.

Welfare-to-Work Job Applicants

An individual may be certified as a long-term family assistance recipient if he or she is a member of a family that:

- Has received assistance payments from AFDC or TANF for at least 18 consecutive months ending on the hiring date, OR
- Receives assistance payments from AFDC or TANF for any 18 months (whether or not consecutive) beginning after August 5, 1997, OR
- After August 5, 1997, stops being eligible for assistance payments because Federal or state law limits the maximum period such assistance is payable, and the individual is hired not more than 2 years after such eligibility for assistance ends.

EDD Employment Development Department
State of California

This form will be the basic record of YOUR ACCOUNT. **DO NOT FILE THIS FORM UNTIL YOU HAVE PAID WAGES THAT EXCEED $100.00.** Please read the **INSTRUCTIONS** on page 2 before completing this form. **PLEASE PRINT OR TYPE.** Return this form to: ➤	EMPLOYMENT DEVELOPMENT DEPARTMENT ACCOUNT SERVICES GROUP MIC 28 PO BOX 826880 SACRAMENTO CA 94280-0001 **(916) 654-7041 FAX (916) 654-9211**

REGISTRATION FORM FOR COMMERCIAL EMPLOYERS

DEPT USE	ACCOUNT NUMBER	QUARTER	ETCSO	FED CODE	ON-LINE PROCESS DATE	TAS CODE

A. BUSINESS NAME		OWNERSHIP BEGAN OPERATING	FEDERAL I.D. NUMBER
		MONTH: DAY: YEAR:	
B. OWNER, CORPORATION, LLC, LLP NAME		SSA/CORP/LLC/LLP I.D. NO.	DRIVER'S LICENSE NUMBER

List all partners* or corporate officers or LLC members/managers/officers	TITLE (partner, officer title, LLC member/manager)	SOCIAL SECURITY NUMBER	DRIVER'S LICENSE NUMBER

*If entity is a **Limited Partnership**, indicate General Partner with an (*). List additional partners, LLC members/officers/managers on a separate sheet.

C. BUSINESS LOCATION Street and Number (see instructions)	CITY OR TOWN	STATE	ZIP CODE	COUNTY
MAILING ADDRESS (in care of P.O. Box or Street and Number)	CITY OR TOWN	STATE	ZIP CODE	PHONE NUMBER ( )

D. HAVE YOU EVER BEEN REGISTERED WITH THE DEPARTMENT? ☐ No ☐ Yes	IF YES, ENTER EMPLOYER ACCOUNT NUMBER, BUSINESS NAME AND ADDRESS ACCT NUMBER BUSINESS NAME ADDRESS

E. INDICATE FIRST QUARTER AND YEAR IN WHICH WAGES EXCEED $100. ☐ Jan.-Mar. 20___ ☐ Apr.-June 20___ ☐ July-Sept. 20___ ☐Oct.-Dec. 20___	**F.** WILL YOU BE SUBJECT TO FEDERAL MONTHLY/SEMI-WEEKLY DEPOSITS? ☐ No ☐ Yes

G. ORGANIZATION TYPE

☐ (IN) INDIVIDUAL OWNER	☐ (JV) JOINT VENTURE	☐ (LQ) LIQUIDATION	☐ (LC) LIMITED LIABILITY CO.
☐ (HW) HUS/WIFE CO-OWNERSHIP	☐ (RC) RECEIVERSHIP	☐ (LP) LIMITED PARTNERSHIP	☐ (PL) LIMITED LIABILITY PARTNERSHIP
☐ (GP) GENERAL PARTNERSHIP	☐ (BK) BANKRUPTCY	☐ (TR) TRUSTEESHIP	
☐ (CP) CORPORATION	☐ (AS) ASSOCIATION	☐ (EA) ESTATE ADMINISTRATION	☐ (OT) OTHER (Specify)

H. EMPLOYER TYPE (see instructions) ☐ (01) Commercial ☐ (10) Church ☐ (11) Indian Reservation ☐ (22) Pacific Maritime ☐ (25) Fishing Boat	NUMBER OF EMPLOYEES

I. BUSINESS TYPE	1) Describe kind of product or type of service:
☐ (N) Mining ☐ (F) Finance ☐ (I) Insurance ☐ (C) Construction ☐ (B) Communications ☐ (E) Real Estate ☐ (M) Manufacturing ☐ (S) Services ☐ (O) Other ☐ (T) Transportation ☐ (L) Utilities ☐ (R) Retail Trade ☐ (W) Wholesale Trade	2) If MANUFACTURING, list principal products in order of importance.

J. CONTACT PERSON FOR BUSINESS NAME	ADDRESS	PHONE ( )

K. SUPPORTIVE SERVICES

If you are part of a larger organization and you are primarily engaged in providing supportive services to other establishments of the larger organization, check one of these boxes.

(1) ☐ Control Administrative (headquarters, etc.)   (3) ☐ Storage (warehouse)   (5) ☐ Does not apply
(2) ☐ Research, development, or testing   (4) ☐ Other (specify) _____

L. IS THIS A(N):

☐ New business   ☐ On-going business just purchased ☐ All ☐ Part   ☐ Other _____
☐ Change of partner(s)   ☐ Change in form - (Sole proprietor to partnership; partnership to corporation; merger; corporation to LLC, etc.)
IF THE BUSINESS WAS PREVIOUSLY OWNED, PROVIDE THE FOLLOWING INFORMATION:

Previous Owner	Business Name	Purchase Price	Date of Transfer	EDD Account Number

M. DECLARATION

These Statements are hereby declared to be correct to the best knowledge and belief of the undersigned.

Signature _____ Date _____ Residence Phone (___)_____

Title _____ Residence Address _____
(Owner, Partner, Officer, Member, Manager, etc.)   Street   City   State   ZIP Code

DE 1 Rev. 68 (1-00) **(INTERNET)**   CU

INSTRUCTIONS FOR REGISTRATION FORM FOR COMMERCIAL EMPLOYERS

An employer is required by law to file a registration form with the Employment Development Department (EDD) within **fifteen (15) calendar days** after paying over $100 in wages for employment in a calendar quarter, or whenever a change in ownership occurs. Complete this DE 1 and file at address shown on page 1 of form.

A. BUSINESS NAME - Give the name by which your business is known to the public. Enter "None" if no business name is used. Enter the date the new ownership began operating. Enter Federal Employer Identification Number(s). If not assigned, enter "Applied For."

B. OWNER, CORPORATION, LIMITED LIABILITY COMPANY (LLC) OR LIMITED LIABILITY PARTNERSHIP (LLP) NAME - Enter the full given name, middle initial, surname, title, social security account number, and driver's license number for each individual, partner, corporate officer, LLC member/officer/manager. Enter a corporation, LLC or LLP name exactly as spelled and registered with the Secretary of State. Include California corporate, LLC or LLP identification number.

C. BUSINESS LOCATION - Enter the California address and county where the business in A is physically conducted. If more than one California location, list on a separate sheet and attach to this form. In Mailing Address, enter the address where EDD correspondence and forms should be sent. If this address is the same as the business location, enter "Same." Provide daytime business phone number.

D. PRIOR REGISTRATION - If any part of the ownership in B is operating or has ever operated at another location, check "Yes" and provide account number, business name and address.

E. WAGES - Check the appropriate box when you first paid over $100 in wages.

F. PIT WITHHOLDING - Check appropriate box. If you are not sure if you are subject to federal monthly/semi-weekly Personal Income Tax deposits, contact your local Employment Tax Customer Service Office (ETCSO).

G. ORGANIZATION TYPE - Check the box which best describes the legal form of the ownership in B.

H. EMPLOYER TYPE - Check the box which best describes your employer type. Enter the total number of employees for the ownership in B.

I. BUSINESS TYPE - Check the box which best describes your business type. Describe the particular product or service rendered.

J. CONTACT PERSON - Enter the name and phone number of the person authorized by the ownership shown in B to provide information to EDD staff.

K. SUPPORTIVE SERVICES - Check the box which best describes the supportive services provided by B.

L. STATUS OF BUSINESS - Check the box that best describes why you are completing this form. If the business was previously owned, provide owner and business name, purchase price, date ownership was transferred to this ownership and EDD account number.

M. DECLARATION - This declaration should be signed by one of the names shown in B.

NEED MORE HELP OR INFORMATION? Call Account Services Group (ASG) in Sacramento at (916) 654-7041 with questions regarding this form or the registration and account number assignment process. If you have questions about whether your business entity is subject to reporting and paying state payroll taxes, contact the nearest Employment Tax Customer Service Office (ETCSO) listed in your local telephone directory under State Government, Employment Development Department or call the Sacramento ETCSO at (916) 464-3502.

Three options for obtaining a new employer account number are available: by mail, by calling (916) 654-8706 to obtain your account number over the phone or by fax service at (916) 654-0211. All three options require that a registration form be completed and mailed to: Employment Development Department, Account Services Group MIC 28, PO Box 826880, Sacramento, CA 94280-0001.

We will **notify** you of your **EDD Account Number** by mail. To help you understand your tax withholding and filing responsibilities, you will be sent a **California Employer's Guide, DE 44**. Please keep your account status current by notifying ASG of all future changes to the original registration information.

DE 1 Rev. 68 (1-00) **(INTERNET)**

INDEX

SPHINX® PUBLISHING ORDER FORM

BILL TO:		SHIP TO:	
Phone #	Terms	F.O.B. Chicago, IL	Ship Date

Charge my: ☐ VISA ☐ MasterCard ☐ American Express

☐ **Money Order or Personal Check**

Credit Card Number

Expiration Date

Qty	ISBN	Title	Retail	Ext.
		SPHINX PUBLISHING NATIONAL TITLES		
	1-57248-148-X	Cómo Hacer su Propio Testamento	$16.95	
	1-57248-147-1	Cómo Solicitar su Propio Divorcio	$24.95	
	1-57248-226-5	Cómo Restablecer su propio Crédito y Renegociar sus Deudas	$21.95	
	1-57248-166-8	The Complete Book of Corporate Forms	$24.95	
	1-57248-163-3	Crime Victim's Guide to Justice (2E)	$21.95	
	1-57248-159-5	Essential Guide to Real Estate Contracts	$18.95	
	1-57248-160-9	Essential Guide to Real Estate Leases	$18.95	
	1-57248-139-0	Grandparents' Rights (3E)	$24.95	
	1-57248-188-9	Guía de Inmigración a Estados Unidos (3E)	$24.95	
	1-57248-187-0	Guía de Justicia para Víctimas del Crimen	$21.95	
	1-57248-103-X	Help Your Lawyer Win Your Case (2E)	$14.95	
	1-57248-164-1	How to Buy a Condominium or Townhome (2E)	$19.95	
	1-57248-191-9	How to File Your Own Bankruptcy (5E)	$21.95	
	1-57248-132-3	How to File Your Own Divorce (4E)	$24.95	
	1-57248-100-5	How to Form a DE Corporation from Any State	$24.95	
	1-57248-083-1	How to Form a Limited Liability Company	$22.95	
	1-57248-099-8	How to Form a Nonprofit Corporation	$24.95	
	1-57248-133-1	How to Form Your Own Corporation (3E)	$24.95	
	1-57248-224-9	How to Form Your Own Partnership (2E)	$24.95	
	1-57248-119-6	How to Make Your Own Will (2E)	$16.95	
	1-57248-200-1	How to Register Your Own Copyright (4E)	$24.95	
	1-57248-104-8	How to Register Your Own Trademark (3E)	$21.95	
	1-57071-349-9	How to Win Your Unemployment Compensation Claim	$21.95	
	1-57248-118-8	How to Write Your Own Living Will (2E)	$16.95	
	1-57248-156-0	How to Write Your Own Premarital Agreement (3E)	$24.95	
	1-57248-158-7	Incorporate in Nevada from Any State	$24.95	
	1-57071-333-2	Jurors' Rights (2E)	$12.95	
	1-57071-400-2	Legal Research Made Easy (2E)	$16.95	
	1-57248-165-X	Living Trusts and Other Ways to Avoid Probate (3E)	$24.95	

Qty	ISBN	Title	Retail	Ext.
	1-57248-186-2	Manual de Beneficios para el Seguro Social	$18.95	
	1-57248-220-6	Mastering the MBE	$16.95	
	1-57248-167-6	Most Valuable Bus. Legal Forms You'll Ever Need (3E)	$21.95	
	1-57248-130-7	Most Valuable Personal Legal Forms You'll Ever Need	$24.95	
	1-57248-098-X	The Nanny and Domestic Help Legal Kit	$22.95	
	1-57248-089-0	Neighbor v. Neighbor (2E)	$16.95	
	1-57248-169-2	The Power of Attorney Handbook (4E)	$19.95	
	1-57248-149-8	Repair Your Own Credit and Deal with Debt	$18.95	
	1-57248-168-4	The Social Security Benefits Handbook (3E)	$18.95	
	1-57071-399-5	Unmarried Parents' Rights	$19.95	
	1-57071-354-5	U.S.A. Immigration Guide (3E)	$19.95	
	1-57071-192-7	The Visitation Handbook	$18.95	
	1-57248-138-2	Winning Your Personal Injury Claim (2E)	$24.95	
	1-57248-162-5	Your Right to Child Custody, Visitation and Support (2E)	$24.95	
	1-57248-157-9	Your Rights When You Owe Too Much	$16.95	
		CALIFORNIA TITLES		
	1-57248-150-1	CA Power of Attorney Handbook (2E)	$18.95	
	1-57248-151-X	How to File for Divorce in CA (3E)	$26.95	
	1-57071-356-1	How to Make a CA Will	$16.95	
	1-57248-145-5	How to Probate and Settle an Estate in California	$26.95	
	1-57248-146-3	How to Start a Business in CA	$18.95	
	1-57248-194-3	How to Win in Small Claims Court in CA (2E)	$18.95	
	1-57248-196-X	The Landlord's Legal Guide in CA	$24.95	
		FLORIDA TITLES		
	1-57071-363-4	Florida Power of Attorney Handbook (2E)	$16.95	
	1-57248-176-5	How to File for Divorce in FL (7E)	$26.95	
	1-57248-177-3	How to Form a Corporation in FL (5E)	$24.95	
	1-57248-203-6	How to Form a Limited Liability Co. in FL (2E)	$24.95	
	1-57071-401-0	How to Form a Partnership in FL	$22.95	

Form Continued on Following Page   **SUBTOTAL**

To order, call Sourcebooks at 1-800-432-7444 or FAX (630) 961-2168 (Bookstores, libraries, wholesalers—please call for discount)

Prices are subject to change without notice.

Find more legal information at: www.SphinxLegal.com

SPHINX® PUBLISHING ORDER FORM

Qty	ISBN	Title	Retail	Ext.
____	1-57248-113-7	How to Make a FL Will (6E)	$16.95	____
____	1-57248-088-2	How to Modify Your FL Divorce Judgment (4E)	$24.95	____
____	1-57248-144-7	How to Probate and Settle an Estate in FL (4E)	$26.95	____
____	1-57248-081-5	How to Start a Business in FL (5E)	$16.95	____
____	1-57071-362-6	How to Win in Small Claims Court in FL (6E)	$16.95	____
____	1-57248-202-8	Land Trusts in Florida (6E)	$29.95	____
____	1-57248-123-4	Landlords' Rights and Duties in FL (8E)	$21.95	____
		GEORGIA TITLES		
____	1-57248-137-4	How to File for Divorce in GA (4E)	$21.95	____
____	1-57248-180-3	How to Make a GA Will (4E)	$21.95	____
____	1-57248-140-4	How to Start a Business in Georgia (2E)	$16.95	____
		ILLINOIS TITLES		
____	1-57071-405-3	How to File for Divorce in IL (2E)	$21.95	____
____	1-57248-170-6	How to Make an IL Will (3E)	$16.95	____
____	1-57071-416-9	How to Start a Business in IL (2E)	$18.95	____
____	1-57248-078-5	Landlords' Rights & Duties in IL	$21.95	____
		MASSACHUSETTS TITLES		
____	1-57248-128-5	How to File for Divorce in MA (3E)	$24.95	____
____	1-57248-115-3	How to Form a Corporation in MA	$24.95	____
____	1-57248-108-0	How to Make a MA Will (2E)	$16.95	____
____	1-57248-106-4	How to Start a Business in MA (2E)	$18.95	____
____	1-57248-209-5	The Landlord's Legal Guide in MA	$24.95	____
		MICHIGAN TITLES		
____	1-57071-409-6	How to File for Divorce in MI (2E)	$21.95	____
____	1-57248-182-X	How to Make a MI Will (3E)	$16.95	____
____	1-57248-183-8	How to Start a Business in MI (3E)	$18.95	____
		MINNESOTA TITLES		
____	1-57248-142-0	How to File for Divorce in MN	$21.95	____
____	1-57248-179-X	How to Form a Corporation in MN	$24.95	____
____	1-57248-178-1	How to Make a MN Will (2E)	$16.95	____
		NEW YORK TITLES		
____	1-57248-193-5	Child Custody, Visitation and Support in NY	$26.95	____
____	1-57248-141-2	How to File for Divorce in NY (2E)	$26.95	____
____	1-57248-105-6	How to Form a Corporation in NY	$24.95	____
____	1-57248-095-5	How to Make a NY Will (2E)	$16.95	____
____	1-57248-199-4	How to Start a Business in NY (2E)	$18.95	____

Qty	ISBN	Title	Retail	Ext.
____	1-57248-198-6	How to Win in Small Claims Court in NY (2E)	$18.95	____
____	1-57071-186-0	Landlords' Rights and Duties in NY	$21.95	____
____	1-57071-188-7	New York Power of Attorney Handbook	$19.95	____
____	1-57248-122-6	Tenants' Rights in NY	$21.95	____
		NORTH CAROLINA TITLES		
____	1-57248-185-4	How to File for Divorce in NC (3E)	$22.95	____
____	1-57248-129-3	How to Make a NC Will (3E)	$16.95	____
____	1-57248-184-6	How to Start a Business in NC (3E)	$18.95	____
____	1-57248-091-2	Landlords' Rights & Duties in NC	$21.95	____
		OHIO TITLES		
____	1-57248-190-0	How to File for Divorce in OH (2E)	$24.95	____
____	1-57248-174-9	How to Form a Corporation in OH	$24.95	____
____	1-57248-173-0	How to Make an OH Will	$16.95	____
		PENNSYLVANIA TITLES		
____	1-57248-211-7	How to File for Divorce in PA (3E)	$26.95	____
____	1-57248-094-7	How to Make a PA Will (2E)	$16.95	____
____	1-57248-112-9	How to Start a Business in PA (2E)	$18.95	____
____	1-57071-179-8	Landlords' Rights and Duties in PA	$19.95	____
		TEXAS TITLES		
____	1-57248-171-4	Child Custody, Visitation, and Support in TX	$22.95	____
____	1-57248-172-2	How to File for Divorce in TX (3E)	$24.95	____
____	1-57248-114-5	How to Form a Corporation in TX (2E)	$24.95	____
____	1-57071-417-7	How to Make a TX Will (2E)	$16.95	____
____	1-57248-214-1	How to Probate and Settle an Estate in TX (3E)	$26.95	____
____	1-57248-228-1	How to Start a Business in TX (3E)	$18.95	____
____	1-57248-111-0	How to Win in Small Claims Court in TX (2E)	$16.95	____
____	1-57248-110-2	Landlords' Rights and Duties in TX (2E)	$21.95	____

SUBTOTAL THIS PAGE _____

SUBTOTAL PREVIOUS PAGE _____

Shipping — $5.00 for 1st book, $1.00 each additional _____

Illinois residents add 6.75% sales tax _____

Connecticut residents add 6.00% sales tax _____

TOTAL _____

To order, call Sourcebooks at 1-800-432-7444 or FAX (630) 961-2168 (Bookstores, libraries, wholesalers—please call for discount)
Prices are subject to change without notice.
Find more legal information at: www.SphinxLegal.com